C000220592

The Best of 'BB'

The Best of 'BB'

ILLUSTRATED BY

D.J. Watkins-Pitchford ARCA FRSA

MERLIN UNWIN BOOKS

Merlin Unwin Books
Palmers House
7 Corve Street
Ludlow
Shropshire SY8 1DB
Tel: (01584) 877456 Fax: (01584) 877457
www.merlinunwin.co.uk

This anthology was first published in Great Britain by Michael Joseph Ltd, 1985
This edition is published by Merlin Unwin Books, 2010

The Best of 'BB' © The Estate of D.J. Watkins-Pitchford
Illustrations as specified on pages vii–viii © The Estate of D.J. Watkins-Pitchford

All rights reserved. No part of this publication may be reproduced, stored in a retrieval system, or transmitted, in any form or by any means, electronic, mechanical, photocopying, recording or otherwise, without the prior permission of the copyright owners.

British Library Cataloguing in Publication Data
A catalogue record for this book is available from the British Library

ISBN 978-1-906122-12-6

Printed and bound in England by TJ International, Padstow, Cornwall.

Contents

Acknowledgements

The extracts included in this anthology are taken from the following books, listed in order of publication:

THE SPORTSMAN'S BEDSIDE BOOK:
    Eyre & Spottiswoode (1937)
WILD LONE – The Story of a Pytchley Fox:
    Eyre & Spottiswoode (1939)
MANKA, THE SKY GIPSY – The Story of a Wild
    Goose: Eyre & Spottiswoode (1939)
THE COUNTRYMAN'S BEDSIDE BOOK:
    Eyre & Spottiswoode (1941)
THE LITTLE GREY MEN:
    Eyre & Spottiswoode (1942)
THE IDLE COUNTRYMAN:
    Eyre & Spottiswoode (1943)
BRENDON CHASE:
    Hollis & Carter (1944)
THE FISHERMAN'S BEDSIDE BOOK:
    Eyre & Spottiswoode (1945)
THE WAYFARING TREE:
    Hollis & Carter (1945)
DOWN THE BRIGHT STREAM:
    Eyre & Spottiswoode (1948)
THE SHOOTING MAN'S BEDSIDE BOOK:
    Eyre & Spottiswoode (1948)
CONFESSIONS OF A CARP FISHER:
    Eyre & Spottiswoode (1950)
LETTERS FROM COMPTON DEVERELL:
    Eyre & Spottiswoode (1950)

TIDE'S ENDING:
    Hollis & Carter (1950)
DARK ESTUARY:
    Hollis & Carter (1953)
THE AUTUMN ROAD TO THE ISLES:
    Nicholas Kaye (1959)
THE WHITE ROAD WESTWARDS:
    Nicholas Kaye (1961)
SEPTEMBER ROAD TO CAITHNESS:
    Nicholas Kaye (1962)
LEPUS THE BROWN HARE:
    Ernest Benn (1962)
SUMMER ROAD TO WALES:
    Nicholas Kaye (1964)
A SUMMER ON THE NENE:
    Kaye & Ward (1967)
LORD OF THE FOREST:
    Methuen (1975)
RECOLLECTIONS OF A 'LONGSHORE GUNNER:
    The Boydell Press (1976)
A CHILD ALONE – The Memoirs of 'BB'
    Michael Joseph (1978)
RAMBLINGS OF A SPORTSMAN-NATURALIST:
    Michael Joseph (1979)
THE NATURALIST'S BEDSIDE BOOK:
    Michael Joseph (1980)
THE QUIET FIELDS:
    Michael Joseph (1981)
INDIAN SUMMER:
    Michael Joseph (1984)

The publishers wish to specially thank Chris Coles for kindly allowing some original BB scraperboards in his ownership to be reproduced in this edition (pp. 19, 111, 159, 241, 251, 256, 258). Two of them, on pages 159 and 256 have probably not been reproduced in book form before.

Illustrations

Indented captions indicate small illustrations which appear between sections; all other captions refer to full-page illustrations.

For CC from 'BB'

'The wonder of the world, the beauty and
the power, the shapes of things, their colours,
lights, and shades; these I saw.
Look ye also while life lasts.'

From the Foreword to A Child Alone

I was born at a fortunate time in a beautiful home set in the heart of the country. Had I arrived on the scene a matter of five or ten years earlier I would not be writing this, which shows what a great gamble life is, and how grossly unfair is the fortune of birth. As a double bonus, for which I take no credit, I had two 'gifts': an ability to write, after a fashion, and to paint and draw, with a modest degree of skill. I cannot claim to have made the most of these gifts. With hindsight, I could have done a lot better, but they have enabled me to realise a few of my ambitions so I cannot grumble. I hope the reader will find things of interest in these recollections; I've certainly enjoyed writing them and that's the main thing.

Part One

A CHILD ALONE

The small boy in the big bed

I sometimes wish there were no such things as clocks to give audible reminder of the passing seconds and no such things as calendars or diaries. Then I remember the rising and setting of the sun is a measuring stick; each nightfall, a tick of the clock.

Youth, that glorious dawning does not notice time. We never gave it a thought, and rightly so. To the child, time is non-existent. It is only when we realise our own life must end that it takes on a new significance. That knowledge came as a terrible shock to me. I was seven or eight at the time, and for days a cloud hung over me which has never gone away completely. I have described this realisation in my book A Child Alone.

(From *THE QUIET FIELDS*)

1.

A CHILD ALONE

The small boy in the big bed was staring at the lighted candles on the dressing-table. The four flames were solemn spires of radiance, their pointed wavy tips were reflected on the backs of the brushes and silver fittings below the oval mirror.

In that seemingly vast room the ceiling was barely illuminated, dark shadows were thrown on the wall behind the dressing-table mirror. The boy could see the tall wooden shutters, which were fitted to all the principal rooms and closed by a black metal bar which fastened into a buttoned catch. Every night at dusk the under-housemaid made a tour of the house, closing those hinged shutters and, in the lower rooms, drawing the heavy velvet curtains.

There was a low stool in front of the dressing-table where his mother sat night and morning to comb her long dark hair – hair so long that she could sit upon it. This ritual brushing and combing was a constant source of interest to the small boy for it took some ten minutes to plait those long tresses in the morning and then to wind them cunningly round the top of the head. A 'fall' of dark hair at the back was left to last when it was back-combed and fastened into place with numerous pins. When she had married, her hair had been corn gold.

Alone now in the big room, the boy stared at the four motionless flames and he felt himself becoming afraid, dreadfully afraid, for he was going to die.

He was sorry about this. In his ten years of life he had found it a fascinating existence with new delights and surprises every day, and though he had been assured beyond all doubt that there was an infinitely more beautiful world awaiting him when he departed, the prospect was becoming increasingly alarming.

And the more he stared at those candle flames the greater his fear.

He had been ill and uncomfortable many times before with the usual complaints of babyhood and childhood – horrid colds in the head when he had been unable to breathe and his nose creaked and squeaked when he tried to breathe through it, irritating coughs which had kept him awake at night with exasperating tickles just when he was dropping off into dreamland.

There had been sore throats – really bad ones, for he had tonsils which were so large they almost met at the back of his throat and were liable to ulcerate every winter.

But this new menace was something much more disturbing and quite different. The first symptoms had begun early in the day, soon after breakfast – a little niggling pain in the middle of his stomach above the navel. He hadn't wanted his breakfast which was unusual for he was a good trencherman. As the day wore on, the pain became more insistent; he felt hot and muzzy in the head.

After tea, his mother put him to bed and took his temperature. The thermometer was put under his armpit and he was told to hold it there. After an interval, his mother took it to the dressing-table and held it close to the candle. He could see the candlelight shining through her hair on to her shoulder.

'Is it up?'

'Just a little, dear, nothing to worry about. I expect you caught a chill playing in the garden.' She looked again at the thermometer, shook it down against her hand, and went out of the room. He could hear her washing it under the tap in the bathroom, and then going down the front stairs.

That was some time ago. The room was very quiet now. The candle flames curtsied, a bead of wax dribbled over and ran down the side of a candlestick.

The boy remembered a story told him by his two brothers who were away at a prep school in Scotland. It concerned a boy called Peters who had died in the Autumn term, how everyone was told to keep very quiet when he was ill and how there had been a special service and prayers in the school chapel. Everyone prayed for Peters but it was no good.

Was he to be like Peters? Perhaps his father would hold a service in the church. The boy began to cry into the pillow – quietly to himself. He dared not look at the candles.

'What's the matter, dear?'

His mother had come quietly into the room. She stood by the bed, her cool hand on his forehead.

'I'm going to die!'

There was a moment's silence.

'Don't say such a thing, you silly boy. Of course, you're not going to die! What an idea!' She went swiftly from the room.

Then his father was there, the tall handsome man with black curly hair. He sat down on the bed – the boy felt it give to his weight. 'What's this nonsense about dying, Tuppeny?'

'I'm going to die, Father.'

'Of course, you're going to die; so is Mother, so am I, and Roger and Engel – we all have to die, but you are not going to, just yet. God has a lot of work for you to do. Tell me where the pain is.'

The boy took the big hand and laid it on the upper part of his stomach. 'There – just there.'

The big hand pressed gently. 'I will make it better. Can't you feel it getting better?'

Somehow the pain lessened. Tuppeny nodded glumly.

'No more nonsense about dying then. You'll be better in the morning and I'll ask Dr Winterbotham to come and have a look at you and he'll give you some medicine to put you right.'

When he had gone out of the room the pain came back, a nasty vicious pain. It was appendicitis which, at the beginning of this century, was a killer.

My life now, without companions in that large house, was depressing. All that February and March I looked forward to the coming of spring and the return of my brothers from Scotland.

Time to a child seems endless, an obvious statement but so true and so easily forgotten. I mooned about the gardens and played on the swing under the great cedar on the lawn.

This fine tree, planted when the house was built, was full of interest,

A child alone

beloved by birds as well as by me. In its lower spreading branches, supported and re-inforced by forked poles against the weight of winter snows, the small birds loved to build their nests: the golden crested wrens, their beautiful little hammock-fashioned nests almost as wonderful as the lichen-decorated nests of chaffinch and goldfinch, and in the dark interlacing crown high overhead, the wood-pigeons built each year, and soothed us with their cooings on summer mornings. Sometimes too, looking upwards as I swung to and fro, I saw a great striped tawny owl regarding me with bent head and huge melancholy eyes, an uncanny unbirdlike creature. Other birds seemed faceless, but the owl had a true face with the eyes to the front and a nose.

Tiring of the swing, I would go into the kitchen garden to talk to old Gunn the gardener, a bearded gnome-like fellow, the only male companion I had apart from my father, who was always too busy composing on the piano to play with me. Or I would go through the little iron gate which led to the orchard where Gunn kept his white geese. One awful day I went down to the orchard gate and all the geese lay dead, their big white motionless bodies strewn around on the green grass. No mark was upon them but Gunn, carrying out a post mortem, found the brilliant berries of the deadly nightshade in the gizzards.

As winter faded into that spring of 1914, I felt strong again and the prospect of the Easter holidays and the return of my brothers gave me a new zest for life. Green points showed on the rows of gooseberry bushes in the kitchen garden and in the lengthening twilights I heard my beloved blackbirds warbling quietly.

The memory of those dark hours so recently left behind, the pain and fear, was over. My brothers would soon be home and my loneliness be ended.

I used to come back from Rugby at weekends, gobble some supper, and sit down to write and write. The story unfolded with a strange and quite frightening intensity – I could not write fast enough, it was as though my hand was guided by an invisible driving force. Time was unimportant. I wrote on and on into the early hours of the morning – page after page.

Once the door of the morning-room opened. My father came in, in his dressing-gown, and wanted to know what I was doing. When I told him I was writing the story of a fox, he said I was wasting my time and that I should be in bed. 'Your work at Rugby will suffer if you go on like this. Anyway, nobody will publish it!'

I had no advance idea of how my story was to end, no plot whatsoever, but as each page was finished, the story seemed to write itself. I suppose I completed the book in a little under eight weeks – writing mostly at weekends and sometimes in my digs at Rugby. I had it typed professionally and, together with the reprints of my Shooting Man's Diary, I sent the manuscript off to David Higham, the London agent who had been recommended to me.

The weeks went by with no verdict from Eyre & Spottiswoode, the publishers to which my agent had sent the manuscripts. Then one day, Bob Dickens, the postman, brought me a letter with a London post-mark – a letter I have carefully preserved for it was to me like a gleam of light at the end of a long tunnel. My secret ambition to be a writer as well as artist seemed to be not so impossible after all.

The letter read as follows: 'Dear Sir, We have received your two manuscripts and if you would care to call at a date convenient to yourself, we may have something to offer you.'

Accordingly, I went up to London to the office of Eyre & Spottiswoode in Great New Street and was shown into the office of Douglas Jerrold and his colleague Mr Cave. To my utter astonishment, they told me that they would like to publish both manuscripts – first The Sportsman's Bedside Book and Wild Lone afterwards.

I was to do my own illustrations for Wild Lone. I promised them within a couple of months as the publishers wanted Wild Lone for their autumn list. I think I enjoyed doing the illustrations almost as much as the writing – for I seemed to live with Rufus in all his hunting and being hunted, his loves, and his enjoyment of his surroundings, his nights and days. I knew every field, spring, spinney and tree in the neighbourhood of Lamport, every rabbit run almost, so this was not difficult.

(From *A CHILD ALONE*)

2.

THE SPORTSMAN'S BEDSIDE BOOK

We had a splendid run yesterday from Gibbet wood, and after a hunt of an hour and five minutes ran into our fox near Miller's spinney, a point of six miles and a splendid line of country.

First... the meet on the village green, below the tall elms. The sun shining like an April morning and a bustle of cars and horse boxes, grooms and second horsemen, pink and white, black and white; as busy as an ant's nest under the trees. Across the road and the village green, blue shadows patterning, and a host of foot people, all moving hither and thither, laughing and chattering. High in the elm tops the twiggy bundles of the rooks' nests, and jackdaws busy about the holes as though they were contemplating nest building at mid-winter. Then comes the ring of hooves and the sound of hounds being called by name, and here they come with their huntsman, through the interlacing shadows; fleeting shadows that turn for a second the vivid pink of the huntsman's coat to a cool rose red. The hounds, friendly and nuzzling, cropped ears as soft as velvet to the touch. Orator I see, strong of loin and straight of back, with many a straight-necked fox to his credit, making acquaintance, in gentlemanly fashion, with a small child hardly a head taller than himself.

The waving sterns are like peeled willow wands through which the breeze is playing. Some hounds sit apart in contemplation, happily smiling to themselves. Others are scrounging on the chance of a tit-bit; and one, Emperor I think, but I cannot be sure from here, is investigating the roots of one of the elms, where he eventually leaves a note.

With every moment more riders come to swell the whirlpool of colour, this open green space is as busy as a springtime pond where frogs are spawning. For every road and lane is filled with horsemen,

Jogging to the meet

cars, and people, all converging to the same spot. The wheeling daws must have a wonderful view, circling in the sunlight, appearing like metal-clad birds as they turn. Below them this hub of changing colour and every radiating road dotted with people and cars, drawn by some mysterious impulse to the spot.

And then, still taking the wheeling jackdaws' view, a change comes about. The stream begins to flow down the village street (where, in the June evenings, the swifts scream past the thatched eaves), a stream narrow at the head, a pink spot at the fore, the waving sterns filling the lane from brim to brim, and then the mass of the field behind.

A mile away Gibbet wood dreams in a false security in the pale sunshine; a flock of wood-pigeons feeding in the green fields below is unaware of the approaching host. Within the wood the birds are going about their daily business and two 'hairies' are peacefully grazing near the rusty beech hedge, hair over eyes, and their sturdy legs, wide like sailors' trousers, matted with earth.

One of the wood-pigeons on the outskirts of the flock has raised its head, listening, and his white collar shows in the sunlight. The two hairies have likewise stopped their tearing of the grass and are waiting with ears a-cock by the side of the russet hedge.

High above Gibbet wood a kestrel is crucified against the soft blue of the sky. It wheels and slides away, downwards and slanting, for it sees the river flooding towards the wood. A ragged rascal of a magpie goes away, with wavering flight and backward glance over his white shoulder; Gibbet wood is uneasy this lovely morning.

Charles James slipped out from the north corner, where the crab apples lie rotting green in the ditch, and the hollow pipes of hemlock stand stiffly and sharp. And then hounds were running in the glorious morning, exultant and musical.

The pigeons fly away as a blue cloud of smoke drifts from a gun. I can see them now against the purple tones of the wood. Every gateway is a dam, holding for a fleeting minute, but unavailingly, the surging of the torrent. With the grace of sable swallows skimming a roof tree, some of the field take the beech hedge. One man on a big chestnut takes a nasty toss and rolls into the ditch, and for a moment lies with a horrid inertness, his horse galloping on with swinging stirrup and staring foolish eyes. The nearest horsemen wheel about and come to the figure, stirring now like a drunken insect in the ditch.

On, on past Dingle mill and the osier beds… rose-red in the sunlight – across the glittering Marly brook as it winds through intimate little meadows, oak studded and remote, haunts of otter and moorhen. Across the main road to the gorse on the hill and here there is a check of some minutes, and we fear he has gone to ground. But the earth was well stopped – Jim Corfield will get drunk on this – and so to the village of Hinton Hine with its squat little church sitting like a hen partridge on its nest, and the white-haired rector watching from the kitchen garden.

In the park behind we lost him for a space but he was 'halloaed' away by a roadman, and for the first time I saw the fox, muddy of brush and with hanging head, crossing, for an instant, a gap in a tall bullfinch. How strange that it is so seldom the majority of the field ever views the fox from start to finish! Led it seems by an invisible thread, the whole mass of the field is drawn along, over hill and down dale, as though they had gone completely mad.

The end was sad, and I saw it and was troubled. The main body of the pack were running down one side of the hedge when the fox doubled back. But Orator and two trusty henchmen had elected to go through to the other side and met the fox as it doubled. The fox saw the hounds running in at him, and slipped like a stoat through a gap between two stout laid thorns. And there he met his end, swiftly it is true, and gamely withal. The mass of hounds engulfed him and turned, then the sterns were waving in a ring and a minute later there floated back a trembling note of horn music.

Far away, by Gibbet wood, the hairies were again at graze, giving no thought for what had passed nor caring where the hunt had gone. The winter sward was poached and cut by the hoof marks of the host, gashes in the hedge and broken sticks showed where flying hooves had caught and blundered, and a big speckled thrush was pulling out a worm that had come up inside a hoof mark to see what all the thunder was about.

And the gentleman on the big chestnut, with his top hat over his ears, was drinking something out of a flask by Miller's spinney. His little finger was broken and it was painful.

Wild Lone *was now going into new editions and reprints. I began to get letters and visits from people who had found the story absorbing; some even visited the 'Rufus' country to trace the way he ran before the hounds and the woods he loved so well.*

To begin with, I was puzzled by this, but I think its attraction lay in the setting of the story and the feel of the seasons, the mists of autumn and the heats of summer.

In my tale, I had described the tragic loss of some of the Pytchley pack when they went through the ice at Fawsley Park – in pursuit of 'my' Rufus, of course. This actually happened, and a stone was erected in the park with the names of the drowned hounds engraved upon it. When Fawsley fell into decay, the stone was hidden in a tangled shrubbery but I found it and copied the names of the hounds from it.

Some years after the publication of Wild Lone, *an enthusiastic 'BB' fan discovered the stone and it is now erected by the huntsman's house at the Pytchley Kennels at Brixworth – a fitting last resting place.*

(From *A CHILD ALONE*)

3.
WILD LONE

Mid–October in Coldhanger… pearly mornings and mushrooms, dying hues of leaf and fern, mists coming up from the river, and longer nights for hunting! Rufus was well grown now; a lithe, clean-run fox without a trace of mange.

In the woodland rides the gold-red leaves lay deep, and with every sigh of air, more would tick and waver down as though loath to join the earth. Most beautiful of all were the pink, almost incandescent, fires of the sloe bushes, and the vivid autumn fungi that grew round the bases of the big trees.

The field maples flamed a lovely salmony orange; the exquisitely cut leaves, borne on the slender pinkish stems, seemed to mock the paintings of a Japanese artist, and the ditches were full to over-flowing with millions of such little beauties, each one a picture in itself. The trees that already showed their bare bones revealed also new and hidden loveliness, yet men went about this world and were blind to it all.

There was a new exciting mystery in the woods, too; nay, in every little spinney, wherever trees gathered together. The lower veils of foliage had not yet dropped, but let through the light in a magical way, and the earth, strewn with the damp fresh-fallen leaves, took on a new smell, sweeter far than the rarest incense. This rusty wealth and range of colour blended with an enchanting rareness the hues of the fox's coat as he padded about his secret ways.

To a black pool in the centre of the woods, some wild duck came in the evenings. The pool was not deep, though it appeared so because the water was so dark and peaty-looking, due to unburdening of many autumns such as this, generations of trees shedding their leaves into its mirror. To this pool came a drake mallard, a duck and three young-sters born in April by Wildwood pool, four miles away across the

17

fields. Every evening, when the smoke from the cottage chimneys was sending up soft blue signals, they circled the wood and came in to this dark water, and Rufus knew of this arrangement. For three nights he had lain in the dying brambles close to the water's edge at the upper end of the pond. From this ambush he had caught moorhens, young ones, as they quested about on the black evil-smelling ooze, in which a bullock would have sunk to his middle.

On the fourth night Rufus went again and hid in his favourite ambush. For a long while nothing came but a cock bullfinch that had been piping in the maple bushes, and he came for a sip before going to bed. He was a lovely little bird, with a breast the colour of some of the hawthorn leaves and a cap as blue as a crow's wing. 'Wit, Wit!' he flew up again, and only his white rump was visible as he flew away through the dark thickets.

'Hoo, hoo, hoohoo!' the owls awoke, mothy and with mothy eyes, birds of the touchwood and the night.

A wee mouse rustled, ever so quietly, making no more sound than a little brown sprite, but Rufus heard it and his eyes took on a watchful expression and both ears cocked right forward. He sat up slowly with bent head, staring through the veil of bramble leaves to where the maple bushes formed a fairy screen. But the mouse disappeared, and the fox lay down again and resumed his watch on the pond.

Whenever the shadows began to fall in the woods, the blackbirds made much bother, zinking like a pair of rusty shears.

Sometimes they had cause for alarm, especially when the owls awoke. There was nothing they liked more than teasing the owls awoke. There was nothing they liked more than teasing the owls, and they drove the poor big-headed things to distraction.

All kinds of sounds came to Rufus as he lay under the brambles, and all manner of smells, all far beyond the range of human ear and nose. He could smell a rabbit that was hopping along beyond a fallen tree-trunk on the other side of the pond; he could smell the yellow-lipped sinister fungi that grew on the underside of the fallen tree. He could recognise a moorhen scent coming from the rushes on his right, and a dead water-rat was lying on the edge of the mud, where a little trickle of water fed the pool. He could smell other things, the scents of different plants and

Bullfinch

trees, and he sorted them all out with a twitch of his nose.

He could hear a beast scratching itself against a rubbing post outside the wood (the post was all shiny on one side and had given pleasure to countless tough hides now long perished) and the men talking over their spades in the village allotments right on the other side of the hill.

And all about there was a pattering, as of little furtive feet. This was the sound of the falling leaves, millions of them, falling all over the wood in a ceaseless flurry of yellow and amber snow. Whenever a breath of wind came over the hill the rustling would grow, and it sounded as if fairy armies were on the march. This pattering would have made a man uneasy if he had lain there long, but Rufus knew them for lifeless things.

Far singing came to him. It was a party of cyclists on the Harboro' road. They were bent over their handlebars with eyes fixed on the ground, blind to all beauty of earth and sky. They were singing a sexy American jazz song, 'D'you love your baby like I love ma baby, or do you simply say, Meet me at twilight, little Miss Eyebright, then that'll be OK.' One of the cyclists was a beefy girl, and her bare lobster-tinted thighs worked like pistons. How could they guess a little red fox heard them, as he lay under the pink bramble leaves by a wood pool!

The sounds died away, and then a cow began to call, a faint horn-like sound like a man calling a moose.

Across the pool a big white owl suddenly flew, quite silently, and two blackbirds chased it. One, in its excitement, let fall a white spot into the water and the consequent rings took quite a minute to subside. Losing their quarry, the excited blackbirds came back into the holly tree close by, and one of them, dropping to the leaves for a moment, saw this new enemy. For a minute it sat there, tail slightly up and its privetberry eye fixed on the fox. Then, with a scream, 'zink, zink, zink,' it flew up into the tree and the other blackbird saw the fox as well. Both birds hopped low in the holly, scolding and shaking the leaves. Before very long, a missel-thrush – a big handsome masculine bird, that feared no man nor beast, and who built in the most absurdly naked positions with such infinite scorn – came and joined the blackbirds, and his long, drawn-out rasping call was louder than the blackbirds'. As Rufus showed no sign of life they soon went away. There was no fun in teasing a thing that would not move, and perhaps the fox was dead.

'Whi, whi, whi, whi,' the sound of pinions circling! Rufus became alert, his eyes glowing and tail twitching ever so slightly. The circling mallards kept on coming round and round past the holly, trying to make up their minds to land. With exasperating indecision they kept this up for two minutes; then the drake, feeling perhaps a little tired of the business, landed with a splash in mid-pond. Immediately he turned round, backing water, his neck very straight and rigid, and a semi-smile on his face, which was not really a smile at all. The other mallards immediately landed, too, and for a full minute they took stock of their surroundings. Then they began to swim slowly about, preening, questing the weeds and mud, and feeling more and more at home. But they did not come near the holly.

In the centre of the pond was a stump of a tree, very green because fresh grass was sprouting on it, and the edge of the stump was quite shiny, trodden by the feet of resting waterfowl. A few grey feathers were there too; it was an ideal preening place. The drake mallard climbed on to this with sturdy greenish-yellow legs, the colour of the rushes, and stretching his head right out and raising the feathers on his head he gave himself a good shake, just as a farmyard duck will do. Several small feathers dropped out of his person. He preened carefully, first his madder breast and then his tail, twisting round and pulling at his white outer tail-feathers.

Rufus drinking in the woods

There drifted across to Rufus the most appetising smell of wild duck and with every exertion of the preening mallard this scent seemed redoubled. It was agony for Rufus. He was ravenous, and he felt much as a hungry man would feel if a steaming turkey were put before him, and he were unable to touch it. The saliva dribbled out of the corner of his mouth, but he never moved. After a lengthy toilet, the mallard pushed off into the pond, passing some remarks in a low, watery voice to his duck. They swam about together, throwing the beads of moisture over their backs with evident abandon. But they did not come near the holly.

In the water was the reflection of a star, and soon a wondrous thing appeared. Over the tops of the thick crowding trees, rose a misty glow, and soon the moon, red and large, swam clear – the Hunter's Moon. It was reflected in the water, not as a whole, but in little shaking pieces as the ducks swam about.

Rufus was puzzled at this light and was at first a little nervous, but he soon thought of nothing but 'duck' again, and how to capture one. The young mallards now landed on the muddy margin of the pond and began to waddle about, and soon the old birds joined them. But they did not come near the holly.

Suddenly all heads were lifted, fox and ducks alike. Something was coming up to the pond, for a stick had cracked. It was some lumbering person who did not care a damn how much noise he made. The mallard sprang into the air, 'quacking, quacking,' and Rufus heard their voices die away over the wood. The old boar badger came through the bushes, and drank noisily at the pond. Rufus discreetly went over the bank and trotted down through the blackthorn thickets. He left the cover of Coldhangar, and went over the Market Harboro'-Leicester road, heading for Old Poors Gorse.

This was a paradise for foxes; indeed, as far as Rufus was concerned, too much so, as the place was full of them, mostly youngsters of the year. Acres of impenetrable thorn, beloved by the bullfinch and nightingale, and, in season, starred with tender dog-roses and sweet honeysuckle; it was a wilderness of joy. Rare birds, too, were found there, and the red-backed shrike impaled his beetles on the sharp thorns. The great round moon, now no longer red-faced, was clear and bright, and in the

Rufus went along at an easy lope

hollows, the mist lay like dense white blankets, cutting off cleanly at the base all herbage that was of any height.

Rufus went along at an easy swinging lope, crossing the metals above Lamport station, and stopping for a moment to gaze at the light of the distant signal. In the signal box Robertson was reading the account of a gentleman who had won four thousand pounds in a 'penny pool', and his brain reeled at the idea of such wealth. It was cosy in the cabin, and an alarm clock ticked loudly. Below, behind the 'Box,' he kept his fowls, white leghorns, which were the apple of his eye. He had housed them in an old rabbit hutch, until what time he could get some more wood to make them a better home. Rufus, two hundred yards up the line, smelt FOWL, and he came to investigate. The sight of the lighted signal cabin alarmed him, but after watching a while and finding all was still, he came up to the fowl-house.

The smell of fowl was strong and Rufus was very hungry. Moreover, he had missed the duck up in Coldhangar, and he had grown somewhat rash. He began to dig under the wall of the coop, sending the earth back between his legs. Some of the fowls awoke and began to make remarks. Rufus dug on until he could get his head into the hole. The hens began to complain querulously....

Up in the cabin Robertson was nodding by the stove. The paper lay on the floor, and a mouse was eating the canary seed under the hanging cage. The moon shone white on the slated roof of the signal box... and down below, something was digging in the inky shadow. Rufus was definitely 'getting on'. He could now get his shoulders into the hole, between the edge of the wood and the chicken-saturated earth. One final squeeze and he was inside. A second to look round and then... In an instant, pandemonium. Fluttering hens, screams and clucks, white bodies banging and bustling. Rufus seized the nearest hen by the neck, and squeezed under the edge of the wood. The hen proclaimed loudly, and vehemently, and Mr Robertson heard.

In the corner of the Box he kept a 'four-ten', which he used for shooting rats and sparrows that came to raid the chicken run for corn. He seized the gun and rammed a cartridge home, then he flung wide the door. In the moonlight he saw a trail of white feathers leading to the hedge, and something like a brown shadow with a white flapping head was moving by the fence.

BANG! A little cone of red flame jetted against the tarred wall of the signal box, and a singing cloud of lead rattled about Rufus. One pellet stung him on the bottom, and he dropped the fowl and fled up the rails.

Inside the fowl-house there was great to-do, and some of the leghorns were still banging about hysterically.

Rufus followed the railway until he came to the distant signal, then cut across the Draughton fields for Shortwood, still hungry and with injured pride. Passing a flock of sheep, that all bunched and first ran away, and then came trotting after, he went over the wide, rolling fields of Wold. He put up a hare on top of the wolds, but after chasing for a few yards, resumed his trail. A fox will not course his game for any distance. He came to deserted Faxton, the lonely forgotten village in the fields, with its jackdaw-haunted elms and owl-ridden belfry. It lay ghostly in the moonlight, and some black-and-white cattle were rubbing themselves against the posts round the churchyard wall. In a rough, ant-hill-strewn field beyond, he stalked a watchful peewit. This was a great field for them, and in the spring they bred there, but they were very hard to catch. In the moonlight he had not got a chance, and the bird arose 'pee-weeing' keenly, and waking others which were encamped among the ant-hills. He entered Old Poors Gorse and hunted it all through without result. But near the hedge he found a rabbit in a snare, partly eaten. This he devoured and, as dawn was greying, he laid up in a dense thicket of blackthorn and went to sleep....

I had lessons each day from my father – arithmetic, Latin (quite useless), some French and history, and twice a week in summer, I went to the house of Mr Abbott, the village schoolmaster, who lived in a little cottage beyond some turkey oak trees in the village of Hanging Houghton.

Mr Abbott was a big man from Derbyshire with a very precise way of speaking – a mannerism which fascinated me. He wrote a fine longhand, like a bank clerk's. He gave me a book on the English countryside illustrated by coloured pictures – one of which I copied, a picture of an open-air market. He paid me seven and sixpence for it – my first commission. It was quite a good copy too. I had already begun to show signs of artistic talent. Both my father and mother could draw well and much of my time was spent with brush and pencil. But most of all I loved to get away, rambling about the fields around the rectory. My favourite walk was beside the fishponds which were visible from the windows of the house.

Of all the most favoured haunts for me were the three pools, the fishponds, in the valley below the house. I have written of them in The Countryman's Bedside Book.

(From *A CHILD ALONE*)

4.

THE COUNTRYMAN'S BEDSIDE BOOK

I stood tonight at the top of the little marsh on my shoot, waiting for duck.

The long hot summer is over, many of the bushes were beginning to turn colour and a few pale slivers had dropped on to the boggy margin of the brook, others had fallen in and been carried away downstream. The dry weather has shrunk the water courses and most of the field ponds are dry. As I waited there I thought of all the sunshiny hours we have had during the last twelve weeks and how the glorious rays must have poured on to this quiet little backwater in the meadows. There was a strand of sheep's wool caught on the wire of the fence and above it leaned a twisted crab tree laden with fruit, bright green apples, some of them blushing a clear pink on the side which had faced the sun. A great many had fallen into the ditch and had rolled together into a solid mass so that from a distance they showed up very distinctly. What a pity it is that the crab is so sour to the taste. I picked one of the red apples and bit it, surely with that red skin it must be sweet! Yet its juices dried up my mouth, though there was a wild tang about it which was not unpleasant.

Out in the mead, about forty yards from the hedge, grows a may tree. Like the crab it leans at an angle and the ground beneath is bare of grass, rammed hard by the feet of cattle and horses, quite a little hollow sunk below the level of the surrounding sward.

On examination the trunk has a definite gloss on one side and the tough bark is badly worn, polished like an old gunstock from constant friction of rubbing beasts. This tree is a natural 'cow comfort', which is the rustic name for trees and posts used by cattle. Here and there a few wisps of coarse hair are caught in the crevices of the bark and the chaffinches will hunt these out next spring. Horsehair is a favourite nest lining for many birds.

On the hot days the cattle stand for hours at a time beneath the tree, rubbing their hairy flanks against the iron-barked stem. How did this tree grow and survive, out in the open field, why was it not bitten off in its early years by cattle and sheep? A few of its upper leaves are now a beautiful rose red, later all will drop and collect in the hollow beneath and the fieldfares will come for the red berries.

All summer long the wind has whispered in the leaves of the willow, it has rustled the tall poplars yonder and the bright brooklet has chuckled onwards, every hour, every day, every year, on its journey to the remote sea.

What millions of gallons must have flowed away, a whole ocean of water. Whence came it? Surely not from the condensation of the clouds, all those tons and tons of water! There is no high ground about here, no lofty hill which would attract the rain and break the clouds.

Not so long ago the cuckoo's chime was ringing from coppice to hedge and all the meads were white with hawthorn snow; shy warblers swung on the willow wands, timorous moorhens have quested along the boggy margin of the brook, whitethroats have built in the nettle brake by the fence gap. There has been nobody to see, only the clouds have gone over and perhaps a passing shower pattered in the night.

This quiet angle of the meadow was a beautiful place, untidily perfect after Nature's own way. What a jolly time the water voles must have had, plopping in and out among the sturdy sedge swords whose sharp edges can cut the incautious hand! The wild iris have bloomed in their season and no-one has come to gather them; wild animals, little wild animals, have come to drink in the grey before the dawn.

Swallows and martins have come, gathering plaster for their homes built in shed and under eave, walking awkwardly on their puny feathered feet, flying away with wee balls of mud in their bills, twittering happily despite the fact of their mouths being so full.

So, thought I, must there be untold millions of little meadows such as this all over the kingdom where nobody comes near all summer long, save birdnesting boys of a Sunday.

The field pond

Now the warblers have gone and the leaves are going, the autumn dusk steals down the valley and the sun sinks low.

Whatever man can do so will it always be; this stream will run onwards to the sea, the simple plovers camp on yonder rushy slope. Peace here always and the passionless march of the years will go on.

I went back to see if the stream* had changed much. It flowed as strongly as ever, looping on itself with its bays and re-entrants, its purling shillets, its deep brown pools. The old oak was still there with the dark and shadowed hollows under its roots where the spring and autumn floods had washed away the soil and gravel.

Surely, if gnomes there be, here was their dwelling place! Here they lived unseen, unknown, more wary than any four-legged or two-legged creature, never showing themselves to mortal gaze, only to their wild neighbours which were their kinsmen.

So I thought up a story of four little creatures, Sneezewort, Dodder, Cloud-berry and Baldmoney who lived under that oak and how, years before, Cloud-berry, the restless, more adventurous gnome, had gone up the Folly Brook to find its source, and had never come back. Then his brothers decide to go in search of him. It was an unusual fairy story – a fairy story without any hint of the 'tinsel fairy' rubbish which is only fit for toddlers. The sturdy self-sufficient little men hunt for game, eat fish, and make their coats from moleskins.

I did all the illustrations for the book, which I called The Little Grey Men, *with decorated capitals to the chapters and heads and tails.*

Shortly after it appeared in 1942, I was dumbfounded one day at Rugby to have a note from the Headmaster complimenting me on winning the Carnegie Medal, which is awarded for the most outstanding children's book of the year. This was the first I heard of the award; Hugh Lyon must have seen the announcement in the Press. I had to go up to London to receive the award and make a speech to the large assembled audience, an ordeal I was glad to get over with.

(From *A CHILD ALONE*)

**The Nene Brook at Lamport*

5.

THE LITTLE GREY MEN

It was one of those days at the tail end of the winter when spring, in some subtle way, announced its presence. The hedges were still purple and bristly, the fields bleached and bitten, full of quarrelling starling flocks; but there was no doubt about it, the winter was virtually over and done with for another seven months. The great tide was on the turn, to creep so slowly at first and then to rise ever higher to culminate in the glorious flood, the top of the tide, at midsummer.

Think of it! All that power, all those millions of leaves, those extra inches to be added to bushes, trees, and flowers. It was all there under the earth, though you would never have guessed it.

After a soft grey morning, the sun had slowly broken through the clouds, and every blackbird and thrush in Lucking's Meadow began to warble and tune up; the first opening bars of a great symphony in praise of Life.

The willow bush by the Folly brook showed silver buttons up every slender wand and on the rough grey bark of the leaning oak tree on the other side of the pool three sleepy flies were sidling about, enjoying the warm rays.

At this spot, for some reason known only to itself, the Folly brook turned at a right angle.

Beneath the oak the water had washed away the sandy bank, and many winter floods had laid bare some of the massive hawser roots which projected in a twisted tangle from the soil of the bank. The sun, shining full on the steep bluff, threw shadows from the overhanging roots, so that underneath all was darkness.

Close to the margin of the glittering water, there was a miniature beach of coloured shingle and white sand; and from the glare on the stream, wavering bars of reflected light played to and fro on the bulging trunk of the oak. These light bars moved up and down in ripples, fading away when the sun was dimmed for an instant by a passing cloud.

It had been a dry winter and the Folly brook was running fresh and clear, higher than in summer, of course, but quite undimmed by flood-cloud. It was so clear that near the beach every stone and pebble on the bottom could be seen, though where the water was deeper, all was tawny obscurity, the colour of ripe old ale.

Near the bank, the tangled reeds were as white as bleached bone, though if you had looked more closely, sharp green sword points could have been seen just beginning to pierce the dead vegetation. Later these reeds formed a deep green thicket, the strong juicy blades growing so close together that only a water-vole could slip between. The bank on the side opposite to the oak shelved gradually to the water's edge, and here Farmer Lucking's cattle came to drink. They had poached and punched the soil at the 'marge' until it was in an awful mess and the grass for some way up the bank was quite worn away. But in the stream itself there was little mud, for the bottom was hard sand and shingle. Most of the mud which the heavy stolid beasts had collected to their knees was soon washed off by the current if they stood long enough in the stream.

Something moved in the shadow under the root. At first you might have thought it was a water-rat or a mouse; then, if you had waited long enough, keeping very still (for the Little People usually know when any mortal is about) you might have been lucky enough to see Baldmoney. He came out from under the root very slowly, peeping first one way and then another, listening.

Up among the silver willow studs swung a tit, a beautiful little sprite splashed with a blue as azure as the patch of spring sky above.

'Tit tee, tit tee, tit tee!'

It was the 'all clear' for Baldmoney. The little man ran, like a mouse, out on to the coloured shingle.

You must remember that Baldmoney and his brothers were (as far as I know) the last gnomes left in England. Rather surprisingly, he was extraordinarily like the pictures of gnomes in fairy books, even to the pointed skin hat and long beard. He wore a short coat and waistcoat of mouse-skin with a strip of snake-skin round his middle; moleskin breeches tied in below the knee, but no shoes or stockings. He had no need of these, for gnomes are hairy little folk; in summer time they sometimes dispense with clothes altogether. Their bodies are not naked like ours, but clothed in long hair, and as to their feet, if you had not worn boots or shoes since you were born, you would have no need of them either. He carried a hunting knife in his belt, made of hammered iron, part of an old hinge which he had found in the stream.

Bluebutton, the bluetit, flipped down, leaflike, to the lowest wand of the willow which projected a little way over the pool and watched the gnome with his beady eye.

'Well, Bluebutton, it's good to see you again; what sort of winter have you had?'

'Not too bad, Baldmoney,' replied the tit, hopping about among the soft willow buds.

Before I proceed I must tell you that of course the wild things did not talk to the gnomes in our language. They had one of their own which the gnomes understood. Naturally in this book I have made them talk in our language, otherwise you would not make head or tail of what they were saying.

'And your wife, Bluebutton, how is she?'

Here the bluetit looked very sorrowful. He said nothing.

'Oh, I'm sorry, Bluebutton, so sorry,' said Baldmoney sympathetically. 'I know, it has been a terrible winter, one of the worst since we've been on the stream… poor, poor Bluebutton. Never mind,' he added lightly, 'spring is here again, think what that means, plenty of food, no more frost and… and… you must find another wife. After all, you've still got your children.'

But Bluebutton would not be comforted and indeed was so overcome with grief that he could stay no longer, but flew away up the Folly brook.

Baldmoney sat down in the sun. It was warm on the shingle, and he found his mouse-skin waistcoat irksome, so he took it off and hung it on an old withered stalk of beaked hedge-parsley that grew out of the bank nearby.

His little red face, the colour of an old hip berry, was puckered and

34

creased like the palm of a monkey's hand. His whiskers were whitish grey, the beard hanging down almost to his middle. The tiny hands with their grubby nails were like moles' hands, though smaller. Gnomes have large hands for their size, larger in comparison with those of a mortal. His ears were long, sharply pointed, and covered with silky hair. After sitting a minute or two on the smooth stones he half turned round, looking towards the root. 'Come on, you two, it's lovely out here in the sun… wake up, spring is here again.'

Two more gnomes immediately emerged; one, Sneezewort, rubbing his eyes, the other, Dodder, blinking in the strong sun. Sneezewort, the youngest, was a little shorter than Baldmoney and was also clad in a mouse-skin coat and moleskin breeches, though, strange to say, he was without whiskers, which is unusual in a gnome. For some reason nobody could ever understand (by 'nobody' I do not mean people like you and me, but the animals, birds and the Stream People generally) Sneezewort had never grown whiskers. It was not because he shaved, for no gnome would think of doing such a thing. Beards keep you warm in the winter. As I say, nobody knew why he had never grown whiskers, not even Sneezewort himself. But his round little face was just as red and puckered as Baldmoney's, and in some ways he looked older for he had lost most of his teeth and gnomes don't know how to make false teeth.

Dodder, the eldest and wisest of the three, was the shortest in stature, but that was because he had a wooden leg. It was a very cleverly designed leg made out of an acorn cup into which the leg stump fitted neatly, with a stout thorn twig morticed firmly into the outside end. The trouble was that this leg was always wearing out and in the summer-time poor Dodder had to make a new one every month. His beard was a beauty, it hung below his belt, almost to his knees, and would have been snow white if he had not dyed it with walnut juice, for white beards would be too conspicuous, and that would never do. Secrecy was of utmost importance, especially in these modern days when discovery would mean the end of everything. Why these little creatures had survived for so long is puzzling, because, though they lived in this rural country-side, it was by no means 'wild' in the sense that some parts of Devon and Cornwall are wild, and there are, to my knowledge, no gnomes left now in either of these last two localities, though I understand they are still to be found in some parts of Ireland.

Perhaps the reason is that nobody in their senses (and only a few out of them) would dream of looking for a gnome in Warwickshire, a country intersected in all directions by roads and railways, with modern villas and towns everywhere.

Unlike the others, Dodder wore a coat and breeches of batskin, with the ears left on. He drew this almost over his head in cold weather, so that he looked like a very curious elongated bat without wings. He always maintained that batskins were more supple than those of mice, and allowed greater freedom of movement.

As soon as he joined Sneezewort and Baldmoney he sat down and took off his wooden leg, laying it on the shingle beside him.

'I shall have to make another leg, Baldmoney,' he said in a sorrowful voice, 'this peg is wearing out and I shall want another one now the spring is coming. I do wish I could find something that would wear better.'

Baldmoney took up the leg and examined the end, rubbing his beard and puckering his already wrinkled forehead until his eyes seemed to disappear.

'I believe we could find something better. I'll ask the King of Fishers.'

Just at that moment, as if in answer to a prayer, a streak of flashing blue darted round the bend of the stream and a kingfisher came to rest just above their heads on a branch of the oak tree, close to five little round oak-apples.

The gorgeous bird glanced below him with side-cocked head, and every now and then bobbed up and down, gulping something.

'Our respects, your Majesty,' said Baldmoney humbly (he always seemed to be the spokesman of the party); 'you're just the one we wanted to see. Brother Dodder here requires a new leg of more durable stuff than thorn. What can you suggest, humbly begging your pardon?'

But for a moment or two the kingfisher could not reply for the very good reason he had just swallowed six sticklebacks and his gullet was crammed.

The gnome waited politely for him to digest his meal, and at last he spoke. 'Wood is no good, it's bone you want. What I don't know about bone isn't worth knowing, seeing that we build our nests of them.'

The gnomes remained silent for they knew kingfishers' nests of old; did not they have to hold their noses every time they passed them? Kingfishers are filthy birds in their nesting habits, and it was always a source of utmost amazement that such gorgeous and kingly beings could be so dirty. Why kingfishers possess such lovely plumage, the most lovely of any British bird, is another story.

'That's an idea,' said Dodder; 'I never thought of bone.'

'Fishbone isn't tough enough,' said the kingfisher; 'I'll keep a look out and bring you something stronger.'

Lulled by the music of the babbling stream, all sat silent for a space. Just above the bend it ran over the shillets, creased and full of broken sky reflections. It was so shallow there that the gnomes could wade across, but it soon deepened and ran smooth and polished into the sherry-brown deeps under the oak root.

'Well, your Majesty, and how goes the fishing?' asked one of the gnomes.

'Rotten, never had worse, though it's better up above Moss Mill. But the miller's brats catch a lot – they're at it all day long. One of them tried to hit me with a stone from his catapult yesterday. You'll be starting fishing soon, I suppose? Excuse me...' (and here the kingfisher made rather a rude noise in his throat, for his meal was not yet quite digested). 'Yes,' said Dodder, politely pretending not to notice, 'I shall be starting soon, but we've fished the stream out about here, and that's the truth. The minnows and sticklebacks don't seem to run up as far as they used to. I don't know what we shall do now that the tar is coming in off the new road. Beastly stuff, it kills the fish. It was bad enough when they used to dip the sheep up above Moss Mill. The poison killed off several gnomes when they began it, that was many Cuckoo summers ago, before your Majesty was born. Do you remember that, Sneezewort?' But the little gnome did not reply, he was gazing wistfully upstream. 'He's thinking of poor Cloudberry, our lost brother, you know,' said Baldmoney in an undertone to the kingfisher. 'Cloudberry went up the stream to find the Folly Source and never came back. That's months ago now,' Baldmoney sighed, and they all sighed. For a space there was nothing but the undertone of the brook, and the wind in the trees.

'Did you ever go to look for him, Baldmoney?' the kingfisher asked, glancing down at the three sorrowful little gnomes sitting below him on the shingle. 'Yes,' whispered Baldmoney, 'we went upstream below Moss Mill and Joppa but we could find no trace. The water-voles said they saw him up above the mill, but nobody saw him after that. Your Majesty's father saw him too, walking through the Dock forest by Lucking's water meadows, but nobody else could help us. Your Majesty's father went all the way to the wood of Giant Grum, but could not find him.' 'Perhaps Giant Grum saw him, though,' said the kingfisher darkly; 'there's been a Giant Grum in Crow Wood for years. He tried to shoot me once, but missed, and I give the place a wide berth now, though the fishing's the best in the stream.' 'Have you ever been right up, beyond the wood?' asked Baldmoney in an awed voice.

'No, not right up. Beyond Crow Wood is the Big Sea and an Island, and then the Folly gets very narrow, and the fishing's poor; it goes on for miles and miles. Perhaps I will go one day, though.'

Baldmoney sighed again. 'I wish I had wings like your Majesty, then I could go right up to the Birth of the Folly. Our people have always wanted to go, but it's such a long weary way, and our legs are so small.'

The sun had gone in and the wind began to rise, ruffling the water. Baldmoney reached for his waistcoat and put it on and Dodder strapped on his wooden leg again.

'Well,' said the kingfisher, shaking himself, 'I must be off; my wife is downstream somewhere. I won't forget your leg, Dodder,' and with a flick he left the branch and arrowed away like a blue bolt across the angle of the meadow.

The three gnomes, left alone, began to collect some dead twigs from under the bank. It would be cold when the sun went down. Baldmoney went up the shingle to search for flints, and the others crept back into the shadow of the root, carrying their fuel with them.

Lucking's cows came trooping across the meadow in a long line on their way to the ford. They waded in, the water dribbling from their mouths, their pale-lashed eyes gazing stupidly at the current as they sucked in long draughts.

Baldmoney came back along the shingle carrying a dead branch. The cows saw him but paid no heed. They went on sucking in long draughts of cold water and the mudsmoke rolled away from their huge hairy legs, dimming the clear stream. They had seen the gnomes many times and took no more notice of them than if they had been water-voles. Why should they? For all wild creatures were the same to them. After all, the little wild people *are* fairies and gnomes; birds and beasts alike.

As each one finished drinking it stood for a moment or two with dribbling mouth and then wheeled round, hoisting itself up the bank and wandering off into the pasture, where it began noisily to crop the grass.

When Baldmoney entered the hollow under the oak root he pulled the branch in after him. Though it was only sixteen inches long it was all he could manage.

There was quite a large space of trampled sand under the root (in the high floods of winter the water sometimes came right up to the door of their house). This door was not more than eight inches high but excessively thick. It was part of an old Sunlight soap box that had been washed down the stream years before and it had taken the gnomes many weeks to cut through with the blade of a pocket knife which belonged to Cloudberry. He had found the knife in the Willow Meadow below Moss Mill, and when he went away he had taken it with him. The hinges of the door were made of wire, filched from a fencing post. Holes had been bored in the door and the wire passed through and the whole contraption was hinged to the living root of the oak.

Baldmoney broke up the stick as well as he could and, shouldering the bundle, opened the door and passed inside, shutting it behind him. Before him the earth sloped upwards between two cheeks of oak root through which he had to squeeze, and beyond he found himself in the actual living space. This was cosy enough and gave them ample room, for under the root there was a great chamber, fully three feet across. The floor was lined with dried rush, gathered from the stream, and the smoke from the gnomes' fire went right up inside the tree, coming out through a knothole in the top.

39

When their fire was burning there was only a filmy thread of smoke, but they took the wise precaution of never lighting it save on a windy night when the smoke would not be noticed, or during bad weather when people would be indoors. On calm nights when there was no breeze, even the tiniest wisp might have been observed by any mortal outside.

As it was a windy evening the gnomes had a good blaze burning and the ruddy light of the flames lit up the interior of the tree, throwing dark shadows everywhere. Looking upwards, a tiny point of dim light was seen where the tree was open to the sky.

Sneezewort was seated cross-legged, making fish-hooks out of a mouse's bone, Dodder was slitting the stomach of a fat minnow. He had seven other little fish in a pile beside him. When all were cleaned he hung them in a row in the smoke from the fire to kipper them. Baldmoney flung down the faggots and stacked them neatly at the side of the cave.

They all worked without speaking, each at his own job. Dodder, owing to his wooden leg, was the chief fisherman of the three, and he was also the cook, and no mean cook either, as he often said. Certainly his kippered minnow and beechnut girdle cakes were *very* good indeed.

After a meal, taken in silence round the fire, the gnomes lay down, each snuggling into his moleskin sleeping bag. They lay gazing at the embers which now smouldered redly. The wind was rising outside and they heard Ben the owl leave the tree and go a-hunting. It was Ben who provided them with skins, as many as they wanted, for gnomes do not kill warm-blooded things save in self-defence; all birds and animals with the exception of stoats and foxes (wood dogs, as the gnomes called the latter) were their friends.

For a while nobody said a word; they lay stretched out under their moleskins, their tiny eyes glowing like moths' eyes in the red glow of the dying fire. At last Baldmoney spoke.

'I've been thinking over what the King of Fishers was saying about going up the stream and looking for Cloudberry. Well, why shouldn't we? We've got the whole summer for the trip and can get back here before the fall of the leaf. I don't see why we shouldn't try it.' Nobody replied, indeed the other two were so silent that Baldmoney thought

Baldmoney carries firewood into Oak Tree House

they must be asleep. But on looking at his companions he saw their eyes as brilliant points in the dusky interior of the cave.

Diamonds flashed from Sneezewort's eyes for he was weeping silently. Of the three gnomes he was the most easily moved and Cloudberry had been his favourite brother. At last Dodder burst out, rather irritably.

'You know, Baldmoney, you're as bad as Cloudberry, always restless, always wanting to leave the Folly and find a better place, always talking, like poor Cloudberry, of the Folly Source. We should never find him or meet any other gnomes up the stream who could help us. The fishing is poor here I know, but we still get enough to eat and the oak has been a good friend to us. Besides, what about my leg? I can't go with you. Still,' he added in an injured tone, 'leave me behind, I don't care. I shall be all right, but if you never came back, like poor Cloudberry, I should be all alone, but... I suppose I could manage very well by myself,' and he sniffed in an aggrieved way.

'Oh, we shouldn't leave you, Dodder, you'd have to come with us, wouldn't he, Sneezewort?'

'I'll go, Baldmoney, if Dodder comes. I've always wanted to go up the stream to find Cloudberry, always...'

There was a short silence again; the wind piped in the shadowy cavern above and sang a song in the twisted branches of the old tree.

Dodder growled, 'Absurd, it's sheer stupidity, and we will never come home again. How can we go all that way? Why, it takes us hours to reach Moss Mill!'

'Ah, but I've been thinking,' said Baldmoney, 'thinking a lot just lately. Why shouldn't we build a boat, not a fishing boat (they used coracles made of frogs' skins stretched over a withy frame, Indian-wise), but a proper boat with paddles. I've got it all planned out in my mind.'

Dodder snorted angrily.

'And do you suppose, my dear Baldmoney, that we could ever paddle against the current of the Folly? Why, it's all we can do now to manage our fishing boats!'

'Well, I think we could in *my* boat,' observed Baldmoney. 'I've got it all planned out. At any rate we could manage in the smooth reaches and we might carry it over the rapids, like the Dartmoor gnomes used to do in the old days, in the country of Running Waters.'

'I've got a better idea than that,' broke in Sneezewort. 'Let's get Watervole to tow us up the rough water, or if he won't, Otter would.'

'What a splendid notion, Otter and Watervole! They'll help us; why, they might take us right up to the Folly Source if we wanted to go. Why ever didn't we think of that before?' Sneezewort and Baldmoney were warming to their subject.

Dodder snorted again. 'Well, you can go, the pair of you, and I'll stay behind and live a few years more. What about Giant Grum and Crow Wood? You're fools, the pair of ye, and I'll have nothing to do with the madcap scheme. You can go, *I* won't come with you. It's all very well for you, with two good legs, but I've only one, and that won't help me run away from any Giants, or swim if I fall in the Folly.'

But the other two gnomes argued on until the last spark of the fire winked out and they were left in the intense darkness with the wind 'bluntering' round outside. Soon even Baldmoney was tired out and a silence fell in the dark cave under the old oak.

Out in the cold meadow the cows had lain down one by one, and from beyond Hallfields spinney a wood dog (fox) was barking. Half veiled by the scudding clouds, the stars glimmered through ragged gaps, and under the root, which smelt of oak smoke and kippered minnow, three tiny snores rose up like elfin horns. The sun was on the other side of the big round world, the soft tide of darkness cloaked every living thing. Only the night hunters, like the red wood dogs, and Bub'ms (as the gnomes called the rabbits) were out, and as for Ben, why, he was away beyond Collinson Church, hunting the new plough!

The gnomes went back down the Folly with a great company. Each tree as they passed it flung some dead leaves down to them, the stream was full; hawthorn, maple, chestnut, elm, oak, lime, willow, ash, and alder, poplar and wild apple, all were drifting with the current, smoothly and silently, in a coloured carpet.

There was nothing to do all day but stand about the deck, smoke and gossip, admire the scenery, and lean over the side to watch the endless procession of coloured leaves sliding past, to watch the darting fish in the clear water, and wave to astonished water-voles.

It is a strange thing that before the floods in late autumn, rivers, streams, and ponds become crystal clear.

It was possible for the gnomes to see every pebble and leaf on the stream bed, and the waving cresses, some like green hair, and neat pillows of tight, green weeds, seemed to belong to a fantastic submarine fairyland.

A friendly wind helped them across the lake and they could not suppress a shudder when they saw hated Poplar Island, barren and wild, on the starboard side, half hidden by mist. Were it not for the *Jeanie Deans*, perhaps their bones would be bleaching on its grim shore. And so they went on, past places hardly recognisable now that the trees were stripped almost bare.

They dropped anchor in Crow Wood and paid Squirrel a visit. They felt they could not go past without looking him up. He was overjoyed to see them back again, and many a yarn they exchanged with him up in Tree Top House.

There, in Crow Wood, were the marks of their old fires, recalling the night of the animal banquet, when Owl told them ghost stories, and, as for the gibbet, it had been torn down by the animals and the poor bones given a decent burial by the moles and sexton beetles. No other Giant had been seen in Crow Wood since the gnomes had left, and everybody lived in peace and harmony.

As Squirrel was a lonely soul they persuaded him to go back to the Oak Pool with them. I think he was a little regretful at saying goodbye to Tree Top House, but the picture the gnomes painted of the Oak Pool proved irresistible. And when he saw the *Jeanie Deans* anchored to a pine

A view of the Jeanie Deans as she ploughs on her way

branch he was too excited to speak.

Soon after leaving Crow Wood it began to snow, so that the conifers seemed like trees on a Christmas card and the gnomes like little snow men. Hundreds of fieldfares and redwings feasting on the scarlet berries in a hedgerow stopped their banquet to watch the *Jeanie Deans* drift by. The sky was a heavy ochre-grey, promising snow for days and days, but nobody minded.

They managed the Folly Falls with ease because more water was coming down than in summer, and though the steamer was buffeted out of her usual stately dignity by the swift rush, she was soon serenely gliding on towards the Oak Pool.

What a happy party it was on board, to be sure! It was good to see the familiar landmarks, and it wasn't long before they fell in with many old acquaintances. Some, like the hedgepigs, dormice, and fernbears, missed the fun, for they were tucked up for the winter and would not appear again until the spring. But kingfishers, moorhens, Bub'ms, watervoles, moles, Spink and Bluebutton, all recognised them and gave them a warm welcome as they went past. As you can well imagine, they were speechless at the sight of the *Jeanie Deans*. Truly this homecoming was going to give the Stream People much to talk about for many a long winter's night. Dodder, Sneezewort, Baldmoney and Squirrel all waving frantically from the bridge of the big ship, the snow falling thickly, all the animals running along the bank, trying to keep up with her, why, it was as good as a play!

Sneezewort had found a little Union Jack in one of the cabin lockers, and this was run up to the forepeak. They didn't care who saw them, even the miller's brats, or the peppery old Colonel from Joppa!

Snow was still falling in big feathery flakes when they passed Moss Mill, and ice daggers a yard long were hanging from the now motion-less buckets of the giant wheel. The mill pool was partly frozen over too, but in midstream the water was clear, which was a lucky thing for the *Jeanie Deans*. And just as dusk was falling they passed Lucking's meadows. A cosy light was burning in the farmhouse window, where Farmer Lucking was just sitting down to discuss an enormous ham of his own curing, and presently they came to the rapids above the Oak Pool.

How strange it seemed, this silent white landscape. Last time they were here all was dressed in summer finery. Now the trees were black and bare and hardly a rush blade was to be seen along the banks.

'If only we had found Cloudberry,' said Dodder sadly to Squirrel, his eyes greedily taking in each dear familiar landmark, 'it would have made this trip just perfect. But we've at least found one thing, this lovely ship. Baldmoney will soon mend the engine – he's as clever as anything at making and mending things. Perhaps one day we'll go up the Folly again – who knows?'

The *Jeanie Deans* glided on, ice tinkling along her sides. In another moment they had rounded the bend, and there was the oak and the Oak Pool. What a moment! What a picture! The snow-covered branches hanging over the inky stream, each twig encrusted with frost, the dear old oak tree sturdily awaiting them, and the excited cries of the crowds on either shore!

All at once Dodder uttered an exclamation, his hands gripped the wheel of the *Jeanie Deans* convulsively. 'Sneezewort! Baldmoney! Squirrel! *Someone's lit a fire in our house!*'

'Who can it be, in our house?' exclaimed Baldmoney.

'Perhaps the Stream People heard we were coming and lit a fire to welcome us home,' suggested Sneezewort nervously.

'Nobody's any business in our house,' shouted Dodder, getting very excited; 'not even the Stream People.'

Slowly they drew nearer, the Folly bearing them ever onward until they were close to the oak root.

'Let go the anchor,' called Dodder, and it went tumbling down into the icy water. The *Jeanie Deans* swung her nose round and Sneezewort lowered the gangway. The next instant they had the greatest thrill of the whole adventure.

The door opened and there, waving frantically, was Cloudberry, dear old Cloudberry, beaming all over his face. He looked just the same (though perhaps a trifle thinner) as when he left the Oak Pool two years before!

The door of Oak Pool House is shut fast and a merry fire is blazing within; never has the old oak re-echoed to such uproarious merriment. Outside, the snow-flakes whirl, and the Folly is still hurrying on between jagged ice floes.

The *Jeanie Deans*, safely anchored, lifts slightly to the ripples talking under her keel, small fragments of floating ice dwell lovingly along her sides and are then swept onwards on their cold and lonely journey. The snow lies thick on her decks, darkness is cloaking the wild winter fields.

But within the oak root all is high revelry and fun. Most of the Stream People who can squeeze in are there – nobody has been left out in the cold. Truly the finest animal banquet ever! And with them round the blaze, full of supper and toasting their toes, sit Dodder, Sneezewort, Cloudberry, Baldmoney and Squirrel. Cloudberry, with his mouth full of peppermint cream, is telling them of his adventures.

'After scratching my name on the bridge,' he is saying, 'I went on up the side of the big lake, and who do you think I met? Why, the Heaven Hounds! They were resting there before their long journey back to Spitzbergen. They asked me to go with them – how could I refuse such an offer? Ever since Dodder and I met them up the Folly years before I had always longed to go. So I went, and came back on Hallowe'en!'

'We heard the Heaven Hounds passing over,' exclaimed Dodder, 'when we were right up the Folly – then you must have been with them!'

'Yes, I was with them; and now I come to think of it, I saw a little bright spark far below us which looked like a fire. I thought it was some lonely old tramp cooking his supper' (here Dodder grunted indignantly) 'or a Lantern Man. It was very cold up there, I can tell you, tucked up on the old leader's back, with my arms round his neck. They put me down in Lucking's water meadow. It gave me quite a turn when I found this house empty – I couldn't think what had happened to you.'

'So you never went up to the Folly Source after all!' exclaimed Baldmoney.

'Of course not. I knew I would never get such a chance again so I took it. But I've done with wandering now, I've seen Spitzbergen and the Land of Northern Lights, and it will take me the rest of the winter to tell you of all my adventures and the strange things I've seen.'

'And to think we've been all those miles up the Folly for nothing,' grunted Dodder in an aggrieved tone, half laughing in spite of himself; 'it's just the same old Cloudberry, he hasn't changed a bit – has he, gnomes?'

There was a slight movement above them and a piece of bark fell down. It was only Ben, staring down at them, his eyes like carriage-lamps in the firelight, listening with all his ears.

So here we will leave the Little Grey Men, for they have much to talk about. Baldmoney has spread out his waistcoat map and is tracing, with a grubby finger, the course of their adventurous journey. Dodder, with great ceremony, has produced a shell of his precious Elderberry 1905, with the result that already Squirrel and Cloudberry are a little too unreserved, having no 'head' for elderberry wine, and (though I hardly like to mention it) Sneezewort can be observed making ineffectual efforts to stifle a hiccup, as tipsy as a bumble bee in a foxglove finger.

Our last glimpse of them is in the cosy flamelight, with their crooked shadows thrown on the interior of the old hollow oak. And the last sound we hear is of the Folly Brook, chuckling on past the Oak Tree Pool as it has done for a thousand, thousand cuckoo years, on its long journey to the distant sea.

I followed up The Little Grey Men *with a sequel,* Down The Bright Stream. *In this, the Folly Brook dries up, due to the meddling of humans, and the little men have to depart from their ancestral home under the oak. So they set off down-stream and, after many adventures, and with the help of their friend, Mr Ben the owl, they fly from Britain in a home-made glider, the towing agency being, of course, Mr Ben.*

(From *A CHILD ALONE*)

6.
DOWN THE BRIGHT STREAM

Now the gnomes found themselves once more back in possession of their beloved ship their joy knew no bounds. The unhappy Mr Shoebottom had done his work well and the *Jeanie Deans* was apparently as good as the day Dodder came upon her reposing on the white sand of Poplar Island.

True, she had lost some of her pristine glory, her paint-work had suffered through what she had undergone, but she pulled along through the water with all her old fire and glided as gracefully as any swan upon the ample bosom of this new river. It cannot be expected, or pretended, that the gnomes found her interior fittings as smart as they used to be, nor that they found everything intact. There was some splintered woodwork in the cabin, several panels had suffered, either from the attentions of Master Shoebottom, or from the fall from the garage window. But the clumsy fingers of old Shoebottom had been unable to force an entry into the cabin and even Master Shoebottom had not had the leisure to explore all the hidden treasure below decks.

The wine was untouched, though one shell was broken and the precious liquid had drained away with the bilge water. Also the glass in the pictures was shattered but the pictures themselves were happily undamaged.

Baldmoney soon got busy putting everything to rights, mending the broken panelling and so forth. Even their new mole skin coats were found hanging up in the little cupboard by the bunks quite unharmed.

You may be sure that they put a good many miles between them and the scene of their alarming adventures. They journeyed unceasingly from dusk to dawn and as they went the river widened and widened. Sometimes they passed under bolted railway bridges. Some came aslant to the path of the river, as though they were out of drawing, as the artists say, some were of steel, others were of brick. Once they passed a big town with many bridges and factory chimneys. And once too, a puzzled policeman, yawning on his beat, saw the shadowy outline of the *Jeanie Deans* pass below him as he stood on a road bridge, but he thought it was a large rat and yawned again and looked eagerly for the dawn.

In passing these Man Dwellings the gnomes were assailed by the many foreign smells which quite swamped the natural smells of reed bed and osier. They were always glad to be past them and out among the open country once again.

They quite lost count of the watermills and villages which went gliding by them. By day they sought the sanctuary of deep osiers, where the wind sang tunes among the slender wands and swallows twittered at close of day. Sometimes they pushed their way into dense reed beds, those graceful slender forests which were ever a-whispering their mysterious secrets to one another and where the little reedy bird people slung their neat ball-like nests anchored from stem to stem.

There was no urgent hurry; when they came to some restful spot, an eyot or backwater, they stayed for a day or so, quietly fishing and now and again having a refreshing swim. For now the country was at its loveliest. Never before had they seen such water-lily beds or such magnificent cup-shaped flowers. Never before had they seen such black poplars, bigger by far than those which they remembered at Moss Mill. And as for the fish they caught – why, Dodder had his tackle broken many times a day by leviathans of the deep, as big or bigger than the perch he caught when he travelled up the folly. There was no lack of good fresh food. Watercress was abundant and all sorts of tender water salads which Mortals do not know of. How pleasant it was to lie in your bunk and listen to the reed warblers all a-singing, to hear the sweet bell-like voice of the cuckoo sounding across those spacious evening meads. Sometimes oak woods, bluebell floored, came right down to the river's brim, and in those soft summer evenings, delicious with the scent of hay-fields and meadowsweet, they watched the big river bats hawking to and fro and heard the monotonous 'crake crake' of land rails among the thick green mowing grass and branching buttercups.

Ben and his wife shadowed them, quiet and watchful ghosts. The two devoted birds were never far away. By day they went to sleep in some thick meadow elm or churchyard yew, but evening always found them floating along the misty river within sight and hail of the *Jeanie Deans,* noting their steady progress.

The gnomes made many new friends in their daily stopping places. The quaint little fluffy corks of dabchicks were a familiar sight, birds who have, as they told Dodder with great pride, no 'parsons' noses', and they met also the graceful and aristocratic crested grebes who glided by with dignified mien. Swans, of course, they met, but these creatures were as vain as peacocks. Once they had an encounter with a particularly bad-tempered bird.

They foolishly anchored near a swan's nest, and in a very short while the cob came alongside and ordered Dodder to move on. 'We don't allow gipsies, land *or* water, on this stretch of river,' he said. Dodder answered with some heat that they had as much right, and more, than he to the river. Whereupon the cob waxed wroth and threatened to drown them and sink the boat. He would have done so had not Dodder, thinking 'discretion the better part of valour', weighed anchor and gone on.

'As spoilt and vain-glorious as the Crow Wood Chinaman,' was Dodder's verdict, and long after they were out of earshot everyone shouted uncomplimentary remarks to the hissing angry bird.

One beautiful evening late in May they were anchored in a dense bed of reeds surrounding a calm backwater. Lily-beds stretched on either hand and blue dragon-flies hawked about the stern of the *Jeanie Deans* as keenly as the swallows and martins, which latter birds were seeking for larger game in that quiet retreat close beside the main river.

There is a particular charm about such places. Hidden away by pallisades of graceful whispering reeds and willows one can dream the hours away and nothing but the sleepy twitter of birds or the splash of a fat fish breaks the quietness. Dodder was up on the bridge, contentedly smoking a pipe, his elbows resting on the rail, watching the blue-black swallows and the white spots of the martins' rumps as they weaved about the ship.

Baldmoney and Squirrel were playing Acorn Hop on the fore-deck and Cloudberry was fishing over the stern. From the faint clinks and clanks from the galley it appeared that Sneezewort was preparing the evening repast.

'It's quite like old times,' said Baldmoney, sweeping the pieces off the board and leaning on the deck rail. 'Quite like the old days when we were going up the Folly to look for Cloudberry, only we don't seem so hurried now.'

'Yes,' said Squirrel, falling in with Baldmoney's idle mood, 'it's sad we'll never sail the Folly again. We've had some tough times since then. I often wondered what would have happened to me if I'd stayed on in Crow Wood. Not that I ever want to go back there. Seems as if I've been living along with you fellows all my life somehow.' And he yawned.

'Young Cloudberry seems more contented these days,' said Baldmoney after a while. 'Seems to me he's been more subdued too after that business with the Shoebottom's.'

'Yes, I was a fool to be led on by him like that, but *you* know what he is, and as it turned out it was the best possible thing that could have happened, otherwise we should never have got the spring mended.'

'No,' replied Baldmoney, 'that job was beyond me I must confess, Squirrel. Doesn't it make you think, looking back on it all, that Pan must have engineered the whole thing?'

'P'raps so,' agreed Squirrel. 'There's a lot of things we can't figure out, but plans don't always come out right. Talking of plans, you have a Plan, so Dodder tells me, about getting to Woodcock's Island?'

'Oh *that*,' said Baldmoney. 'Yes, I've got a Plan, of sorts; at least, Ben and I have one between us, but we've got to reach the Sea first before we tell anyone about it.'

As Baldmoney talked Squirrel saw him looking very intently at the reeds which swayed about all around them. Squirrel was a very sharp animal and seldom missed much. And this interest of Baldmoney's intrigued him enormously. Now, if he had been a little less subtle he might have remarked upon it, but instead he held his peace and pretended to be watching the swallows curvetting and circling about them. 'Look at the martins and swallows, they're having a high old time just here, catching no end of flies!'

'What about a row in the dinghy?' suggested Baldmoney, ignoring Squirrel's last remark.

'Good idea!' said Squirrel eagerly, who was, truth to say, just a little bored. 'But won't we have to get Dodder's permission?'

'He looks in a good mood,' observed Baldmoney, 'he's always in a good mood on an evening like this and he's smoking a pipe, which is a good sign. I'll give the old chap a hail. Hi! Dodder!'

'Hullo below there! What d'ye want?'

'May Squirrel and I take out the dinghy for a row?'

'What for?'

'Just for a row – we won't go far!'

There was a pause as Dodder took his pipe out of his mouth and pointed the stem at Squirrel. 'No more tricks then, you mustn't go out in the main river.'

'All right,' shouted Baldmoney, 'we won't.'

Full of excitement they lowered the boat into the water – luckily the Shoebottoms had not taken it off the deck davits – and a moment later both were safely aboard and rowing away. 'Don't make too much row,' whispered Baldmoney, 'we don't want Cloudberry bothering to come. I think he's so busy fishing he won't notice us.'

55

But at that moment Cloudberry, sensing in his uncanny restless way there was fun afoot, called out in his piping voice, 'Hey! come back for me, I'd like a row too!'

'Sorry,' called Squirrel, 'sorry, Cloudberry, old chap, but we can't come back now. Go on, row fast, Baldmoney,' he added in an aside, 'we don't want him with us.'

In a moment or two they had drawn away and were threading between the stout green stems of the reeds and the *Jeanie Deans*, with the gesticulating Cloudberry standing in the stern, was lost to view.

'What fun it is,' said Squirrel, looking about him and settling himself on the cushions, 'this is *real* fun, this is!' and he leant back luxuriously and closed his eyes, sniffing the air, for he could smell the hawthorn wind. There comes a day in early summer when the air becomes charged with the scent of the newly-opened hawthorn flowers. This lovely perfume, not unlike bean flowers, is wafted for miles o'er hill and dale. It needs a warm wind to bring it out and only on one day is it possible to notice it. Mortals sniff and say, 'What a lovely smell, what can it be?' That is the wind that the Little People name the hawthorn wind.

After awhile, when they had pushed well into the reed bed, Baldmoney stopped rowing. He pulled the little dinghy against one of the stout stems and began cutting at it with his knife.

'What's the idea?' asked Squirrel, watching his friend with interest.

'O, I just want to test out something,' said Baldmoney. He hacked away at the stout reed stem and in a minute or two its feathery top trembled and it toppled across the prow like a falling tree.

Baldmoney worked away and soon cut off a length. This was, of course, hollow and quite strong. Baldmoney examined it with care, shaking his head now and again, and passing low remarks, hardly audible to Squirrel. 'Not strong enough by half... wouldn't stand the strain, no... they won't do at all... must find something else ...' and such like observations which so tickled Squirrel's curiosity that he could contain himself no longer.

'Whatever *are* you about, Baldmoney, muttering away like that? Do tell me. Is it something to do with that Plan of yours?'

'P'raps it is, p'raps it isn't,' said Baldmoney mysteriously. 'They're no good anyway, not strong enough.'

'Not strong enough for *what*?'

'For my purpose.'

'O, all *right*,' said Squirrel testily, 'I don't want to know your precious secret, but I think you might tell me!'

But Baldmoney would not be drawn.

He lay back and paddled slowly along with half-shut eyes. 'This is the sort of thing I just enjoy,' he murmured, gently guiding the dinghy between two water-lily leaves, 'just gliding about like this. What huge fun we're having.' He sighed again.

'I believe Dodder is keeping a log every night,' said Squirrel, 'ever since we started from the Oak Tree he's kept a diary.'

'All Captains have to keep a log,' said Baldmoney. 'Surely you know that? The trouble is, Squirrel, I'm no hand at writing myself, engineering's more in my line. I say,' he cried, half sitting up, 'what a jolly place we're coming to!'

They had glided out of the reed bed into another smaller backwater. It really *was* the most fairy-like place, with the dark green water studded with pure white lilies, each with a yellow centre, a small pool not more than ten yards across.

The willows, in a lovely silver tangle, formed a wall on all sides, shutting out the distant views of river and meadows. The low sunbeams pouring down into that well-like place were gilding the tops of the bushes but the water itself was in cool shade. All manner of beautiful riverside flowers grew among the reeds and vegetation: willow herb, milk parsley, water betony and dock, and many another moisture-loving plant; each added its quota of scent, which lay heavily on the evening air.

From under some water-lily leaves they saw the trembling tails of several large fishes. To fish, the flat lily leaves were like parasols.

Waterhens swam about very busily, but when they saw the boat appear they shyly took refuge in the reed pallisades and passed watery remarks to one another.

'Now, if we had only brought our fishing lines,' said Squirrel, 'we might have caught some of those big fellows hiding under the lily pads there.'

'O, it's too hot, even to fish,' murmured Baldmoney, yawning widely and letting the little boat bump gently among the lilies. 'I believe I'm enjoying this trip more than the one we had up the Folly. Hullo! See who comes!'

Squirrel turned about and saw, high above them, the huge extended vanes of grey wings, the pinions spread like fingers. It was Sir Herne the heron. He wheeled round in a wide arc and seeing the little opening below he checked himself and plunged down at a surprising speed, almost as if he had been shot. They could hear the still air burring through his feathers. When he came just above them they saw his long green legs suddenly drop down and he alighted with infinite grace a few yards away on a half-submerged willow root. It was quite remarkable to see how his silver-grey plumage toned with the willows all about them.

'Sir Herne!' exclaimed Baldmoney, and doffed his cap politely. Squirrel, having no cap to take off, bowed distantly.

'Hey ho! if it isn't the gnomes again! Why, I haven't seen any of you since I gave your friend Dodder a lift up the Folly, let me see … how long ago was that? Last summer, wasn't it?'

'Yes, he was following after us and he told us how good you'd been,' said Baldmoney, beaming broadly.

'But gnomes, what *has* happened to you? I've been thinking a lot about you lately. All the Stream People have left the Folly and the stream is dry. Your tree is down too. You wouldn't recognise the place. But I said to myself, I'll bet a pound roach to an ounce minnow the gnomes have not been caught napping, I'll wager they've gone off in that boat of theirs, I've heard so much about!'

Baldmoney grinned from ear to ear. 'We *were* caught napping, Sir Herne, we were all asleep when Watervole came and woke us up!'

'Ah! a good friend is Watervole,' said Sir Herne, drawing up one long leg. 'Poor things, they've had to pack up too, I suppose?'

'Indeed they have,' said Squirrel.

'Pardon me,' said Sir Herne, noticing Squirrel for the first time, 'I don't seem to have met you before!'

'No, he came with us down the Folly last autumn, he lived in Crow Wood, you know,' said Baldmoney.

'Ah… How's Dodder?' asked Sir Herne, after a pause.

'O, he's well *and* flourishing.'

58

'Are you living close by?'

'O no, we're on our way down-river to a place Woodcock called the "Severn Sea", wherever that may be.'

'And what, may I ask, are you going to do when you get to the Severn Sea?' asked Sir Herne, looking rather surprised.

'We're going to Woodcock's Island, where a hermit or a saint lies buried, and no Mortals will bother us. It's right in the middle of a grey, grey loch, so Woodcock said; Ben knows the way, Woodcock told him.'

'I expect,' said the heron, 'it's Ireland that Woodcock's talking of, he thinks a lot of the country, swears by it, says there's no place like it! I've never been there. I'm rather a home-lover, I'm afraid, England's good enough for me.'

'It's good enough for us,' said Baldmoney earnestly, 'if only the Mortals would behave themselves, but they can't. We just can't stand them, and now the Folly's gone and our tree too, we feel we must clear out and find some peace before we die!'

The heron nodded gravely. '*I* know. I can quite see your point. I, too, sometimes feel the same way myself. But you've still some way to go to reach the Severn, and when you get there I don't see how you're going to get over the Irish Sea to Woodcock's Island.'

'We don't quite know ourselves yet,' confessed Baldmoney, 'but the Bens and I have a plan, and I think we might do it.'

'The *Bens*, did you say?' asked Sir Herne. 'Not Ben from Oak Tree House?'

'Yes, *the* Ben, *you* know!'

'Well I never, and where are the Bens? I haven't seen them for ages.'

'O, I expect they're somewhere close-by, roosting in an oak or an elm. Anyway, they always show up at night when we do all our travelling.'

'So they are going too, are they?'

'O yes, we've decided we'll stick together, come what may. You see, we've always lived in the same tree. Ben's ancestors did too, *you* know what it is with old friends.'

The heron nodded wistfully. He was rather a lonely old bird and truth to say, he often ate a fat water-rat on the sly. And as for frogs, he fairly wolfed them down.

'Well, I wish I was coming with you,' he said after a pause. 'I do indeed. But I've got a wife and we've had a fine family this year on Poplar Island, two girls and a boy; fine children,' he said proudly.

The sun was now well down and Baldmoney realised that, without their knowing it, the evening had advanced surprisingly quickly.

The tops of the willows were no longer bathed in light and the backwater was full of green gloom and shadow. Everywhere arose the sweetly rank scent of the herbage and a bat began to hawk about overhead.

'Well,' said Baldmoney, 'goodbye, Sir Herne. We must be going. As it is, I fear we shall get in an awful row from Dodder for stopping out so late, time passes quickly with friends.'

They turned the boat about and began to paddle softly away. Baldmoney waved his cap to Sir Herne and Squirrel raised a paw.

Looking back they saw his grey form standing on one leg, his head sunk in his shoulders, and his spear couched in readiness.

'Good hunting, brother,' called Baldmoney. 'Good hunting and a good trip,' called back Sir Herne, and the next moment the clustering reeds hid him from view.

It was nearly dark when they reached the larger backwater and saw the *Jeanie Deans* anchored against the wall of reeds. She looked indescribably cosy, her every line reflected in the still water between the lily islands. Appetising smells were wafted from the galley stove and a dim slit of light showed through a porthole of the cabin.

They tied up the dinghy, and a minute later had scrambled aboard, hungry and tired, but feeling as though they had spent a thoroughly enjoyable evening.

★ ★ ★ ★ ★

For the two days following the trials of Wonderbird, the gnomes set to work to make extra flying equipment. The Bens hunted as they had never done before and brought them mole and mouse skins and the little men stitched and stitched all day long and half the night.

They made thick fur gloves and helmets, and warm duffle coats, and even fur boots. Even then they found time to collect together a store of food to take with them on the journey. Squirrel made a completely new set of fishing gear and Yaffle seemed very busy also and they saw little of him.

At last all was ready and one evening a crowd again assembled one the flying field at the top of Sperrywell Lane, only this time an even larger number of animals and birds were gathered together. They meant to give the gnomes a grand send-off. And early in the evening who should appear but two of the Otters from Rumbling Mill *and* the King of Fishers, *and* dear old Watervole!

It was a perfect night for the take-off. A gentle breeze was blowing from the west right on to the top of the hill. The Wonderbird had never looked so trim and workmanlike. Squirrel went round her and examined the skids and tested them, Baldmoney tested the controls, and Sneezewort went round her with a duster, removing invisible specks of dirt from her sides and wings. And of course, just before the take-off, a starling must needs make a mess on one of the wings! The poor bird did not mean to, it was sheer excitement. But it had to be washed off and Baldmoney was fuming to be off.

'I can't believe you are *really* going to leave us and this Island of ours,' said the King of Fishers. 'I only hope you will find the fishing as good on Woodcock's Island!'

'Think of us sometimes,' cried the Otters from Rumbling Mill. 'Give a thought to us back here in the old country!'

'Don't forget the old days by the Folly,' squeaked Watervole. 'Pan keep you, give you an easy journey and bring you back again safe and sound!'

Baldmoney climbed aboard first, putting on his new fur gloves in a professional manner and giving a jaunty wave to the assembled multitude. Then followed Dodder (he had to be helped up into the plane by Sneezewort) then came Squirrel, carrying a bag of nuts in his teeth, and finally Sneezewort, who raised both thumbs at the crowd. The door was shut to and Ben, who all this time had been looking over his shoulder like a restive greyhound, settled himself grimly into the towing harness.

Just at that moment a breathless Yaffle appeared with swift and dipping flight over the bushes. He was carrying something square in his bill. He came breathlessly through the crowd and lo! and behold, he presented Sneezewort with a new Acorn Hop Board, which he had made all himself!

The door of the plane shut-to again and now the heads of Dodder and Baldmoney could be seen peering out of the windows, laughing and nodding and waving their hands.

First Mrs Ben took off in front, then Ben put down his head and charged like a bull along the hilltop. The tow rope dipped and tightened and the Wonderbird began to move swiftly forward over the grass.

Breathless, the crowd watched, never a sound was heard as the glider left the ground and then a great cheer went up, the animals waved, the birds flew hither and thither over and above the moving plane.

Away they went, out over the valley, dwindling smaller and smaller, heading for the last glow of the sunset sky.

'I can still see them!' squeaked a field vole, dancing up and down on tiptoes. 'Goodbye! Goodbye!' shouted the Rumbling Mill Otters, and then, when the two tiny specks melted into the infinite distance, the crowd dispersed their several ways, feeling life was very tame for stay-at-homes.

Baldmoney at the controls had hardly time to glance out of the windows. His eyes were on the tow rope and the flying shape of Ben. The old owl was flying with slow and measured beats and ahead, acting as pilot, was Mrs Ben.

Dodder and Squirrel, who had good seats, both with windows, gazed down like Lords on the landscape below. They saw the steeple of Chilcote Church swim under; they looked down into the tops of the rounded elms and neat cottage gardens, all very dim in the gathering darkness.

In a short while, a matter of minutes, the village and river had been left behind. They did not catch a glimpse of the goats because of the apple trees. The poor beasts had been unable to attend the final send-off.

Woods and parklands, mansions and hamlets, ponds and streams, all passed below in slow succession. The ponds, reflecting the last light in the sky, shone like crystals, the rivers and streams as silver threads.

Ben was climbing. Baldmoney, his eyes on the chart and on his instrument panel (it was too dark to see Ben now) felt exultant. How smoothly the plane rode the air! There was no thump of screw nor jarring of machinery, only faint squeaks in the framework and the low hiss of the wind about the windows.

Poor Sneezewort was in the dark interior at the back; he could see nothing but the portly back of Squirrel and a bit of Dodder's fur cap.

Making the most of his opportunities he slyly opened one of the cupboards close behind him but was disgusted to find only spare clothing. He tried another which he was sure contained food, but it was locked. The cunning Baldmoney had seen to that.

Dodder leant back in his seat and sighed, half in relief and half in sorrow.

'Well, it was a grand send-off, Squirrel.'

'Yes indeed, the best we've ever had.'

'But it's sad saying goodbye. I *hate* goodbyes!'

'So do I,' replied Squirrel heartily. 'that's the worst of making friends.'

'Where are we now, Baldmoney?' asked Dodder, trying to peep over the pilot's shoulder.

'Getting near the sea, I should say. Keep a look out for it, any minute now!'

The moon was rising and very soon they saw the land below grow dark and then lines of white appeared. They were the breakers beating on a lonely beach.

The gnomes had never seen the sea, nor had Squirrel; and the spectacle was awe-inspiring. Soon the land was left behind and beneath them was nothing but sea, which looked as solid as the land. A ship was visible here and there, very small and far-away, trailing a long streamer of white behind it like a snail on a garden path.

And then veils of moonlit cloud began to hide the void beneath, massed woolly blankets hid everything and they seemed to be flying through an unreal dream-world. Ahead of the Wonderbird the Bens were now invisible, flying with measured beats. And soon (thrilling sight!) they passed a flock of birds, they knew not what, flying in the same direction as themselves.

Dodder poked Squirrel and pointed, but at that moment the fog hid them from view.

More cloud and yet more clouds swam by, over them sometimes, veiling the forms of the Bens. It was eerie for Baldmoney, sitting forward in his pilot's seat, to see the tow rope disappearing into nothingness ahead, and to feel the invisible agency gently towing them along.

Occasionally they felt the jar of a wind pocket, the plane lurched and dropped a foot or so, and Baldmoney felt his heart jump into his throat. The sensation was very like that of a boy who is flying a kite in a high wind who feels the line slacken and then pull taut again.

The whitish clouds grew more sombre and soon they seemed to dive into a blackness as of moonless night. Sharp raps smote the windows and the sides of the Wonderbird. It was rain. Ben, out in front, began to be a little weary. They were heading straight into the storm, and his feathers began to feel heavy, the tow rope to chafe his shoulders.

But in a moment or so they were through the cloud and, once more, there was the shining limitless sea all green and grey, and crinkled in the moonlight, while overhead the stars shone bright and clear.

I thought up a tale of three boys whose parents were abroad and who had been put in the charge of a maiden aunt – Aunt Ellen. Chafing under petticoat govern-ment, they decide to run away to a large forest. I based this on Salcey Forest and Geddington Chase in Northamptonshire, places I knew intimately and where I had hunted for the lovely rare Purple Emperor butterfly. The boys' school was based on Rugby. I also drew on my own experiences as a boy when, with my brother, we used to camp in the wilds of Blueberry Bushes in the long summer holidays, taking with us a rifle with which we hunted for our meat which we cooked over open fires.

The amusing thing is I have had letters from irate headmasters blaming me for putting ideas into boys' heads as several of their pupils, having read my book, had also taken to the woods, defying their parents and the law. It appeals to boys, especially country boys, because it is about throwing over the traces and cocking a snoot at authority, and going back to the primitive life of hunting, and living free in the open air.

(From *A CHILD ALONE*)

7.

BRENDON CHASE

A house, even one so friendly and well-loved as was the Dower house, is an eerie place at dead of night. Some miraculous change seems to take place when the last light goes out as though a magic spell has been pronounced and every living moving thing frozen into immobility.

Familiar corridors and rooms, which, during the daylight hours were full of laughter and bustle, the clatter of feet, and merry clink clank of distant kitchen activity, are horribly silent, as silent as a vault; with shadows and vagueness everywhere.

The boys, healthy young animals, had no knowledge of this transformation. Their bright days were full of activity and sunlight. At nightfall, they, with other mortals, retired like fowls to their respective roosts, and left the old Dower house to its own ghostly devices.

So that when, with thumping hearts, Robin and John found themselves tiptoeing out into the landing, they sensed this new phenomenon and were momentarily appalled.

In some strange way they felt the hostility in their surroundings and for a few seconds they stood still, listening and watching like startled rabbits. But in all the old sleeping Dower house there was no sound, save for the sotto voce 'tick tock' of the grandfather clock on the stairs.

'Come on,' whispered Robin, startling John out of a trance, and they slid silently to the head of the front stairs. Aunt Ellen's shoes were outside her door waiting for the morning maid and there was light glowing dimly from Harold's sick room, a long narrow strip of light between the bottom of the door and the curly black carpet on the threshold. But even the patient must have slept, his mind perhaps busy with feverish dreams connected with the escapade. He would not know what course his brothers had decided to take, perhaps he had guessed that now he had fallen ill with the measles they would carry out the original plan. It was easy to imagine his discreet probings on the morrow, his seemingly innocent enquiries as to what his brothers were doing. Knowing Aunt Ellen and Miss Holcome, and thereby knowing the ways of women, Robin and John surmised that even when their disappearance became known Harold would not be told for fear of heightening his fever.

Robin cocked his thigh over the smooth oak banister and the next second had plunged from sight into the dark well of the front hall with no more sound than that of a stealthy snake. John followed suit, landing silently beside him on the Persian carpet. For a moment they again paused and listened but there was nothing but the subdued 'tick tock' of the stair clock.

'John!' – this in a whisper.

'Yes?'

'We've gone and forgotten the blankets!'

'O Lord!'

'One of us must go back,' he whispered again. 'We'd better have them. Pop back and get them, it won't take a minute.'

Obediently, but with a quaking heart, John made to ascend the stairs but at the first cautious tread a board squeaked agonisingly and the boys shrank back against the hall curtains.

To John's annoyance he found his limbs trembling violently as though he had an ague. It was not fear but excitement.

'It's no good, we must leave them, we shall be warm enough! Besides they will be awfully awkward things to carry,' he said weakly.

'All right, leave them. Come on!'

They tiptoed down the stone-flagged passage to the kitchen door. Inch by inch Robin turned the brass knob. There was a loud click from the lock. Again they stood. In the silence of the sleeping house these sounds assumed titanic proportions.

TING! chimed the grandfather clock way back on the stairs and the boys jumped. One o'clock in the morning! and they must make the forest before dawn! There was not a moment to lose!

It was unbelievably dark in the kitchen. John, feeling his way along the scrubbed white table, encountered a chair leg. It fell over with a hideous crash which seemed to echo through the house.

'Clumsy owl,' hissed Robin. 'Look where you're going!'

'How can I when it's dark?' that worthy growled. The sweat was standing in beads on his forehead. 'Hist!'

They were both again frozen into immobility. From upstairs was heard the unmistakable noise of Harold's door being opened. It had a squeak which the boys knew well.

'O Lord!' groaned Robin, 'somebody's heard us now. If they come down the front stairs we must bolt for it. Listen!'

But the guilty consciences were soothed by the sound of bold steps bound for the bathroom. It was Miss Holcome, or possibly their Aunt, going to fill a water jug. They heard water running from the tap and steps returning along the passage. Then Harold's door shut quietly.

Perhaps the poor feverish patient was thirsty.

Breathing again they softly undid the bolts of the back door and the next moment were out in the garden and all the sleeping beauty of the summer night. The stars shone clear and bright and the crisp bow of the moon in its first quarter was cocked jauntily over the stable roof.

It was the work of a moment to undo the door of the tool-shed and secure the rook rifle and ammunition, scaring a rat as big as a rabbit which was sitting on the bottom stair.

And in the leafy nut walk they collected together their simple needs, the frying pan, saucepan and plates, the matches and waterproof match box, the Quaker Oats and salt. John made sure that the fishing lines and snares were in his pocket and after feeling about inside the root to discover if anything had been overlooked, they jumped the ivied sunken wall and struck off across the fields.

They passed the churchyard, crammed with its glimmering white tombstones which made them avert their eyes for fear of what they should see, they passed the ivied bulk of the old church tower framed against the luminosity of the sky.

A dog barked at them from Baldrick's farm and the noise roused every village cur within hearing. Worse still, from the direction of the Dower house, the boys heard Tilly uplifting her voice in plaintive howls. 'Blast the dog, she'll raise the place,' growled Robin as they hurried along in the shadow of a thick thorn hedge. 'I believe she knows it's us, doing a midnight flit.'

'By the way she's barking, she's trying to tear down the stable door,' said John. 'The sooner we're clear of the village the better for us.'

'It's all the fault of Baldrick's beastly cur...'

The barking dwindled behind them, fainter and fainter, until it was on the edge of hearing.

They passed cows asleep among the buttercups, they smelt their sweet meadow breath and heard their subdued rustling in the shadows. Something of the eeriness of the silent Dower house lingered even here, out of doors. The landscape which, during hours of daylight was so dearly familiar – I think they knew every tree and bush within a radius of a couple of miles about Cherry Walden – seemed now entirely changed and foreign. The big chestnuts along the lane, for instance, bulked large and forbidding, like couched monsters, yet in staring day they were friendly trees with many treasures in the shape of conkers and owls' nests.

Stealthy wild life was revealed as they passed upon their silent way, the dim scut of a rabbit bobbed and wavered across the turf, splashings and ploppings sounded from the horse pond where Harold in his happier days was wont to fish for polly-woggles and nameless revolting worms – horse leeches he called them – and where even Robin and John had found much magic in the days of their extreme youth.

They felt like burglars or poachers as they nipped across the Brendon road and dived into the sinister shadow of the hawthorn hedge, and the dim ribbon lay vacant and horribly remote to right and left.

In early May the dawn soon comes and it was not long before the boys saw the sky paling to the east of them and trees and bushes becoming more distinct. And soon they heard the first lark singing over the Weald, its far-away music threadlike and cold, matching the silver light.

They took it in turns to carry the cooking utensils and the rifle, for they had not thought to make a sling for the latter before they started. From a blossom-smothered hawthorn a blackbird began to warble richly and soon bird songs were echoing on every hand, from blackbirds and thrushes, chaffinches and wrens.

As the boys stood for a moment under the dim hawthorns all the birds could be heard getting into their full stride and soon a cuckoo joined

70

Tracking in the winter woods

71

the chorus, dominating even the blackbird's rich warbling notes.

It was strange to think of Cherry Walden, yet asleep. Aunt Ellen's shoes would still be patiently waiting outside her door, everyone in the house and village would be wrapped in slumber. Yet in an hour or two their disappearance would be discovered and the hue and cry would begin.

It did not seem so very long before the boys caught sight of the Chase. It lay all along the horizon, a dense band of darkness against the dim sky. And ere the sun rose at last over the rim of the Weald they were crossing the last field – where some cattle were grouped round a salt lick – for the shelter of the trees. Though it was now little after four in the morning – they had been walking continuously since one o'clock – the light was steadily increasing and they gained the forest edge not a moment too soon. For, on looking back the way they had come, they saw the first sign of life, a labourer with a rush skip on his back, cycling to work along a distant lane.

Robin turned in the shadow of the bushes and a strange expression passed across his face as he looked back at his brother, an expression of triumph and excitement.

'We've done it!' he exclaimed, 'we've done it, Big John!'

And then they capered and danced, Robin waving the rifle over his head like a wild Indian Brave celebrating a victory and as they danced they chanted curious half-formed words. 'No more Aunt Ellen! No more lessons, no more school!'

Carried away by their high spirits they even vowed they would never return to Cherry Walden, they would live in the forest, like outlaws, hunting and fishing like true wild woodmen, for ever and ever. The birds sang joyously, the scent of fern and leaf drove them nearly demented with delight. They rolled among the bracken and buried their faces in the dew wet grass, they pelted each other with sticks and turned somersaults. They were drunk with the glory of living, they were the happiest beings in the world!

Part Two

A FISHING MAN

A fishing man

From A Child Alone

Captain Muntz, the squire, lived at Umberslade – a fine big Georgian mansion with a lake where he let us fish. He also let us fish in the Blythe Brook – a lovely winding stream near Henley-in-Arden. I have described in *The Fisherman's Bedside Book* how I caught the big trout in the Blythe Brook. But we caught other good fish near Danzey Mill in the mill leat.

The fishing belonged to Captain Muntz and though we had his permission, the old miller, if he saw us coming, would open the sluice and ruin our chances. Sometimes, however, with true cunning we slipped secretly with our tin of worms and under cover of bushes had many a good fish out of the tawny depths, though I doubt if Captain Muntz would have approved of worms as bait. Indeed, one day in conversation with Gippy, he said, 'I hope they are fishing *with the fly?*' Gippy had to make some diplomatic reply.

The great trout I caught one lovely April morning below Danzey Mill was carried in triumph to Gippy who greatly admired it. However, under the influence of Granny Wilson, he said I must on no account have it mounted as I wished to do.

But I reckoned that it was *my* fish – I had caught it, after much labour and guile and was *determined* to have it stuffed. So I smuggled it out of the larder at Tanworth when the cook was not looking, packed it up and sent it to a taxidermist called Geo. Bazley in Northampton.

Years later, when I went to London, I actually carted it up by train to my digs where I hung it on the wall.

When I reached the age of discretion (which is infinitely more dull) I realised that the trout was really a hideous old cannibal, big in the head and lean in the body and not worthy of a glass case. It was replaced by a truly magnificent sea trout I caught one early morning in Loch Arkaig in Scotland and I still have it on my wall.

75

8.

THE FISHERMAN'S BEDSIDE BOOK

A WARWICKSHIRE TROUT

I have never captured a record fish but I have caught two 'notable' fish, one a trout and the other a tench. The trout came out of a brook in Warwickshire where no trout were supposed to be, but I afterwards found out this supposition had been cleverly bruited abroad by those whose lands adjoined the brook. The stream was certainly unprepossessing to the uneducated eye. It was very narrow, much overgrown with bushes and the banks patrolled by bulls. The latter, I have no doubt, had been placed there by riparian owners. But what are such trifles to a small boy? Any active and healthy boy is a match for a bull if he keeps his head and as for keepers and farm bailiffs...

When I was about thirteen years of age I went to stay one spring with my grandfather, who, in his day, had been a keen fisherman. He had a coachman named Dickon, who wore a glass eye, always an object of morbid fascination to the young. Dickon had lost his eye one winter afternoon when he was chopping wood, a chip flying up had almost gouged it out.

But I digress. One spring morning I was with Dickon in his harness-room watching him polishing the brass fittings to a collar. I remember that harness-room very well, it smelt of saddle soap, leather, horses, and, of course, Dickon. The combination of all four odours was not unpleasing to my juvenile tastes as I sat swinging my legs on a high stool.

The conversation turned to fishing. 'Ah,' said Dickon, polishing away at a buckle, 'there *are* trout if you knows where to look for 'em.

Didn't Mr Free used to get up at five in the morning when he stayed here, and go out and catch them?'

'Trout?' I asked incredulously.

'Aye, trout. Good 'uns too!'

'Where did he go?' I asked.

'Why, Pedder's Mill, of course.'

'But the Commander told me that there were *no* trout there!' I exclaimed. (The Commander being the chief 'riparian owner'.)

Dickon smiled and went on polishing. That was enough. I would go to Pedder's Mill as soon as I could get my tackle together.

The next day I developed a roaring cold in the head. But despite this, and managing to conceal my malady from adult eyes, I set off soon after breakfast with my trout rod, neatly dodging my grand-father who was talking to Dickon by the coach-house.

It was a wild April morning, grey and blowing hard, with occasional showers. Though the wind was cold it was one of those days when you feel the spring everywhere, you hear it too, and smell it.

I reached Pedder's Mill and had barely rigged up my tackle in the shelter of the hawthorns by the old mill pool (they were speckled all over with bursting green buds and a thrush had built a very new emerald nest in the heart of one of them) when the miller up at the mill opened the hatch and the still water at my feet became alive with thundering turmoil, dead leaves appeared and drowned sticks turned over and over in the muddy maelstrom.

Then came the miller and ordered me off. I went out on the road, walked down it for a quarter of a mile and rejoined the brook.

I lay low under a willow stump until I saw the Commander come down the drive in his neat trap, complete with cockaded coachman, and then began to fish. Soon a man appeared up by the Dower House kitchen garden fence, and bawled at me at intervals. I took no notice for a time until he began to purposefully climb the fence. Bailiffs and bulls are best left to themselves. He meant business so I stood not upon the order of my going.

These interruptions were tiresome and this latest interference made me impatient. I made another détour and came upon the stream again. Here, under a pallisade of alder trees I at last got my fly on the water and fished the brook down for some two hundred yards without the sign of a rise. Then the stream took a sharp turn to the left in a sort of elbow.

Under the far bank the current was swift and the fly tittupped round on the ripples and was engulfed. The reel sang as a big fish made upstream and I had to follow. He made for a biggish pool some twenty yards above and there we fought it out for twenty minutes. I had no net (the very young do not carry nets) and I had to play my fish right out and beach him on the shingle at the pool head.

He was a beauty and I took no chances with him, he was practically drowned when I towed him ashore and fell upon him, a trout of three and a half pounds.

The battle won I wrapped it up in dock leaves and put it in my pocket, though the tail flapped under my right arm. I regained the road and almost at once heard the sound of a fast-trotting horse. It was as I had feared, the Commander was returning.

I raised my cap respectfully, and then I heard the clatter of hooves mingle and stop as the trap was pulled up. The Commander was a red-faced man, clean-shaven, of course. He glowered at my rod. I endeavoured to keep my right side turned from him lest he should see the 'tell-tale tail'. I wished the ground would open and engulf me but at that moment Providence took a hand. There came again the sound of trotting hooves and just as the Commander was about to cast aside his carriage rug and descend upon me, no doubt with the object of searching my small person, there swept round the corner my grandfather, likewise in his trap, with Dickon beside him. Under the confusion of the meeting I bolted through the hedge and ran all the way home.

Now, by hook or crook, I had made up my mind to have that fish 'set up'. As bad luck would have it my grandmother met me in the drive and I foolishly showed her my trout, telling her I was going to have it stuffed.

She said nothing, probably because she knew I was a determined young devil, but when my grandfather returned, having calmed the Commander, she told him I was going to have my big trout 'stuffed'.

'That trout will be eaten here!' he thundered, and, as I was afraid of my grandfather, I said no word. Next day I was due to leave for home and without saying anything to anyone I raided the larder, procured my

A Warwickshire stream

trout and wrapped it up in paper, posting it off from the post office 'ere I left for the train.

In the queer way grown-ups have, the trout was forgotten in the business of seeing me off to the station and on the way thither I confided in Dickon what I had done, and he gave his unqualified approval. That is why that three-and-a-half pound brook trout still surveys me as I write these lines, superbly mounted in an ebony framed case, a pleasant reminder of boyhood's triumphant victory over elders and betters, and an aldermanic fish.

9.

SUMMER ROAD TO WALES

THE GREAT TROUT OF PONT BERWI

This chapter is about the great trout of Pont Berwi: such an epic fish deserves one all to itself. Even if you are no angler, the sight of this majestic sea trout would have filled you with awe and reverence, and a desire to encompass his end.

We have, in fact, already met this monster for it was the same fish the angler was playing from the Pont Berwi, and which he lost by its dashing up under the arch. It was the same that took a fly, according to the fisherman's story, under the self-same bridge, though I can't believe that sea trout would have even looked at a fly in that particular river.

I was assured at the post office that nobody had yet started to fish and that I should be wasting my time and money. But, if one angler, in broad daylight, could tempt and hook a sea trout, estimated weight nine pounds upwards, then I might conceivably do the same.

Accordingly, on the eighth of June, at five-thirty in the morning, I was standing on Pont Berwi looking down into the pool below. I had not been leaning over the parapet for more than five minutes before the water bailiff, Richards, joined me.

'He's still there,' said he, looking downwards to the foot of an ashen shelf some five feet under the water.

Cuddled at its foot was a long dark dumb-bell shape. Occasionally a white blur showed when he opened his mouth, the only part of a sea trout's anatomy, seen from above, that betrays its presence.

'You might annoy him with a worm,' said the bailiff, 'he'll look at nothing else, he's been there for six weeks, since the last flood.'

A Welsh trout stream

I rigged up my spinning rod and with one shot on the cast and two lively worms on the hook I dropped the bait in front of his nose. The water was so clear you could see the wriggling pink worms resting on the ledge just in front of him, and the white bar of his mouth puffing now and then.

For a while Richards leaned on the bridge watching me and the fish, then he stumped away to patrol his beat. 'I hope you catch him,' he called over his shoulder.

I went on annoying the dark dumb-bell shape at the foot of the ledge. I 'annoyed him' for half an hour. Quite suddenly a white mouth opened in a blur and at that instant the line went as taut as a bow string; he had succumbed to temptation at last! My big reel screamed. Straight down the pool he went like an express train, coming clean out of the water in one gigantic leap which showed all his massive form. There was a boil at the tail of the pool. My line came back with the hook still on!

Sadly I reeled in. I had just missed the biggest sea trout it had been my lot to see – for ten glorious seconds I had had him on! There was nothing to be done but go home.

The day was very hot with thunder about and in the afternoon I decided to return to the bridge to see if there was any sign of my fish.

I found the bailiff leaning over the parapet.

'He's back, look you, there in the same place, under the ledge.' Cecily and Angela were with me, they leaned over the bridge too and saw it, the dim dumb-bell shape at the foot of the ashy ledge of stone, the occasional whitish gleam of an opening mouth, a paleness which is always as surprising as the glimpse of the palms of a Negro's hands.

Again I dangled a worm before his nose, again and yet again, but he lay sullen with mouth shut. All at once he seemed to wake up. He left his berth and shouldered his way round the pool. I cast my worm in his path, twice he swam over it, the third time he paused in his digni-fied procession, and tilted his big nose. For the second time the line tightened!

Now there was a large stone which lay at the head of the pool. It was called the 'pig' by the locals, partly because it was shaped like a sucking pig but partly, I suspect, for other reasons, as we shall see.

My rod bent in an arc as the great fish re-enacted his run of the morning. He went straight down the pool and leapt. But this time the hook held, and I knew that I had him fast, that, barring accidents, he was mine. Back he came, racing, with me frantically reeling in the slack to keep up with him. He took several turns round the pool, boring deeply and turning on his side to show a glorious gleam of silver. I had seen the angler broken on the evening of the sixth by the fish running up under the bridge and sawing the line through on the arch. I was determined not to be caught by the same trick. I leapt down from the parapet just as he executed that very manoeuvre, a big charge right under the arch into the white water of the fall.

Now, if only Cecily and Angela had been there to turn him by throwing stones he might have been mine, for he was firmly held and my line was 8 lb. BS perlon. It was the *pig* that beat us. The great fish went straight round the rock. The line twanged. It broke!

I still had a chance. My ticket did not expire until midnight and I was determined to try my fortune once again. For, believe it or not, within an hour the great fish was back once more tucked under his ledge! So, at seven o'clock that evening, we again went to the bridge.

If I could persuade him to take just once more, I would get Cecily and Angela to leap the wall and by scare tactics turn him before he reached the 'pig'. But could I deceive him a third time? For two hours I dangled juicy wrigglers in front of his big nose (*pace* you purist fly-fishers) but he heeded them not.

Then Cecily suggested bread-paste, common bread-paste, more indecent as a bait for such a royal fish than even a worm, and she despatched Angela back up the road to the caravan for some bread.

So it came about that I put on the hook a knob of well-kneaded paste. After all, I had caught a two-pound trout with bread-paste whilst fishing for carp in the lake at home.

As soon as the blob of dough came dangling in front of his nose the white mouth gaped like a lizard's. Once, twice, thrice it gaped, then the bread vanished! For the third time that day the line tightened. As it did so I shouted to the girls, 'To the pig!' They were over the wall like gazelles, though one of them laddered a nylon in the process. My fish charged down the pool but this time did not leap. He turned and came back. I was just jumping over the parapet when he rushed past me for the arch and the line slackened for a moment. When I tried to tighten up on him the cast came in slack. The hook was intact, he had not been firmly held.

Within a minute we looked over the arch and he was back in his station once more. 'Good luck to you,' I said as I reeled in my line, 'you deserve to get away – but all the same, it was the pig which saved you!'

Alas! This story has a sad but inevitable ending. On the Sunday morning I went to see if he was back under the ledge. He was. Round his neck was an ugly noose of wire. Richards was watching him.

'Someone tried to snare him in the night, see the broken wire?' I thought to myself, how could that be, how could a poacher take the great fish from right under the windows of the bailiff's cottage? I knew then that it would never leave that pool under Pont Berwi alive, only a sudden merciful flood could save him. This cool parlour under the ledge was, in fact, his prison. His hours were numbered.

On the Monday morning I approached the bridge with fear in my heart. Sure enough, his place was empty, no dim dumb-bell shape lay there.

The bailiff, usually so prompt to materialize, was long in coming down to greet me. We thought he looked askance, and seemed ill at ease.

'I see he's gone,' said I.

'Yes, he's gone. Maybe he's hiding somewhere. But he'd be better out of it with that ugly noose round him.' He looked at the sky. 'Thunder about by the feel of it, I want the rain for the garden.'

He seemed (it may have been my imagination) rather unmoved by the disappearance of the great fish which had been in the pool for six weeks. Anyway, whoever took him, I had had my legitimate chance at him. It was the pig that had robbed me of my prize.

So ends this sad tale of the great trout of Pont Berwi.

10.
LETTERS FROM COMPTON DEVERELL

THE JUNE LETTERS

Compton Deverell Priory

My Dear John,

I seem to remember that some while back I promised you a description of the Priors Pool. As the fishing season is upon me and the weather just now is summery I think the time is ripe. I do not know if you have kept these letters, probably not. After all, they would be better employed in spills for your pipe, but if perchance you can refer to a February letter you will find therein, if I mistake not, a description of the Priory. You cannot form any conception of my English home unless you have a mental image of the pool. A pool to me is as important as a house, I vowed that one day, when I looked about for the home of my dreams, when I searched for the spot where I would end my earthly days, I would have some-where close by, where I could view it from my windows, a still lily-studded water full of fish. It is given to few of us to realise our ambitions. By the grace of God I am one of the few.

The Priors Pool must date from the sixteenth century at least. I have, after long research and with the help of friends, discovered old maps and documents which mention this water. It is a natural lake fed by a small deepish brook which later on, at the completion of its eternal journey, joins Shakespeare's Avon.

It is a small affair here but later where it joins the main river it is a considerable stream and at one time turned several mills, indeed there is a ruined mill, Lambert's Mill, a mile below my property. This mill was working up to the end of the last century, the wheel is still there though the mill house is a weedy willow-girt ruin.

The lake, which is not more than a matter of two hundred yards from the house, is of considerable size, very deep in places and is in the form of a pear, the small end where the stream enters being shallow and choked with willow and sallow, a fine breeding place for duck. On the western bank is Priors Wood and a mixed plantation grows at the southern end. This woodland shelters the pool and makes it very attractive to wildfowl who always like a sheet of water which is flanked by trees. That is why most duck decoys are hidden away in woods, the birds gain a sense of privacy and no wild mallard is partial to an open water inland. On the coast of course it is different.

My predecessor here reared a number of mallard (so I am told) but I must say I prefer the wild stock and have always disliked hand-reared and artificially-fed birds. It offends my hunting instincts to shoot creatures which have been half-tamed and I even feel this about pheasants.

Wild duck bred under artificial conditions become pathetically tame and it is sometimes difficult to get them to fly at all.

I do not know how anyone with any love of nature as well as of sport can bring himself to be so treacherous. Carted deer and bagged foxes come into this category and such practices give a handle to the anti-sport brigade.

The shallow end is a mass of water lilies, white and yellow, and there are several large lily beds on the Priors Wood side. I have to keep these lilies in check, as if they were neglected they would cover several acres of the pool. The boat house, which was in a shocking state when I took over the property (roof gone and supporting timbers broken and decayed), I repaired. My craft consist of a punt, row-boat, and a small sailing dinghy in which Diana and I amuse ourselves when we have no better things to do.

The water is never very clear save in the autumn. It is of a rather beautiful tawny hue, the deepest part is at the southern end where, ten feet from the bank, I plumbed a depth of sixteen feet. There are, however, considerable shallow reaches, especially at the northern end where the stream, through the years, has brought down a considerable quantity of silt. I would like to have this dredged out but when I went into the cost I found that it was prohibitive.

The overflow is at the southern end, through an ancient stone hatch. When I first came here the iron grill which had been placed across the outlet had rusted away and I had a new one put in. After leaving the lake the outflow winds away through the plantation where I have made quite a charming walk, planting snow-drops and aconite beside the banks and keeping the grass mown with a scythe. There is no prettier place on the whole of this little estate and this is one of my favourite spots.

This stream is much frequented by roach, though how they got there is rather a puzzle as they cannot get through the hatch and I suppose must either come up from the lower reaches or were already there when I put up the new fish grill. I can always catch a roach in the stream, at all seasons of the year, and they are no mean fish, some of them run up to a pound and a half in weight. The stream through the plantation is about four feet deep with some deeper holes here and there and Dinty Boyle has told me that 'many's the time, when he was a nipper' he had goodly trout out of this stretch of the stream. That was of course many years back. I have never seen or caught one so they must have all gone down to the Avon.

Unless restocking with trout is undertaken every ten years they never seem to remain or thrive in an inland pool unless one lives over or near the Border. For the first five or six years rainbows give good sport but after a time they will vanish whatever you may do. Brown trout are by far the best but will not be a success in a pond. I have no doubt that if I stocked the brook below the lake they might establish themselves but I hold the trout should be caught in the swift waters of the west or north and not in mid-England. I do not care for 'synthetic' trout fishing!

In the Priors Pool are good old monkish fish; carp, rudd, roach, perch, tench, and, I fear, pike as well. There was a time when pike fishing appealed to me and good fun was to be had in the winter, spinning and live baiting, but now I care not for the fish, for its cruel shovel mouth and wicked eye, and the long shark-like body. There are some very large pike in the pool. I have myself caught them up to twenty-five pounds, and some must be a good deal larger. It is the tench and carp which afford me the greatest pleasure and in a day or so I shall be making my first expedition against them.

Last night after dinner I took out the boat and rowed quietly up to the head of the lake. It was one of those magical evenings we frequently get in June after a hot day, absolutely tranquil with not a suggestion of breeze and all the prime trees laden with their new summer foliage, drooping and still. Near the upper end of the lake is a grove of horse chestnuts which are now in full flower. What an entrancing sight they were in the soft light, each spire of blossom, each white candle erect and still, each tree smothered in bloom, throwing a reflection in the moveless dark water!

I rowed quietly along, the rowlocks giving forth a secret squeak, the water at the bows clucking gently as I pulled. Then I would ship oars and let her glide. The tobacco smoke from my pipe hung in a blue cloud over the surface of the water, descending and 'crawling' along it in a curious way. There was in the air a quite indescribable perfume, a mingled bouquet of grass, leaves, elder flowers, dock leaves, reeds, lilies, and the pond's own special flavour, a wild lustral tang which is somehow intensely exciting to me.

Moorhens scuttled when they saw me coming, breaking up the dark reflections by gleaming spears of light; a pair of mallard, always secretive at this time of moulting, were lurking among a bed of reeds. Gnats danced in fairy fountains. I glided through them, saw them scatter and reform, moving sideways now and then as some imperceptible warm air caught them.

At this time of year the bird song is fading but a song thrush or two were singing their vespers and wood pigeons cooed. The turtle doves also were crooning in a dense thicket of hawthorn on the bank. There is no bird voice of summer which tells of such sweet content. As I neared the end of the pond I shipped oars and glided silently along until the boat brushed softly among the lily pads. Some tench were moving about in the shallows where the stream flows in and now and again there arose above the surface a broad black tail, waving gently as the fish foraged for food, standing on its head. The fragrant peace of the place was indescribable, I cannot attempt to tell you how at ease I was with life, how happy I felt. Hidden from the house I was alone and

The lake at Lambert's Mill

still in my little boat with the chestnuts hanging over me and the late evening light fading behind the dark mass of the wood. Now and again a tremendous splash echoed and re-echoed across the pool as one of the giant carp somersaulted into the air. And every time this occurred some waterfowl would complain in an expostulatory shriek. One would have thought that moorhens and coot would have become used to the nightly stirrings of the big fish but it is not so.

Then a sedge-warbler began to sing close by among a lovely jungle of wild rose and reeds. These little birds have a song which fits their habitat exactly, the churrings and raspy sounds, the clicks and clucks are somehow uncannily suitable, in the same way that the call of moorhens, croak of frogs and quacks of ducks are 'watery' noises conjuring up water mills, camp sheathings, and weedy weirs.

The sedge-warbler sings with great vigour for as long as thirty seconds at a stretch and then is quite silent. One imagines the striped little trim reed bird hopping about in his aquatic forest daintily clasping the grey-green tubular reeds with slender feet, peeping at you with his bright eye.

Talking of frogs reminds me that not long ago, soon after dawn, I put on my dressing-gown and had a stroll by my little rockery pond. I was shocked to hear the silvery peace of dawn rent by a horrible human-like scream and looking along the shrubbery I saw a large black cat had pounced at a frog which had been making for the water. As far as I could see the cat missed his stroke for with one prodigious leap the frog landed in the pond and swimming to a stone out in the water it sat there still screaming in a fearful way. To return to the subject of this letter, I frequently see the signs of otters up the stream here and they also chase the fish in the lake. I have found the half-eaten remains of a splendid tench on the bank which must have weighed 6 lbs. Unless there are roots or stones in a pond, however, the otters must find it a difficult matter to corner a fish and they fare better in the brook. Lambert's Mill is a sure holt when the otter hounds come this way.

Yours
James

11.
THE WAYFARING TREE

I am afraid I am still at heart very much a boy; but why should one be ashamed of such a thing? There is still magic for me, thank God, in the seasons; there is still that sense of awesome mystery in a dark wood; I still lie awake with a slight quickening of the pulses when I know that at first streak of dawn I shall be making my way through the reeds to ambush wild ducks and geese. If ever the day comes when I can no longer feel that thrill, then I would be better dead. It is the same the night before some fishing expedition to perhaps an unknown burn or river, or maybe a pool; I lie awake wondering what the morrow will bring forth, and my mind gets busy with fabulous fish and heavy creels.

The other evening the river below the Lodge, which had been running low and clear for weeks, suddenly awoke. The strange thing was that we had had no rain down in the valley, there must have been a cloudburst in the hills. By dark it had become a roaring torrent, muddy and red; familiar rocks, which I had noted as good 'lies' for sea trout disappeared; it was a real spate. Fly fishing was out of the question and I immediately thought of the Byreburn, a merry water which has many good pools, even when the weather is dry.

I knew that if only the spate would last until the morrow I would be sure of good sport there, not the high class sport of the fly fisher, but the sport of the callant and shepherd's bairn.

Now I can almost see and hear the purist, the true fly fisher, ejaculating 'Pish!' and suchlike sounds of supercilious scorn. 'What! this fellow confesses that he intends to go fishing with a *worrm*! and in a *spate*, too! Disgraceful! and he calls himself a sportsman!'

Well, there you are, I have said before I have never grown up, and in truth there is no other way for one of my skill with the rod to bring to grass those fat brown trout which I know have their secret lurking places in the Byreburn.

I have been up there on many a fine summer day when the water is low and bright, and I have seen nothing larger than a 'smout', but I have fished it in spate and... well, I will not spoil my story. At any rate, as I went to bed, and heard the voice of the river growing, I decided that on the morrow I would fish the Byreburn as soon as I could get my breakfast down, and I lay awake and thought about it.

As they say in the novelettes, 'came the dawn' and with it rain, steady, drumming rain from a forbidding sky.

By now the river and the burns were really angry. They roared and swirled, bearing upon their muddy bosoms barrels, trees, old boxes, and dead wild ducks.

It was useless to think of going, the water was too big. But those who know Scotland will know how quickly she changes her moods. She is like a capricious girl, one moment weeping, another radiant and gentle. At the end of the morning the sun came out, by the end of the afternoon the water was dropping and its voice dying. I could not have wished for a more opportune moment, for a dropping river is the time to fish a spate.

As I made my way down the road after tea I saw the shepherd, clad in a flyaway mackintosh with tattered tails and an inverted clay pipe between his teeth, making his way to the river. I noticed his line was tarred twine and his hook big enough to catch a whale.

It took me half an hour to reach the Byreburn by way of the little ivied bridge under which the dippers build every summer. The sun was lowering, gilding the sodden haycocks in the fields, and the low meadows by the river were musical with curlews.

How wonderful were the hills in that low, clean-washed light! There came the 'caw, caw' of rooks and I saw hundreds of the black thieves perched on some corn stooks. And on a fir tree growing in the Auld Kirkyard ten pigeons were sunning themselves. I passed that forsaken burial ground, with its leaning, mossy graves (some of the incised inscriptions on them are full of moss so that each letter is picked out in thick green lines on the lichened stone) and soon I was beside the Byreburn.

Yes, it was as the shepherd had shouted to me, 'a gey watter for hurrling.' It was not too big and not too small, and only lightly coloured.

It came hurrying and stumbling under the bridge and along its banks the butterburr leaves were limp and draggled as though they had been through a good deal of buffeting.

Many sycamores and plane trees crowded the burn just there and the water was swift and rather shallow.

I pushed on up the path which leads beside the Mains o' Kirk, a grey old farmhouse with many outbuildings and a very green lawn before its west windows.

Beyond were more trees, larches and conifers, thick and dark, bunched together in a wall which shut in the Byreburn and made it a gloomy, troubled place. It was here, so the story goes, that a tinker was murdered long ago as he was on his way to Peebles. They say his ghost may still be seen on frosty moonlight nights.

But it was no evening for ghosts, even the Auld Kirkyard had seemed quite a sunny, peaceful spot when I had passed it. I pushed on along the burn edge, picking my way among the boulders where the litter of the flood lay all about. Pigeons cooed and clappered in the firs and a dipper flew direct in front and alighted on a stone, bobbing his white waistcoat at me.

Still I did not fish, for the water was too boisterous, and I knew I should only lose my hooks, there is nothing like 'hurrling' for losing tackle. So I pushed on.

In a minute or two the fir wood was left behind and I was in a rocky gorge, red, red rocks, as red as Devon rocks, draped with ivy and crowned with bracken where rabbits sat a-sunning. There were some nice little pools under the red cliffs and they yielded (very promptly) three fat trout of a quarter-pound each. Of course, there was no art about it, you chucked and chanced it.

Out flew the worm on its shimmering cast, weighted with three leads gimped on the gut, and in a moment there came that thrilling

A buzzard by the burn

little tug and you swung them out, flipping and kicking, on to the stones.

Then, as I climbed higher, the red cliffs were left behind and I was in the silence of the hills, great, rough, but kindly hills which curved grandly down on either side, green with bracken and red with heather, all a-glow in the evening sun. The Byreburn was getting smaller, with long stretches of chattering shallows, useless for anything but 'smouts'.

Then it bore left, the hills became more steep, there were frequent waterfalls and a red-berried rowan here and there off which large spotted missel-thrushes were feeding greedily. And it was there I saw the first grouse whirr up, 'go backing' from the heather, and curve away like a large black partridge round the hill's shoulder.

A little higher and I came to a grand pool, a really spanking pool, at a bend in the burn. On one side grew a stunted willow bush which nearly overhung it, on the other was a ferny bank. At the head of it the water came sliding in at a gradual angle, a furled and almost silent volume of spate water which lost itself in the sleepy bosom of the deeps. Large clots of yellow froth gravely revolved under the willow, some were caught against it, like whipped yellow cream.

I stole up, flicked my worm into the head ripple, and let the current swing it down into the calm.

Almost at once the line tightened and I was into what I knew was either a very big yellow trout or a sea trout.

And what did he do? Why under the willow roots, of course! Under the willow he dashed, like a miniature torpedo, and there neatly hung me up. I pulled and, Ye Gods! he was still on! I could feel him thrilling down the gut, and it was not the thrill of the obstructing branch.

What to do? Aye, there was the rub. I laid down the rod on the shingle with a quiet and reverent prayer, waded the burn with the net, and cautiously approached the shrub willow. There, in the fast clearing current, I saw a swaying, spotted shape like a captive airship tethered by the nose. He was not a sea trout but a big yellow trout, a real 'burn leopard' of about a pound's weight. How that cast held him I cannot imagine, unless it was because the willow twig gave to his frequent and frantic efforts to disengage himself.

I slipped the net down and tried to scoop him up, but as soon as he saw the net ring he dived from sight. I saw the gut (a fleeting glimpse only) wavering free from the willow, and I thought he must be off. Hastily recrossing the burn I retrieved my rod and reeled in. And that trout was still on! There is no more to tell. He was a beaten fish, and soon I had him on the stones admiring his spotted sides of red and blue.

A pound yellow trout is a good one at the best of times, for the Byreburn it was my best.

I tried the pool again and caught four more nice ones (though they did not compare with the pounder), and then fished on up the valley. All the while the merry water babble was decreasing. Various tributaries had helped to swell its lower reaches, besides which the spate was slackening.

Suddenly I was aware I was in shadow. The sun had slipped behind the hill, night was not far distant. I had a long way to retrace my steps, and there was the tinker's ghost to contend with. He might be tempted out on an evening like this!

Opening my basket I laid all my trout out in a row on the smooth, flood-worn stones. What a picture they made! Fourteen burn trout, ranging in size from a fat pilchard to a really big herring. What a breakfast they would make!

Far up on the shadowed slopes a sheep was bleating. I saw it, a pudgy, fat-faced youngster with astonished eyes. No doubt it had lost its mother. I like these Border breed, they have such intelligent faces compared to the dirty grey 'mops' at home.

Rabbits ran about the higher banks, some sat up and watched me, hundreds of rabbits, millions of rabbits! Plenty of good meat here, thought I, plenty of good meat for the getting! No cloud up there above the clear-edged hill, just a soft glaze of daffodil; little sound but the lonely conversation of the burn. I had a sense of great antiquity in my surroundings, far more powerful than that experienced in some ancient cathedral. The very rocks about me were ground and worn by time, polished as smooth as skulls.

Curlee! Curlee! I lifted my eyes and there, high up, flew three curlew with the evening light upon them. Down here I was in a valley of shadow, they were still looking into the eye of the sinking sun.

I was tired of this sunless place. Putting my fish into my basket and taking down my rod, I climbed away up the slope. Very quickly, at every upward step, the voice of the water dwindled, and soon I was in a frightening silence. For the last two hours the tumble and fret of the Byreburn had filled my brain; it was like coming out of a noisy power house into the open air.

Up and up and then I was on the hill top, only a little hill. Below now was the burn, very bright and glittering, reflecting the sky in a cleft of grey shadow.

But unlike those gilded angels, the curlews, which still wheeled high above, crying, crying, I was too late to see the last of the sun.

Homing rooks were strung out across the sky heading for the woods of Westerhall; away there too was the great river, the mother of every burn and burnlet in a hundred hills. It flowed like white-hot metal in the sunset's light, away to south and Solwayside. Not long now, old river, and you will feel the sea and hear the cry of the white gulls about your sandbanks!

I saw the hillsides creased and furrowed by those tributary burns which go to make that river what it is; mere drains they may be from the roof of Britain, but very lovely nevertheless, decked as they are with scarlet-berried rowan, bright green ferns, and purple ling.

All this water, ceaselessly pouring to the sea, for thousands of years.

But it was no time to idle. I had a long march to go, and I set myself to the task. I cut across the Kirkhall fields, shunned the Auld Kirkyard and the tinker's wood, and soon had my feet on the lowland road, where big beetles boomed in the dusk, and an owl called from the gloomy woods of Castle O'er.

12.

CONFESSIONS OF A CARP FISHER

THE KING OF CARP

One of the old philosophers once remarked that fortune favoured everybody at least once in a lifetime, but that most people failed to recognise the right moment: he who ignored the fickle goddess would never be allowed to grasp the chance again.

Such moments tend to occur more than once in the life of an angler or hunter. Let me relate a case that happened to me.

Soon after the 1914–18 War a friend of mine, also a passionate angler, invited me to spend my holidays with him in a village on the shores of Lake Balaton, where we would fish for *fogosh* (the famous pike-perch of Lake Balaton). At that time the fishing possibilities of this vast expanse of water were practically undiscovered by sportsmen, and for a number of years we were undisputed masters of the fishing grounds. Things have changed since then, but we still treasure grateful memories of ten perfect fishing holidays spent there.

By chance I was introduced one day to the art of fishing for carp. We had made an excursion to Keszthely and, on the way back, met an old acquaintance on the train. Noticing my fishing gear he enquired how many carp I had caught.

'We don't fish for carp,' I replied, 'we only catch *fogosh*.'

'And how big are they?'

'Oh, not very big, about 4 to 8 ounces.'

'Isn't it rather boring catching such small fry?' my friend asked.

'Why, do you by any chance catch sharks?'

'Well, not exactly. But in the space of two weeks I have caught

A corner of a carp pond

seventeen carp. None of them weighed less than four pounds, and my bag included two of twelve pounds and one eighteen pounder. I have also hooked some even heavier fish, which I lost again. On the day of my departure I went down to a spot by the edge of the reeds where I had been ground-baiting, and a whale of a carp took my bait. Try as I would, I couldn't tire him. He fought so powerfully and with such determination that he broke my rod and my very strong line and escaped. And that is the third time this has happened to me!'

My friend's tale of the great carp excited my angler's imagination. Perhaps I would never have started to fish for carp, had I not been told of the existence of such a rod-destroying, line-breaking, ferocious fish. It would be worth one's while to pit one's wits against a fellow like that!

I took the first opportunity of buying hooks and a line suitable for carp and returned to Balatongyörök, the village on Lake Balaton.

'From now on I am going to fish for carp,' I told my friend John.

He smiled: 'You are, are you? Better have a talk with Michael Varga, the professional fisherman. He knows the lake like his pocket and is sure to show you a spot where there are carp.'

However, I did not ask Michael, much as I regretted this later on. For a whole week I sought the carp in vain. I did manage to catch four, but none of them scaled more than two pounds.

Rowing back to the boathouse one morning, who should help me out of the boat but Michael Varga. Glancing at my meagre catch he shook his head and said: 'You're fishing at a hopeless spot, sir. The water is too shallow next to the reeds there, and the bottom far too muddy. You'll rarely find a large carp stray to a spot like that.'

'Where would I stand a better chance?' I asked.

'I'm free this afternoon,' Michael volunteered. 'If you like, we'll look for a better spot and also have a look at the old one.'

The sun was very hot that afternoon and no breath of air disturbed the smooth mirror-like surface of the lake. As arranged, Michael appeared at the boathouse at half past two, carrying with him a reedcutter with a long handle.

We got into the boat and Michael took hold of the oars. With quiet, sure strokes he headed out for the reedbeds.

Arriving there, he dipped the oars into the water carefully, avoiding any splashing and rowing very slowly. Keeping a steady distance of eight to ten yards from the edge of the reeds, he silently pointed to a number of different places. In vain did I strain my eyes, I saw nothing. Later on, I at least noticed a slight movement or an almost imperceptible rustling noise among the reeds, whenever the oars slightly stirred the water – although Michael dipped them into it almost noiselessly – and the carp, noticing the approach of something strange, fled into the reedbeds.

Michael let the boat drift and instructed me: 'Look carefully in the direction I am pointing out, sir. There in the shady part of the reeds, near the open water, some eight or ten inches below the surface, you will see the carp; there are many of them enjoying the sun to-day.'

I tried to follow Michael's instructions. For quite a while I saw nothing. Then, gradually, as if my eyes had been enchanted, I began to perceive large, motionless fishes, hugging the edge of the reedbed no more than a couple of hands below the surface.

We continued to row along the edge of the reeds, which stretch as far as Keszthely. I noticed innumerable carp, from four and five up to sixteen and even twenty pounds. Hardly stirring a fin, they seemed to be asleep in the sun. No sooner, however, did the boat get closer to them, when they suddenly allowed themselves to sink into the depths or fled into the rustling reeds. Finally my eyes became so experienced that I even noticed that the larger specimens were the more careful ones and that they dived or fled earlier than their smaller brethren.

In the meantime we had reached my old pitch. Michael thrust one of the oars into the water: the depth hardly exceeded one yard, but it

was no difficult matter to press the oar into the mud for another yard and a half. On lifting the oar back into the boat, we saw that the blade was coated with grey, slimy mud.

'This is a bad spot,' said Michael, 'the mud is too deep and the water too shallow. Carp don't like that. I could find you a better place near here, but I'd like to suggest that we row over to the stretch of water near the houses, where the bottom near the high reeds is clear and the water deep. You'll be sure to find large carp there.'

'All right,' I consented, 'let's try it there.'

After some twenty minutes of rowing, Michael arrived at the chosen spot.

Here the reedbeds extended some sixty or seventy yards from the shores of the lake and were so thick that it would hardly have been possible to penetrate through them with a boat. Small bays cut into them and here the growth was not quite so thick.

Michael stopped the boat in one of these bays and, keeping close to the reeds, tried to measure the depth with the aid of an oar. Although this was nearly three yards long, he failed to reach the bottom.

He was satisfied. 'The water is deep here,' he said, 'and the bottom consists of good, hard clay. There is a thin layer of mud as far as the reeds and after that the clay bottom stretches far into the lake. Carp love to rest in this deep water. Then, when they start to move, they swim up to the reeds and forage for food. This will be a grand pitch for you, sir.'

Michael then began to prepare the pitch for me. First he removed all odd reed stalks which might have got into the way of my line. After that he rowed right up to the edge of the reedbed and, taking hold of some thirty stalks, tied them into a big bunch with the aid of some wire. This process was repeated some four yards further along, and lo and behold! I had a first rate anchorage.

'Those reed bundles will hold the boat even in rough weather,' he assured me.

I thoroughly liked the look of the place. By good fortune – or maybe by the foresight of Michael – it even faced north, so that the sun did not hurt my eyes.

The next step was to bait up the place. I used nearly four pounds of maize, cooked to a nicety, and distributed it along the edge of the reedbed. This I repeated on the following three days.

On the fourth morning, at 6 a.m., I rowed out for the first time with the intention of fishing.

Stealthily I approached my pitch and was most careful to avoid making the slightest sound with my oars. I was practically holding my breath while I baited my hook with maize prior to casting out to the edge of the reedbed on my left.

Hardly a few minutes had passed, when the float suddenly began to move and then disappeared altogether. I struck and the line tightened. The fish was putting up a good fight and felt heavy, but after a few moments the line slackened and came back to me. I had struck too early and the fish had managed to free itself.

On the following day I was more successful. I caught three carp, but their total weight was no more than ten pounds.

With that I had broken the ice. Soon I had caught a mirror carp of eight pounds and a 'wild' carp of eleven pounds. The latter gave me such a tug when I struck him that I nearly fell out of the boat. He fought so fiercely and so tenaciously that I was inclined to mistrust my scales when they showed no more than eleven pounds.

These wild carp,[1] recognisable by the elongated body and the small scales covering the whole of it, generally fight so fiercely that only in the rarest cases is a really big one caught. Usually something breaks or the hook is torn free.

One morning early a mist covered Lake Balaton. The sky was grey

---

[1] Our 'common' carp in England.

106

and hardly a sunbeam penetrated the thick layers of clouds. Noiselessly I approached my usual place and cast out my line. No sooner had the float cocked itself, when it began to give unmistakable signs of the bait having aroused the interest of a fish. Taking up the rod, I prepared to strike but by that time the float once more lay motionless. The fish had removed the bait without touching the hook. I baited up again and made another cast. The bait could have hardly reached the bottom, when my float suddenly disappeared in a most determined manner. I struck at once.

But what has happened? Have I hooked a rock?

My line is tight and it seems as if I have caught the bottom of the lake. Whatever it is, I can't move it, though I try hard enough. Finally the strain eases a little and I am able to regain some line. The fish shows less resistance and allows me to drag him nearer to the boat.

Staring into the slightly coloured water I reel in and… get the fright of my life.

A huge, uncouth apparition slowly surfaces no more than a couple of yards from the boat. The pale mouth gapes, it must be ten inches in diameter. The line disappears in his gullet, only the shaft of the hook is visible somewhere in the depths. The water rushes through the open gills and the pectoral fins move slowly and evenly not unlike a ship's screw. The gleaming scales are the size of silver dollars and the dorsal fin reminds me of a sail. Indeed, a huge, a powerful carp!

Now he has seen me! He makes a sudden flight towards the reeds, but I am prepared.

Suddenly lifting the tip of my rod, I succeed in getting his head up, and, carried forward by his own impetus, he gains the open water.

I breathe again, but I know that my troubles are by no means over yet.

Twenty-five yards are between us now, and it is time to turn him again. Once more I lift the rod, begin to reel in and to slowly lead the fish back to the boat.

Thank heavens that worked! Now I shall have to reel in faster and take care to ensure that the line remains tight, because I know there will be another flight as soon as he feels the slightest loosening.

And now I can also take a side view of my monstrous antagonist. His length is at least four feet and a half!

Once more he begins to work away from me and I can hardly keep him out of the reeds. I feel the cold sweat breaking on my forehead.

Again I prevent him from gaining safety in the reeds. His flight takes him out into the open water; will I be able to land him after all?

He seems to be less sure of himself now, his flights are irregular and he is continuously changing direction. I apply more strain and he shakes his head. Obviously he is beginning to feel vexed.

Now he makes what appears to be a supreme effort. Impetuously he charges into the open water.

I have a notion that something will go wrong, my rod is bent to its utmost and the line sings like a harp-string.

My heart is beating like mad, my throat is parched and I can hardly breathe.

Now I must try and turn him, my reel is nearly empty. He is still tearing away powerfully, fighting for his life and for his freedom. He wallows in the water, jumps, and again pulls with all his might.

All attempts to get some line back on the reel are in vain. I even climb into the bow of the boat in order to regain a yard or two. All to no avail. I can't move him an inch. The fish is fighting furiously, churning up the water. Suddenly the line snaps and I stumble back, nearly falling over the seat.

The line is slack and from the end a length is missing. With it the lead, the trace, the hook and my monster carp...

Discouraged and exhausted I untied the boat, and, knees still atremble, I rowed home.

My lunch was waiting by the time I returned, but I could hardly eat a bite and was seriously thinking of giving up fishing on Lake Balaton and of departing the following day.

That afternoon a thunderstorm broke at about four p.m. and from then till six o'clock it rained continuously. Fishing was out of the question for my friends as well, and, as was usual in such circumstances, we met in the inn. I told them my tale of woe, without, however, arousing much sympathy. On the contrary, they pulled my leg and only John tried to console me. 'Never mind,' he said, 'you'll get many a big 'un yet!'

Their attitude had embittered me even more, and I soon dropped the subject.

I went home, had supper, and went for a walk, ending up near the boathouse, where I sat down and gazed across the lake.

It was a clear, calm night, the moon was nearly full and the air sweet and mild after the rain. I smoked one cigarette after the other as I once more lived through the morning's fight, my nerves still on edge and my eyes unable to forget the sight of that majestic carp.

'Good evening, sir,' Michael's well-known voice suddenly reached me through the darkness.

'Good evening, Michael! Come closer and sit down. I'd like to tell you something.'

Michael joined me and I related the whole story of my adventure in all details: when and how I had hooked the fish, his flights and how I had parried them, how he had finally broken loose, and how vexed I was with myself to have lost him in the end.

'Didn't you see five gleaming, white protuberances on the shoulders of the fish, like a five-pointed crown?' Michael asked, and, thinking back, it really seemed to me as if I had seen a number of protruding white spots near its head.

'If the fish you hooked wore this white crown, you'll never succeed in landing it. It is the biggest fish in the whole of Lake Balaton, the 'King of Carp'. Nobody knows how old it is, it may well be more than a hundred. Twenty-five years ago our most famous harpooner struck him with his great, five-pronged harpoon, whilst the fish was sunning himself in deep water. Even then he was a giant, who fought back with all the power at his command. In the end he succeeded in upsetting the boat, throwing the fisherman into the water. But even then our harpooner held on to his weapon, the fight continued in the water until finally the flesh of the carp gave way, the fish escaped. The fisherman, half drowned, was saved by his friends, and the carp, too, recovered in spite of his wounds. Flesh grew where the prongs of the harpoon had bitten into his body and now it looks as if the fish is wearing a five-pointed crown. He is nearly twice as big as the second largest fish of the lake, and perhaps this is the first time in his life that he has felt a hook. He has often been caught in nets, but each time he has made good his escape, generally by tearing the net to pieces. The fishermen of Lake Balaton know him well and fear him, for they know he will tear their nets to shreds. So don't feel grieved, sir, that you lost him, be grateful that he didn't drag you into the water.'

I gave some thought to what Michael had told me. Many tales of this kind have been born on the shores of Lake Balaton, but there is always a grain of truth at the bottom of them. And so there was in Michael's tale. Don't we anglers forever wait for the monster fish, the king of fish, to take our bait? It is he we dream of when we watch our float for hours on end, whether from the shore or from the boat. And when, finally, he does take our bait, he laughs at our dreams, gives an almighty tug and breaks us.

Michael's tale had given me back my peace of mind. It was late, and so we walked home.

'Nevertheless,' I said to Michael, 'I won't rest until I have caught this King of Carp!'

'You'll never catch him, sir. Many another good one, but the King, the one so many would like to catch, will always elude you!'

Early the following morning I was back on my pitch and ever since I have been waiting for the carp monarch of Lake Balaton.

Already I have caught one carp of twenty-eight pounds, many large ones, and even more smaller ones, but never again have I encountered the giant that broke me on a misty summer morning of 1924.

I have often told my friends this story, and one, a witty fellow, once replied:

'I know a similar story.'

'What would that be?'

'Josef was serving his time in Vienna, way before the war. After his return to his village, his father asked him: "Well, have you seen the old Emperor?" "Once," replied Josef, "but then it wasn't him."'

And yet, I maintain, it *was* him!

THE LAST DAY OF THE SEASON

I have just been putting away my tackle and have held in my hand a little scarlet-tipped quill which has been a faithful friend and lucky talisman for several seasons. Many times it has traversed submarine depths following its prey, like stoat pursues quarry, many times has it explored shadowed fathoms unseen by the eye of man.

It has frequently disappeared from view in the nether pit of Beech-mere and has no doubt witnessed some interesting battles and doings of bulky carp. It has become enmeshed in sunken trees, and has, on many occasions, been tangled in willow branches, lily pads and weed banks. Yet somehow it returns to my basket as faithfully as a homing pigeon and will, I hope, be my cheerful companion in many another carping expedition in the years to come. Only yesterday, at fall of eve, it tracked a mailed and weighty warrior into the depths of a pool. Alas! it was not in at the death, for death there was not; that invisible muscular adversary dismembered my gear among sunken thickets and I had to reel sadly in.

It was the last day of the season, a day in mid-September, by which time carp are thinking of going downstairs and taking up their quarters for the winter. After weeks of hot sunlight, scorched pastures, withering trees and bushes, the rain had come. It came softly, sweetly, in the night watches, a refreshing hissing fall which has so eagerly been awaited by the parched land. At dawn, when I arose, it was still gently falling, making rings in the rockery pool. I stole about the house like a felon so as not to awaken my family; I crept in stockinged feet into the kitchen and grilled myself some kippers, and the rich aroma filled the sleeping, disregarding house.

Outside the sky was growing even lighter. Some young swallows, perched upon my willow, roused themselves and stretched, leaning forward and raising their little wings so that the back of each touched its fellow, which is the way a bird stretches its 'arms'.

Another yawned and tucked in his head again, yet another began to twitter and preen, casting an eye towards the sky where pearl-grey rain-clouds hurried over. I felt a pang of sorrow that they would soon be gone, that I should have to wait for seven long months before I saw them again.

My breakfast done and tackle packed I was away, calling for a friend nine miles distant and going on from there to this unknown pool. Unknown carp pools are always a delight, and this proved to be no exception.

It lay among remote Leicestershire pastures, visible only when you had penetrated a veil of thick trees. Standing in the nearby lane you would not have guessed a pool was there. The way in, through some double gates, was locked and barred, and the confines of the wood hedged about with many strands of barbed wire. I have yet to meet the barbed wire which can keep *me* out and, having a clear conscience as the permit was in my friend's pocket, we wriggled through a rabbit run with the agility and expedition of small unbreeched urchins.

First there was an awful pond, set in a hole, black as the nether pit and upon whose ebony face rotifers gyrated. Heaven knows what depth it was; to me it appeared fathomless! On one side was a cloudy weed cushion, deep under the surface, a fungoid-looking growth with scarlet tentacles, on the other an ashen blasted tree whose writhing naked branches were reflected in the inky waters.

But what a pond for carp! and how impossible it would be to ever get one out! This was not the water where we were to fish however – that lay a hundred yards on and was a much less forbidding place. To reach it we threaded a pleasant wild woodland where blackthorn and teazel flourished and jays scolded. And then, in a step or two, a vista opened both charming and rare, the sight of an irregular pool of about an acre in extent, its banks bushed with thick trees – sycamore, ash, oak. The rain in the night had moistened the leaves which had fallen about their feet, leaves decayed before their time owing to the dry hot summer. From this fallen damp carpet which rustled under our feet there arose the most exquisite perfume which took me back immediately to the days of my babyhood. Each day in the winter our governess, a dear little lady called Miss Nicholson (who is still living, I am glad to say), took us down to the post office in the village about a quarter of a mile from our house. The road at that spot was overhung with elms, limes, and some sycamores, and was never dry from September to May.

Of course, in those days, there was no tarmac, and I well remember the ridges of soft mud left by the pram wheels as we went along. From this moist muddy road where fallen leaves were ground into the mud to form a sort of porridge there used to arise this same smell which I noticed and recognized yesterday.

While we were setting up our rods on a little promontory, whose worn, cracked earth suggested it was a much frequented angling post, an enormous butterfly swooped over the trees and flapped over the water, dipping once into it before soaring over the opposite wood. What it was I had no idea and have never seen any British insect like it.

The water was not very clear and was of considerable depth, close to the bank it was eight feet or so and a much greater depth in the centre. I cannot say that the pool appeared to me exactly 'carpy', it was perhaps too cheerful and tended a spot; the fishermen's seats, hut, and neat paths may have given this impression. However that may be, I had no run on stout ledger tackle and it was not until after lunch, when I was walking round the pond on the wood side, that I saw any sign of carp. Then I spied a common carp of about three pounds swimming in a deep bay half screened by willows. A little farther on a fat mirror, he looked 2 lb and had a most benevolent face, was lazily swimming close to the bank. I noticed him rise now and again to have a look at small floating willow leaves, one of which he actually took into his mouth and swam down with it, expelling it when he had swum a dozen yards or more.

I thought I might have a chance at him with floating bread, and though he did not appear more than 2 lb I took off my ledger and substituted a lighter greased line and roach hook to gut which I tied direct to the line.

The cherub-like mirror disappeared, but about ten minutes later I observed his bluish form swimming below the crust. He did not seem to see it at first. He then came and had a close inspection of a willow leaf two yards from my bait (which by then must have been fairly sodden as it had been immersed for quite a quarter of an hour or more).

He then noticed the bread. He swam round it twice, came close, stared at it, turned away, and came upwind, just as Burton says they do. It was my first experience of this method in open water and the thrill was great even though it was no record fish. He sucked it in, turned swiftly about, and the line slipped through the rings. I never struck him, just tightened, and for ten minutes we had a pretty exhibition. I saw he was bigger than I thought at first and when at last my friend slipped the net under him as I towed him past, head out of water, he was soon kicking in the folds. A second later he was flopping on the grass, a fish of 4 lb exactly, by my pocket scales.

This shows how deceptive it is to judge carp in the water. I should never have guessed it *was* a four pounder. It made me think of a Bedfordshire pool and a huge balloon-like form of a big chap I once saw one summer day. That fish must have been nearer thirty than twenty if this 'mirror' was anything to go by!

When the carp had been returned to the pool the sun went in and I changed to worm, a lob, fished on the same tackle but with my favourite scarlet-tipped quill before mentioned. About an hour later, just before sundown, the scarlet tip sank from sight and a terrific 'pull' ripped off the reel line as the fish made straight across the pond. Against the far bank was a sunken briar bush and into this my carp went – and that was that. I had no 'banjo string' to hold him off and a break was inevitable.

What this fish weighed I have no idea as, of course, I never saw it but I am sure it was a common carp from the power of his rush, mirrors never seem to possess such strength.

As we had used up the last of the 'lobs' and a mournful autumnal wind began to rustle in the trees, we packed up our tackle and came away, threading the winding paths among the thickets where already leaves of sloe were turning salmon-pink.

Such was the last day of the season, a sorrowful occasion but one on which I look back with considerable pleasure.

After September is out most carp go below and stay there until the following spring. I do not think this pretty pool contains any record-breakers, indeed I am not sure many carp are there; they certainly do not breed as there is not enough weed. I also had the impression it was

What a pond for carp!

overstocked. Roach, perch and pike are never the best bed-fellows to carp.

The chief interest for me in yesterday's expedition was the opportunity to try the floating bread method in open water. Without a wind it is difficult to get the crust out. I was fortunate in having a backing breeze from exactly the right quarter, indeed I once floated the crust right across the pool, paying out the line as the wind took the bait. I also experimented with a small raft made from a scrap of bark, resting the bread upon it.

But with the 'boat' method I usually manage to get some tangles in my coiled line; a single blade of grass, a leaf or twig, will cause the moving line to 'snarl', the bait is jerked off the 'boat' and the whole laborious business has to be begun again.

It is an exciting business to see a great fish turn into the wind, grab your bread crust in one sullen salmon-like lunge, and make off with it.

I have little to add to these notes, I have told all I know about big carp. I feel that I have no authority to write a book on carp fishing as I have never caught a very big one. But the reader will, perhaps, have guessed this. It may well be that even now, at this very hour, there is, somewhere in some country, a tough old alderman which is destined to fulfil my lifelong ambition. There he swims in that unknown water, questing perhaps, like a great bronze hog among the dark forest of the lily roots. Our destinies may be united, and my desires will be satisfied! But now the red leaves of autumn whirl, the wind pipes mournfully among the trees, leaden ripples lap on lonely forgotten shores.

I think this autumn night of Beechmere, wrapped in deepest shadow, the beechen tops restless and hissing in the wind, the sinister dark waters brooding and waiting, barely ruffled by an occasional puff of air.

I think of my other well-loved haunts wrapped in the mantle of this same night with the owls calling among the woods and foxes setting out for their evening's hunting.

I think of Woodwater, of how the stars are now shining down on its broad fine acres, whilst high overhead fly the migrating birds.

I heard only the other day that, during the war, a German plane dropped an oil bomb one night into Woodwater, no doubt mistaking the pale glimmering expanse for some cringing town. But I doubt whether the carp suffered much harm.

My rods are laid up in their cases, my tackle put away, the summer has gone.

But summer days will come again, and yet again, and if I am spared I will be there once more, beside the pools I know and love, listening to the cooing of wood pigeons yet unborn, smelling the wild sweet water as it smokes in the summer dawn.

Being an habitual carp fisher, I am content to wait. After all, waiting is part of the game, I am well used to it.

Part Three

A SHOOTING MAN

The fowler

From *A Child Alone*

The next morning I heard the back door bang and saw Bob Dickens crossing the yard by the coach house carrying a long brown paper parcel. *The gun had come!*

I flew downstairs and burst into the kitchen. Bob Dickens was having a cup of tea with the cook. My long parcel was on the kitchen table. With feverish hands, I undid the string, removed the paper – and there beheld a green gun case. Inside was my new gun. Not since 'Gunn's gun' was I so overcome with triumph and delight. My satisfaction was even greater because I had saved up for it so long – well over a year – and now here was a new gleaming double barrel, all my very own, complete with case and cleaning rods.

The young of today, so often shockingly spoilt, can have no idea of what it was to save up for a thing and, by one's own endeavours, achieve one's desire. No more footling about with crazy .22 rifles, or Perkins' ancient and very unsafe .410. No more single barrels with nothing to spare if you missed – which I usually did! I was now well armed and ready. What a day that was to remember.

I showed the gun to Perkins with great pride. I rubbed oil in the cheap wood of the stock. I polished the barrels and oiled the locks. I was *so* happy.

13.

TIDE'S ENDING

SHOOTING PARTY

Most boys begin shooting at an early age and I have described in other books some of my youthful experiences, of how I saved up my pennies week after week to purchase my first weapon, a twelve-bore. (Hitherto I had possessed a crazy .22 rifle and an equally crazy four-ten. The .22 had blown up and injured my eye when I was firing at a tit, a well-deserved punishment, it seems to me now.)

But one's first shooting party, surely, is a great occasion. (In my case it was unusually memorable.) I do not think that this account is out of place in the present book, and it will also serve, perhaps, as a horrible warning to other boys who are referred to by sporting relatives as the 'young entry'.

When I was about fifteen years of age I went to stay with my god-father who was by way of being a sportsman-naturalist and to whom I owe, perhaps, my own love of shooting and wild life generally.

A neighbour of his, whom I will call 'Major Heathcote', was a peppery old gentleman who lived about three miles from my godfa-ther's house. He was as keen and punctilious over shooting matters as are some men over foxhunting. He reared a large number of pheas-ants (he was a very rich man, and employed three keepers on his large estate) and an invitation to one of his shoots was considered an attrac-tive fixture by the sporting gentry of the neighbourhood, especially as the hospitality provided was renowned.

I cannot think what induced my godfather to take me with him on that fateful day unless it was the fact that I had by that time become (though I say it myself) an unusually excellent shot for a youngster. I seem to remember the Major had been let down by a gun at the last minute, and had in a rash moment asked my godfather to find someone to fill his place.

I was quite terrified when I was summoned to the latter's study and told that I was to 'stand in'. The idea of shooting in company did not appeal to me; my idea of the true joy of a gun was to potter about the spinneys at home with Rollo, our spaniel. One saw more of the wild life of field and wood, and one had to work for one's game. Mechanical slaughter was (and is) distasteful to me.

It was with some trepidation, therefore, that I found myself sitting beside my godfather that frosty December morning en route for 'Blaydon Manor', with the guns in the back, and Hughie Bell, my godfather's groom, in his best tweed coat and breeches and mirror-like leggings, looking very neat and spruce. He was to act as my godfather's loader, a rôle in which he was well versed. Between his knees was Bruce, a black labrador which my godfather had recently bought on Bell's recommendation, a 'second season' dog whose parents had been Field Champions and which Bell had pronounced to be a 'grrand worrker'. (Bell was a keeper's son and knew a lot about shooting matters.)

Steam from the pony's nostrils puffed on the keen air as we drove along and I was glad of my thick tweed overcoat and scarf which the housekeeper had insisted on, much to my disgust.

I noticed the puddles in the road were white with cat's ice, the wayside grass crisp and furred with rime. Hedgerow oaks and elms were likewise decorated and in the air was that keen spice of frost which made the blood tingle.

The first drive was outside a big oak wood and when we arrived we found about half a dozen guns already assembled, standing about, talking and smoking. A little distance away was a cluster of keepers and loaders, and a knot of cloth-capped rustics carrying white rags tied to sticks. Major Heathcote's head keeper was giving instructions to the beaters as we came up. He touched his hat to my godfather and I thought he regarded me with rather a jaundiced eye; he was the kind of keeper who views all small boys with distrust.

Major Heathcote came bustling up. He wore a rough brown tweed jacket with leather shoulder pads and cuffs, and a deerstalker.

'Glad to see you, Boy,' he said, giving my hand a terrible grip and looking keenly at me with piercing blue eyes. 'I hear you are a useful shot; good of you to stand in, I'm sure.'

I saw his glance fall upon my new twelve-bore which I carried proudly under my arm. 'Nice little weapon; you ought to be able to shoot with a gun like that.'

My godfather nodded. 'He hasn't really got used to it yet, Major, so don't be too hard on him if he misses a bird or two.'

'Quite right, quite right,' puffed the Major, 'start on a twelve as soon as you can.' He took my gun from me and examined it with a profes-sional air. He opened the breech, looked down the barrels, snapped it to, and handed it back with the verdict – 'a little beauty; you're a lucky feller; better gun than ever I had when I was a boy.' (A remark I did not believe for a moment as it was not a first-class weapon.)

Meanwhile other guns were coming up and exchanging greetings. I looked about me, to see if I could spot Hughie Bell. I saw him a little distance away deep in conversation with a keeper. They were discussing Bruce who was submitting to a close examination. Bell's companion had his hand round the dog's muzzle and was looking at his teeth. Other dogs sat about expectantly, all on leads, with their pink tongues hanging. I noticed a fat Clumber which followed Major Heathcote about with an air of anxious weariness, never leaving his heel, and ignoring the other canine guests with an expression of superiority.

By now the sun had come up and rime began to rustle down from the twigs of the trees; blue shadows lay in the shelter of hedges but in the sunlight the frost was melting. I noticed a few pigeons flying over the big oak wood.

All along the cover side, out in the field, were little sticks with white labels stuck in their tops, and I wondered which my stand was to be. Perhaps I should be 'beater's gun', whatever that entailed, and rather hoped I would be. I did not fancy standing out in the open competing with the 'professionals'.

Major Heathcote was now moving energetically about giving orders in a military manner. The beaters and keepers trailed off round the wood and the guns and their loaders began to sort themselves out.

Then the Major came puffing across to my godfather. He had a habit of blowing out his purple cheeks.

'Ah, there you are. I've put you at the top, number seven, the boy's at number ten. Mind my beaters, Boy,' he added, turning to me, 'and remember – cocks only!'

Bell, with my godfather's second gun under his arm, and carrying a cartridge magazine, came up, and I tagged along after them, wishing myself pottering about with Rollo at home.

My godfather, never a keen shooting man, had not instructed me in the etiquette of shooting parties and the Major's last remark about 'cocks only' was rather mystifying. If I had had more warning I would have confessed my ignorance to Bell who might have enlightened me. As it was I remained mute; there was no chance now to buttonhole him.

I could not for the life of me see how I was to distinguish cocks from hens if they came out of the wood at any height. A pheasant at home, cock or hen, was speedily in the bag. Also I had forgotten my number and pictured myself wandering about trying to find my peg.

I need not have been anxious, however, for when my godfather and Bell reached their position the latter nodded reassuringly to me and said, 'You're number ten, Master Denys,' and I found my place without difficulty. On my right was a very tall thin man in knickerbocker breeches, white spats, and with a drooping moustache. A dour-faced valet was in respectful attendance. My left-hand gun was a stout little Pickwickian man with a merry rubicund face and glasses which glinted in the sun. He looked as if he couldn't shoot a thing. He had no loader with him and I mildly wondered why. A fat liver-and-white spaniel sat bolt upright behind him looking at the wood.

A silence fell. I looked along the line, saw the expectant figures waiting, and sensed the intense drama of the scene.

Beaters and keepers had vanished. Away to the left a kestrel was poised, its outspread wings quivering a little. Then it tilted, slanting away over the wood. The minutes passed. Then a jay screamed somewhere in the cover. It came slyly out with dipping flight to seek the refuge of a small plantation of fir on the side of a hill behind us.

Still nothing happened. My excitement was mounting. My mouth felt 'dried up', I fervently hoped no bird would come anywhere near me. Quite oblivious of the drama being enacted, a man was ploughing on a far slope. The team moved slowly, sluglike, up the tawny stubble, with rooks and a few white gulls clustering and dipping in attendance. Far away a train whistled on the clear keen air, and a party of starlings moved like shiny beetles out in the field behind us, now and again one or two birds would rise up in a jangling quarrel.

Then the first pheasant came straight out of the wood, climbing steadily, its wings whirring and gliding, the long tail streaming straight out behind. It was well away to my right. I watched with interest mingled with a relief that it was not my bird. Looking down the line I saw one man put up his gun in a hesitant way, lower it, then another slender barrel pointed skywards. I saw it swinging and a faint puff of smoke jetted forth a few inches from the muzzle. A second later came the dry thunderclap of the shot.

The steadily flying bird (it was too far for me to see whether cock or hen) seemed to be arrested in mid-air a fraction before I saw the smoke. It fell far back in the meadow. Muffled sounds now came from the wood, far away uncouth noises, and tapping of sticks.

Two more pheasants appeared, right away at the end of the line where my godfather was. One fell, the other went on, followed by a cluster of shots.

Then a bird came out over 'Mr Pickwick'. For one moment I thought it was coming over me and my heart thumped painfully. I half put up my gun but when I saw him aiming I lowered it just in time. It was awfully hard to judge range and direction.

I could see quite clearly it was a cock. The sun shone on its burnished golden mail, the long tail quivered and streamed behind it with the exertion of its wings.

Then it staggered, I saw a puff of feathers fly from its breast and it fell like a stone, hitting the ground with a thump thirty yards behind me, and the wood threw back an echo to the shot.

The little man, to my surprise, never turned round. I heard his gun click and saw the empty, smoking case fly out. He darted one sideways glance at me and gave me a wink which was immensely comforting.

Shots now began to crack out all up the line and the air was fragrant with powder. The pheasants came out now every moment, all high birds. Some fell like stones, one or two slanted down in a steep glide, a few passed steadily on, ignoring the cannonade. Then I saw *my* pheasant coming. There was no doubt about whose bird it was. With two nervous sidelong glances I reassured myself on this point, for the fat little man simply sat on his shooting stick and watched it through his glinting glasses, and the tall aloof person on my right remained standing like a gaunt old heron and took no notice.

I waited as calmly as I could, hoping the bird would swing off either right or left, but it seemed determined to come for me and with an inaudible prayer I lifted my little gun.

It was the easiest of shots, I had many a more difficult one at home when I was shooting on my own, where they usually rose half-screened by bushes in front of the hunting dog.

This pheasant looked as big as a turkey and flew as straight as a bombing plane. I fired. Its tail seemed to disintegrate, its legs dangled, and the bird dropped a foot or so, but still carried on, gradually losing height, in the direction of the fir plantation.

'Too far behind, my boy,' called the fat little man, as I broke the breech and tossed the empty case away. I felt ready to sink into the ground, tears of mortification were in my eyes. I had 'tailored' my bird, and imagined everyone in the line had seen it. I heard the tall aloof man mutter something to his loader.

Then I was horrified to see *two* more pheasants, a cock and a hen, coming dead on the same line. Determined to make amends I swung on to the cock as he came up over me and pulled the trigger. To my horror nothing happened, there was a faint 'click' and I realised I had never re-loaded!

Luckily I thought of my other barrel and after a slight falter I pulled the back trigger. The old cock jerked back, threw his head up, and slumped to the grass behind me. I was so elated I ejaculated 'got him!' and just stopped myself from rushing across and gathering it. After a successful shot at home I invariably pelted headlong to retrieve my game with wild whoops of triumph. But I had not deserved success.

From my left I heard the 'Mr Pickwick' exclaim 'Well done, my boy,' and those four words filled me with pride and gratitude. Assuming an air of having shot high pheasants every day of the week, I looked behind me and saw the still body of my bird half-hidden by the frosted grass, the wind faintly stirring its plumage. I felt immensely gratified. I longed for another chance now. Shots were ringing all along the line in a regular fusillade. Then there was a lull.

The clamour of the beaters was distinctly audible now, rustlings sounded in the underwood. I remembered the Major's words, 'Mind the beaters'.

Then a faint shout of 'Mark!' on my right. I heard a few shots go off but could see nothing in the air and was quite mystified for a moment. Then the tall aloof gentleman faced half-right and I saw him getting ready, his loader crouching down. Still I could see nothing.

Then I spied a little brown round-winger bird coming at a great pace along the line of guns. Everyone was banging off at it. Just before it reached the tall man it jinked outwards behind us and the tall man's shots went bang! bang! without effect.

Instinctively I lifted my gun, it was just the sort of snap shot which I delighted in. I forgot I was at a shooting party, on my best behaviour,

A little brown round-winger bird

the early blunders were forgotten; for one precious moment I was quite unselfconscious. As soon as I pressed the trigger I knew he was mine. The woodcock hit the ground.

The tall man called out in a grudging porty voice, 'Good shot!' 'Mr Pickwick' turned his glinting glasses my way and beamed a wide smile of satisfaction. It was a glorious moment! Then the beaters appeared on the fringe of the wood and I knew the drive was over. I hadn't done too badly despite the shocking start, and I was puffed with pride when Major Heathcote came up to me and clapped me on the back with a 'Well done, young feller, wiped our eyes, eh? you young rascal,' and I saw Hughie Bell grinning at me behind my godfather's back.

Nobody mentioned the 'tailored' bird.

14.
MANKA, THE SKY GIPSY

Out on a lonely point was a ruined wooden hut, relic of some Dutch whalers that had wintered there over a generation before Manka was born. They had been trapped by the savage stealthy ice, and never lived to see the sun again. The rotting timbers had been swollen by the rains and contracted by the frosts, the roof gaped. And down in the black mosses of the foreshore were other remains; a rusty anchor, the broken haft of a harpoon and some Dutch coins.

Manka sometimes came to this lonely point, but the hut aroused suspicion in his mind, and he gave it a wide berth. In some curious way it smelt of danger, though he knew not why. And when he was here, one misty day, something loomed out of the fog close inshore.

A fairy castle in peacock blues and greens, with postern doors and battlemented keeps, and fairy buttresses and embrasures. But no figures manned the ramparts, it drifted silently as though propelled by invisible engines, slowly, slowly past the point, to be swallowed in the mist.

Beyond a honk of alarm, Manka did not move. He stood, a white figure, watching the iceberg dissolve into the fog.

At the beginning of September, more ice appeared in Sassen Bay, and at night the white gleam to the North grew brighter. The pack ice was now only a few miles North, and soon the island would be gripped solid until the spring.

Now the pain grew so strong the geese could hardly rest. They flew in small parties hither and thither, lining the banks in their grey regiments (the white spot of Manka appearing very conspicuous by comparison) awaiting some secret signal we can only dimly comprehend. Humans at times have a faint ghost of this restlessness that the geese felt, that longing to be gone from the old familiar places to seek strange new lands. As we become more civilized we feel this instinct less and less, we become more akin to the machines that govern our little lives. To the geese it was a call that must be obeyed, as strong as life itself. The South drew them as a magnetic pole draws the needle.

The snow came to whiten the marshes, and Manka, flying over the waterfall, bound for Brent Pass, saw bearded icicles shielding the curtain of water that ran clearer now than at any time since the spring. Only the tip of the reindeer's horn peeped above a new-fallen mantle of snow that was spread upon the rocks. A large, yellowish-white object was ambling above the bluffs, a polar bear. Manka was so interested he wheeled about, croaking in alarm. But the bear took no heed, and finally disappeared among the tumbled blocks of ice.

Low clouds hid the cliffs, trailing in fantastic shapes and whirling a ghostly dance about the glaciers, sometimes assuming the forms of giant men and women, fantastic monsters and horned devils. Everywhere there was sense of the lights being turned down; the play was over, and the curtain fast falling. There was a sense too, of preparation. Preparation for what?; for the dark months when only the stars and moon gave fitful light, or when the Northern Lights played upon the ice and frozen plain that was once open sea? For the time when all the birds had gone, when the loomeries on the cliffs were silent, and only the foxes, reindeer, and bears, were left to face the winter through? So must have the world appeared before it was alive, alive with the sunlight and flicker of white wings.

Already the gulls had left the cliffs, the shrieking bustle of auks, puffins, and skuas, had gone. Only the grim sea, doomed to eternal battling with the rocks, boomed and sucked among the ice caverns, or ran its grey ram against the snout of the glaciers. The little purple sandpipers had fled, and no longer did the eider fleets ride the waves within the bay. They were out at sea, among the big green rollers that were playing quoits with numberless little ice floes. In Sassen Bay the sea was oily-still, for Northwards there was a firm-locked barrier that broke all wind and swell. A stilling of everything; of bird voices, of the homely wash of waves along the shore where the terns and sandpipers had nested, a silencing of rivers and streams, of all the laughter of the sun.

Yet still the geese lingered, wings must be strong for the long journey that lay before. Night after night, however, little parties slipped away.

Next morning there were fewer geese ranged along the bars. Manka's parents, unable to bear the pain longer, left with thirty other geese. Their youngsters remained in company with sixty or more others, who still waited for the strength and courage to depart.

Only for a few hours did the sun shine, sometimes not at all when the clouds were low. The sea froze solid in Sassen Bay. For the last time Manka flew up to the fall, with his two sisters, and the voice of the fall was muted by ice pillars as thick round as forest oaks. Snow lay in white bands along the bluffs (the ledge where he was hatched was two feet under) and the reindeer's horn was hidden and would not appear again until the following spring.

Dusky Brent geese, white collared and royal, passed, all one day, high and bugling in compact arrowheads and chevrons, half hidden by low, driving cloud. On top of the ruined hut, the snow was deep, and the lidless coffin had a drift that nearly covered it, the bones had a new winding-sheet. Some animal had taken the skull from the coffin and carried it up the shore. Winds, snow-charged and stinging, raced across the barrens, and then, one night, it ceased to blow.

A fearful silence fell, the sea was mastered at last, no more thundering avalanches startled the quiet of night. The frost had also gripped the elusive streams as an otter grips a slithery trout. Only the red sun moved for a short space above the hills at noon.

The pain, the wild pain that the geese know, was no longer to be borne. Manka, together with fifteen other geese, mostly young of the year like himself, rose for the last time above the Sassendal that lay like a white band upon the dark marsh, and turned South. Whither they were bound they knew not, they had no chart or compass to guide them on their way. Clamouring one to another they wheeled upwards in a vast spiral until the river was a mere thread below and Sassen Bay no larger than a sixpence. They saw the greater part of the island at a glance, and North, the white plain of ice that stretched to the Pole.

Then, with a sudden wild crying that echoed among their ranks, they fell into station, each astern of the other, and wing beats began a deathless tattoo. Flying in so much disturbed air was new to Manka. In addition to the 'whoof' 'whoof' of thirty-two wings all beating in unison, he felt the rush of air past his lores as his bill cleft the sticky air asunder, the suctional pull behind the forward camber of his wings. Higher and yet higher rose the skein, falling into the formation of a big arrowhead, an arrow that pointed to the South, that slowly dwindled beyond the far mountain peaks.

It seemed then that darkness and silence took immediate command. The geese had been the vanguard of the retreating army. Northwards the ice-blink quivered and jumped, not a bird called or a wing beat in all that silent land about Sassen Bay. By the hut on Starvation Point the sightless skull stared upwards, two cavernous spots of shadow with snow for eyes. It could not see the black arrowhead of geese pass over against the stars. No longer did the ice groan and crash out in the bay, or fairy bergs come drifting through the mist. The land was forgotten again and was ready for its long sleep. And somewhere out in Sassen Bay, far below the roof of ice that now stretched for hundreds of miles to the Pole, a half of an egg-shell lay between two rocks. The bright spirit that had once been its tenant was now beating Southwards towards Bear Island, crying the wild cry that tells of the great pain.

Behind, Spitzbergen lay like a little white cloud sitting on the ocean, ahead there was nothing but the dark curve of the seas' horizon. Beneath them were scattered white lumps, of all sizes, so that the sea appeared not unlike Hampstead Heath after a bank holiday. Soon these white lumps (which were ice floes) became less frequent until there was nothing but faint streaks that came and went as the crests of the waves broke downwards into the billows.

Far below, little man-ships toiled along, leaving a smear across the dark plain of the sea as a snail leaves a trail behind it. They toiled so slowly, and with so much labour, across the grey continents of water that the ease of the speeding arrowheads of birds seemed to mock them. Half naked men, down in the white tanks of engine rooms sweated and laboured among the thrusting pistons, surrounded by a network of steel in an atmosphere sickly with oil. And they knew nothing of the geese passing over. Rusty old tramps, their bows white under in the swell; brilliant liners, lit from stem to stern, where in palm-decked ballrooms people danced and made believe they were still on land; all passed under, none knew or cared about the geese. Little atoms of life, puppets drawn by the strings of circumstance, all weaving and inter-weaving, as changeful as the sea. High above, their heads in the stars, the geese drove onwards in a black arrowhead, elemental as the land they had left behind them. By dawn they had passed Bear Island, soon Iceland lay to the West, but they turned not aside.

Manka was glorying in the power of flight. A beautiful bird, like something out of Hans Andersen's fairy tales, as white as a Spitzbergen snow-field, the very embodiment of all that is wild and free, intense with vivid life.

His wings moved rhythmically, responding to every air current, the shaped flight feathers, on which stability depended, spreading like fingers with every downward thrust, closing again as he raised his wings. He rose to the invisible billows as a ship rises to the swell, he sank again into the troughs of air, always steady, always in command of the yielding substance.

To fall, he would have to close his wings and drop his head, as a swimmer in water, but now the air held his quill feathers open like a kite. With every downthrust he rose upwards, sinking gently as his wings finished their sweep. It was circular motion; up (to take hold of the air), round and back and down; up, round, back, and down; up, round, back, and down; his wings a screw that drove him forwards.

Each goose flew in the slipstream of the next ahead at a speed somewhere about ninety miles per hour. Ahead of Manka were eight other geese; the leader was an old bird that had seen twelve Spitzbergen summers. He weighed six-and-a-half pounds. The last summer had been a tragic one for him. He had lost his mate and four goslings to an arctic fox, so he had lingered. But now his sorrow was forgotten in the great pain. As they flew, goose answered goose, the sound rippled down the ranks in a wave of bugle notes. The sky was full of other birds, fleeing before the cold, skein after skein of geese were passing over the grey plain of the sea far below, all flying at an altitude of over ten thousand feet. Now massed banks of vapour appeared below them, solid in appearance as land, Manka was tempted to drop his paddles and alight among the snowy cushions. Now and again, through a ragged, black hole, the sea could be glimpsed, with the surface crinkled and creased like corrugated paper. Then for a space the woolly white blankets dissolved away and the geese sped on in a moonlit world of unreality, darkness below and darkness above, the glitter of the moon on the sea, star dust above them. Then cloud again, a steady blanket. They rose to clear it, but even after their strong wings had borne them seven hundred feet higher, they were soon flying in a dense cloud bank that obscured everything. It was so cold that tiny particles of ice began to form on the vanes of their tails and on the back camber of their wings. On the left, the mist grew lighter and soon came the sun again; they saw the round, bright globe before the ships could see it. 'Woof' 'woof' 'woof' in a gladsome concert the strong pinions sang the flight song, the wind song of the free skyroads. Manka's feet were tucked up out of sight like the retractable landing-gear of modern flying-machines, he felt the suctional pull behind his shoulders, the pull that held him up, and the soft, icy stream of air flowing along his flanks and sliding off his outer tail-coverts. That glorious rush through the dawn air, how can it be described? There was that sense of speed that the airman in his modern enclosed cockpit never feels, the surge of his body forward with every powerful stroke. Like a bullet with wings, or an arrow-shaft with thrilling vanes, the swish, the drive, the speed! South! South! South! 'Here!' called a goose. 'Where?' answered another. 'Here!' called the leader, as he drove at the head of the skein. Whistle of wind, thrum of vanes, effortless motion, effortless speed! Paling stars and warmer air. Dainty wisps of cloud, like veils, passed under their paddles, one moment ahead, another moment they had flashed by; those fleeting wisps of vapour and the streaming wind gave the true sense of speed.

Behind lay the darkness, the cold, the land that was unfinished, ahead lay the warm South and fat fare, a green land of gentler airs, well loved, well known. Beneath them at last, through a rent in the clouds, they saw the Shetland islands, ringed about with white foam, land at last after so long! But they did not set their wings and glide to earth, the journey was far from finished. They saw the angry white of the rollers about Cape Wrath, the bare, bleak hills where wee, white farms crouched to be out of unceasing winds, tapes of roads where specks passed to and fro, valleys, pine-clad, and snow-capped mountains.

Over the white-capped hills

And there was new light now, not the feeble glare of a weary sun, but vivid, sunpatched hillsides, tawny with bracken, rushing rivers (once, three stags fording a torrent) cloud shadows patching a long, stony hillside. The geese lowered now, when they saw the land, but still they were high. Their shadows sped with them like fairy sheep, up hill and down valley; purple woods they saw, and the blue reek from a lodge chimney, belts of dark firs, the sweet trees that were new things to Manka. Then the white ribbon of the Tay and the reek of towns. But still they did not alter course though the sun was westering, turning the hills red and casting great blue shadows where detail was drowned, as the bed of a stream is lost in deep water. They passed high over Holy Island (where the houses were beginning to light their lamps) and long lines of white rollers beat ceaselessly upon the wide sands by Bamburgh.

Still the leader led them on. Manka was tired. He would have liked to let himself sink down and rest on those firm sands, yet still the pain was not spent and he must obey, he must yet beat on, the journey was nearly done.

Then came the Humber with big ships plying, bell buoys and light-ships. For over fifteen hundred miles Manka's wings had beat, now only a few hundred miles remained.

The sun eluded them in his eternal race, darkness was falling and the world below was muffled, starred with lamps and bright with furnace glares. From the mastheads of ships sprang little points of light.

Quite suddenly Manka felt the pain was at an end. The wings of the leader ceased to beat, and calling one to another they lowered, throwing themselves downwards through the air with closed wings, 'tumbling' in all directions. They passed a bell in a cage that clanged wildly in the passing wash of a steamer. At first the sound was faint, then loud as they swept past it, 'clang! clang! CLANG! clang! ...' it died behind them. Round they wheeled, still calling, and Manka saw solid sand beneath, not a foot from his paddles; shells, seaweed, rocks and little pools, rushing under. He saw the grey-green herbage of the marsh and the innumerable 'channers' that split up the dark expanse of sea lavender. He saw the distant blur of the far sea wall and flocks of little silver dunlin rushing along the water edge.

The tide was running out and the sandbanks were exposed. Down on to a bar the geese descended in a grey cloud, wings lifted for the last time as each goose stalled to a standstill, folding wings across tired backs.

The air was so much warmer and softer, the birds noticed this at once, and there was no rush of icy wind past them. Instead of the 'swoosh, swoosh' of wings there was the rustle of the tide on the sand bars and the pipings of flighting waders, curlews, redshanks, and golden plover. From the land came the smell of good, moist earth, farms and woods.

After the long journey the geese were dead weary and no sentries were posted. In a moment or two each goose had tucked in his head. Some drew up one leg, most sat down on the sand and went sound asleep. So much had happened in the last few hours, there was a sense now of overwhelming peace and quietness. Manka's wings ached and his neck was weary. As soon as his eyes were shut he surely must have dreamt of the weary pilgrimage that was now at an end, of the waterfall, the glaciers, of the ruined hut on Starvation Point.

A dull throbbing pulsed through his dreams and became part of them. A steamer was going up the Wash laden with timber. The red and green of her port and starboard lights moved like coloured sparks across the dim waters and long after she had passed the dull bump of her screw persisted. Soon little white wavelets came creaming up the sand, breaking with a soft lullaby on the bar and licking the pink paddles of the sleeping geese.

All down that coast were other tired geese; some, like Manka, had come in that very night, others (including Manka's parents) had been back some days and their wings did not ache as did Manka's wings.

The first chapter of his life had been written. There was a promise of great things to come in the talk of the misty sea and the 'glug, glug' of the tide as it receded across the miles of sand.

And soon perhaps Manka did not dream, but sank down into the blessed quietude of healing sleep, heeding not when the wind, playing across the flats, ruffled his white scapulars. It was journey's end at last.

★ ★ ★ ★ ★

The tide was beginning to ebb, and the frothy suds and bubbles were turning again to the sea that gave them birth. At first that movement was scarcely perceptible, and it would have been hard to say whether the tide was at the ebb or flow.

Second by second the movement became more marked until there was a definite current that bore a gull's feather as fast as a cow can walk, steadily and surely, down the winding path of a creek, towards the sea.

As the water dropped inch by inch under the overhanging fringes of sea lavender, and the slimy walls of clay were laid bare, crabs sidled down from cleft and cranny, and sank into the yellow stream. They left little wavy lines on the mud that would not be washed away until the next tide. From the guts and gullies there came deep gurglings and suckings, and sometimes a wheezing noise that seemed almost a creak, as the clay clefts drained of moisture. Many stranded creatures of the sea sought frantically for water that had unaccountably fallen away beneath them and some would die before the tide brought release and life once more.

Restless pipits, whose thin cheepings were as high as bat squeaks, flitted to and fro over the grey-green marshes, and with them were snow-buntings, newly in from the far North. These birds seemed like scraps of white paper as the wind took them and tossed them this way and that, or like pale leaves that fly before October gales.

As far as the eye could see, North and South, the marshes stretched, a continuous plain of grey-green that melted into the grey of the November sky.

Nothing moved on that sombre expanse save the wiry stems of the sea lavender as the cold wind blew strongly in off the mud flats. In the distance, across the ooze, rose the targets on the Air Force ranges magnified to vast dimensions and misty with distance.

The aeroplanes had gone away, as birds migrate in autumn, and once more there was peace. Wherever man comes he brings noise, and here, on these bleak lands around the Wash, he made the air rock with the crash of gunfire and vibrate with the continual roar of aero engines. With the coming of winter there was peace again and only the cannonade of longshore gunners echoed across the dreary wastes of sand and saltings.

Landwards a line of trees marked the sea wall, bent and twisted trees that had learnt the rude breath of the sea winds, winds that seldom slept. Beyond those trees the flat rich Fenlands stretched, dotted with glasshouses and prosperous farms, with never a hill and scarce a wood; a bitter land of toil and mist, devoid of noble mansions, devoid of beauty, devoted to the making of money and the sweating of labour. Ely lay beyond, a misty finger that brooded over the flat lands and reminded man there was still a God in heaven; Peterborough and Crowland, names that suggest the Viking raiders and the bitterns' boom.

As the tide fell, curlews began to flight in from the fields, calling one to the other in loud bell-like voices that carried some way across the saltings. They flew in formation, in Vs and lines, seven or eight together, sometimes more.

Soon, on the velvet muds, pearly and moist, the tips of the samphire stalks appeared, sticking stiffly out of the cushions that were imprinted with the footmarks and claw marks of many wild creatures.

The winding runnels and creeks were everywhere; haphazard but efficient drains that had served their purpose for many thousands of years. Lying between two samphire stalks was the body of a blackbacked gull, a handsome bird almost as big as a goose. Some shore gunner had shot it on the morning flight and it had journeyed out and in with the tides. It seemed perfect, no stain of blood or broken feather betrayed an injury, but nevertheless one single number four pellet had pierced the heart.

Two hooded crows, beating up the outmarsh, saw the body and circled round, cawing hoarsely, their wicked eyes fixed on the white spot below them. They pitched close beside the body, and after walking round with a waddling gait, took wing and flew away across the muds.

'Wheet, wheet,' reeded the pipits, as they flicked above the sea lavender, pitching in the higher herbage out of the wind. They roosted out on this bleak place, and strangely enough it was warm down in the tangled roots of the lavender. There they could creep like mice, and only the tides disturbed them, or maybe a marsh harrier, hunting up the marshes.

As the light began to dim, toiling figures appeared, making their way across the marsh from the sea wall. Some had dogs at heel and carried guns. It was early yet for the duck flight, but the curlew were coming in now in bigger trips, and along the tide line a bunch of teal sped, whizzing like bullets just over the sand.

By now the gull's feather had cleared the outmarsh and was drifting down the main channel for the open sea. Little trips of wader flew past it, calling all together in thin voices, and two godwits, probing the muds, watched it drift past them. As the tide fell, it seemed to gather speed, for in some of the guts and runnels the water was rushing in a turgid torrent, swirling over the mussel beds and talking about the base of a big weed-strewn buoy that now lay half on its side on the hard sand. Soon this buoy ceased to float and the water left its base. On one side there was a deep pool, hollowed by the action of the tides, and in this trap several dabs were flipping along the surface of the sand. They would have to remain there until the tide came back next morning.

Two redshanks rose shrieking from the bed of a gully and went away across the marsh, orange legs trailing, and their white wing bars showing vividly against the grey-green tones of the marsh.

They had been disturbed as they pattered over the smooth bed of a creek.

A man was coming along the top of the sea bank and as the redshanks flew away he came down from the sloping bank at a run and took a sheep track that wound out to the tide's edge. These sheep tracks were everywhere about the marshes, and served as useful short cuts for fowlers when the tide came in.

As he went along, pipits rose on either hand and flitted away, and a curlew rose from a little brackish pool that had been left by the last tide. 'Curlee! Curlee!' it shrieked in a hoarse voice, and went out to the tide line where others of his kind were clustering in long line at the edge of the receding water.

'Foxy' Fordham knew these marshes like a book, for he had been born in the little village three miles away, where the ruined wind-mill stands. As a young man he had worked on the land and then he took to fowling. He had saved up enough money to buy a punt and after a while he found he could make more by selling his fowl than working for the farmer. 'Foxy' – so called by men because he knew his craft so well, and also because he was the most skilful poacher in the district – was a man of middle height and broad shouldered. Ragged red bristles sprouted from his upper lip and his chin was seldom closely shaved. His eyes were never quite open and he always seemed to be peering out at life as it passed before the windows of his soul.

Not a bird, or a beast, could move without being quietly marked and noted by those keen eyes, and like an old fox that has learnt the craft of hunting, he had within him a sure knowledge of his livelihood. Not many cartridges were wasted when Foxy pulled the trigger, and if he missed his target he felt bad for hours afterwards.

On his head was a tattered cap, turned back to front, and he wore an old seaman's jersey, much darned by his thin little wife. On his legs were rubber thigh boots, the tops turned down so that he could walk more easily through the muds. And under his arm he carried a big rusty eight bore, the dearest thing he possessed – next to his dog.

Foxy treasured three things in life; his gun, his dog, and his gunning-punt. His wife and two pigs came next, and anything that contributed to his welfare was tolerated.

With a swinging gait he soon left the sea wall behind him and the herbage on the marsh grew shorter and the gullies wider. Now and again he would come to a deep drain and he crossed it with a practised leap, landing, well balanced, on the far side. The black and white cocker came after, ears flapping as he jumped.

Foxy

After a while Foxy stopped and looked about him. His head was turned sideways, against the chirrup of the wind, and his eyes were fixed on the far line of water.

'Boomp!' a shot sounded away to the westward, down the marshes, and the screwed-up eyes swivelled round that way.

He noted a tiny figure, no bigger than a beetle, climb out of a gully and run across the salting to pick something up. 'Some b..... shooting a curlew' thought Foxy. Then he turned his face to the sea again.

The light was failing now and all of a sudden it began to drain quickly, almost as he watched.

He looked about him and found a narrow 'gull' scarce two feet across, but quite deep, and he lowered his rubber boots into this and sat down on the edge where the crab grass formed a wiry dry mattress.

His two great feet formed a dam in the trench, and very soon the water, draining from landwards, accumulated into quite a little lake, in which shrimps jerked about and a tiny crab sidled.

He took a well-seasoned pipe from his pocket and began to fill the bowl, pressing the rank shag down firmly with his broad, dirty fingers, with their split nails.

Close by, the dog sat watching every movement with a sulky expression set upon its mouth, because the upper lip had been caught up on a tooth. Now and again its brown eyes would scan the sky and follow the track of a passing gull. Line after line of gulls were now coming in off the fields, flying on set and lazy wings, gliding out to the sand banks where they would pass the night. Hardly had one group passed before another came in view, at first mere specks against the grey sky, and then clear and distinct.

Foxy moved his feet in the mud and released a torrent of water that swept down the gully bed and surprised a crab that was crawling along under the overhanging fringe of sea lavender. The smoke from his pipe was blown spinning away on the cold wind and the interior of the bowl glowed like a tiny forge.

Now a heron came, slow flagging and high, with the wind in his face. He was bound for the high sands and Frieston shore. All day he had been fishing the landward dykes and he was full fed and content. 'Zank!' he cried when he saw the tiny figure far below, and flapped heavily onwards, lofting to each surge of wind.

Foxy now turned round and faced the sea, and one big thumb clicked back the hammers of his gun. The spaniel became more alert and kept on watching his master's face intently, for Foxy's eyes were on the greyness of the sky.

'Boomp!'... 'Boomp, boomp!' Shots began to sound, some near, some far, for the evening flight had begun.

Bang! Close at hand, and the dog jumped. Foxy turned a slow head and glanced idly along the marshes. Jim Barrit, the postman's son, got out of a creek and picked up a redshank. Foxy swore to himself and climbed out of his gully also. He walked away to the big main gully that feeds Long Drove End. A man could not be alone nowadays, there was always some pipit popper to spoil one's sport.... This main gully, known as the 'main', was nearly thirty feet across and only wadable at low tide. Its slimy walls were seamed with glistening runnels that had eaten into the clay so that they were almost miniature gullies in themselves and in some places the mud was up to a man's thigh.

Foxy followed this down, until the gully divided into two channels, forming on one side, a bastion of clay.

This was a favourite spot, known only to Foxy, and he had shot many a duck and goose from this place.

He sat down again and repacked his pipe, and once more he cocked the hammers of the big gun.

Suddenly his eyes narrowed still more and he bent his head so that his eyes were on a level with the rim of the bank.

A hare was loping across the marsh, stopping ever and again to sniff the air with ears in a questioning V. It came nearer, and the heavy barrels crept up until the muzzle was resting among the sea lavender. Eighty yards, seventy... the hare stopped, looking directly in Foxy's direction, with its eyes dilated and nose working. The wind blew its fur so that it showed little blue tufts, but it could only see a distant redshank flickering over a dyke. Boomp!... The gun barrels seemed to jerk upwards and Foxy reeled back against the bank. The hare leapt skywards and fell back quivering, a blade of grass fixed firmly in its rat-like teeth.

From the far drain the cocker came tearing, ears flapping and with open mouth. It got a grip on the big body and went staggering back to Foxy.

Now the light was going fast, and the first mallard came over, high; so high that even the big eight-bore could not reach them, and Foxy's eyes watched them come and go, windborne, for the sea wall. Little stuttering quacks sounded on all sides as party after party came in, all too high with the wind behind them.

But Foxy had a comfortable feeling within, for he felt the warm bulge of the great hare inside his big bag, and knew his tramp had been worth while.

Westwards the sky was now still bright, but over the sea it was dark and darkening, even Foxy's eyes could not see the mallard if he looked that way; he had to turn so that he faced the last lingering light. Over the flats a line of stars began to dance and quiver as the ships and houses on the Boston side lit their lamps, and there came a great sense of loneliness and desolation, intensified by the querulous plainings of a green plover.

And then there came to Foxy a faint sound that was at first only intermittent. But the man seemed to rouse himself and his eyes almost opened wide.

'By Gor, if it ain't the geese!' he muttered, and climbed out of the Main.

The sound which was growing louder with the passing moments was like the far baying of hounds, the most wonderful music in the world. As it grew louder the various voices could be heard, deep-toned old ganders, and high, squeaking yelps intermingled, and yet there was still no sight of the geese. And then, very high against the last glim of the sunset he saw a long line of geese. They scattered as he watched them and seemed to tumble in the air, dropping like smuts from a chimney on to the high sands. As they lit on the banks they redoubled their clamour and then all was silent.

Only the rustle of the wind in the sea lavender and the 'week, wee-week' of the green plover remained.

Foxy opened the door of his little cottage and stood for a moment blinking in the light of the room. His wife was beside the fire, sewing, and when she saw him she got up and went into the kitchen to prepare his supper – Foxy did not like to be kept waiting for his food.

The spaniel, wet and slimed with grey clay, stood patiently while the man rubbed him down with an old sack, and then went and curled up before the fire, watching the sparks burning a little chain on the soot of the chimney.

When Foxy had finished his supper and put his feet into some old slippers he lit his pipe and spoke.

'Th' geese cum in to-night, Mother, I 'eard 'em when I was up in the Main, a good pack on 'em too.'

'Early, ain't they?'

'Ah, I reckon so.'

'Where did 'ee get th' old 'are?'

'Up be the drain, cum runnin' across to me as I sat in the gull ... a good un, ain't 'ee?'

Foxy took the stiff body off the table where grease and beer had stained the newspaper that served as a tablecloth and stroked the fine, handsome fur.

'That Jim Barrit were down on the outmarsh, the – , 'ee's allus bangin' about there at pipits an' shank and such like.'

The spaniel roused himself from the hearth and sniffed at the head of the hare as it hung down between Foxy's knees.

''Ere, don't you dirty my floor, Fred, I cleaned un this afternoon.'

Foxy took no notice, but went on stroking the fur. 'Reckon I'll be after them old geese to-morrow mornin' on the flight, they'll very like be cummin' in over the Drain.'

At that moment, the geese, sixteen tired birds, were asleep in the windy darkness on the high sands. The stars were hidden by scudding clouds and there was no moon.

Like the swallows, they had returned to their winter quarters, and the barrens and rocks of their summer home belonged to another world. For many hours their wings had borne them over countless miles, and they slept as deep as worn-out dogs. Nearly all had their bills tucked into their wings and not a bird was standing. All were resting their grey breasts on the sand and the tides swirled and sucked along the winding creeks unheeded.

Southwards a light grew and waned as the lightship on Boston Deep kept watch and ward, and beyond was the loom of another at the head of Lynn Deeps.

Occasionally a goose would shift his position, withdraw a sleepy head for a second, then tuck in its bill again with a weary gesture. Now and again a wader would flit by in the darkness, only its faint peeps betraying its swift passage, and from seawards came the low, windborne rustle of the flowing tide. Ever ceaseless, ever unwearied, the water was turning again for the land, and right out near Boston Deeps, the gull's feather was swaying this way and that as the tide took it.

Foxy Fordham was asleep, lying beside his thin little wife, his mouth open and softly snoring. He had taken off his trousers and boots, likewise his coat and shirt, but was sleeping in his underpants and vest. These he rarely took off unless he got a wetting in a creek.

The little room was in darkness and a cheap alarm clock ticked loudly on a chair by the bed.

And three miles away, out on the windy sands, buffeted by the sweet airs that came in unsullied from the North Sea, Manka slept, his pale pink bill, banded with black, tucked under the big feathers of his back. Foxy was dreaming of millions of geese that carpeted the sky and he was shooting at them with a pop-gun that fired corks. This enraged him so much he grumbled in his sleep, and stirred. 'Fred, what be you at, carryin' on so, bide quiet can't ye?' Foxy grunted and turned over and a frightened mouse ran under the rickety washstand, for the mattress had squeaked.

The long twilights had come again and the aeroplanes were back on the bombing ranges, making the days hideous with buzzings and bangings. They swept above the marshes with stuttering machine-guns and the red flag flew from the pole on the bank, warning trespassers to keep away.

To Manka and his mate had come the wander pain once more. Already, maybe, they saw in their minds the white-clad peaks and icy glaciers around Sassen Bay and, most impelling of all, the bluffs and breeding-ledges of the Esker river.

Had the weather remained open they would have gone North to the Tay, where thousands of other geese were assembling, but in the last week of February a short snap set in, and the geese dallied. There was little frost, but it snowed fitfully and was bitterly cold.

Out of a dun-coloured sky stray flakes wandered, lonesome and large, thickening soon to a moving curtain that blotted out the marshes and the sea. Moithered by the flakes the geese flew low about the sea wall, for they hated falling snow as much as fog.

Three rooks were sitting in a baby oak tree that grew in the hedge behind Mellons Platt, not far from the sea wall. The rich dark earth was mantled in white, and they had sat thus for over an hour, croaking dismally one to another. It was an unexpected change, for only a week before they had been thinking about house-hold duties in the rookery by the farm. Now winter had come back and hopes were dashed. They sat puffed out, with raised crests, watching the wavering flakes blot out the distant dark line of trees by Mellons Platt.

And then one of them drew itself up and depressed its feathers for it had seen a figure coming along the sea-bank. It croaked an alarm and all three flew leisurely away, to be hidden, in a very few moments, by the driving snow.

Foxy, with collar turned up, was tramping along with bent head, the front of his coat whitened by the blizzard. It was a splendid day, from Foxy's point of view; he might get a shot at a pheasant under cover of the snow.

A hare was crouched, like a clod of earth, beside a gateway. The snow had whitened it and Foxy did not see it until he was on the bank above. Then the hare stretched its legs and made off under the gate. Up came Foxy's gun; for a split second his single rheumy eye squinted down the barrel, then a puff of smoke jetted. The hare rolled over, kicking in the snow, and Foxy darted down the bank, jumped the drain (slipping in and wetting his leg to the thigh) and quickly thrust the limp brown body into his capacious bag. Then he climbed back over the drain and continued his walk down the sea wall.

When he got to the shepherd's hut he struck out across the marshes, heading for Horseshoe gull. There was a lively chance of a duck on such an afternoon and he might have some luck on this, the last day of the season.

On Leader's Drove the geese had been feeding all morning, scraping away the snow to get at the tender blades of wheat. The snow was criss-crossed in every direction by their paddle-prints and greeny-white droppings were everywhere. Manka and his mate were with them; in the snow all looked alike, all appeared to be albino birds, for the flakes settled on their plumage. Late in the afternoon they rose from the field and went away for the marshes.

The snow had ceased, and over the sea was a clear patch of sky of the faintest prussian blue. Mild weather was coming, and the next day the geese would be away for the Tay, and very soon the journey would begin, the long journey to Spitzbergen.

As usual, Manka headed the skein, and with a great clamour they held their course straight over the shepherd's hut.

The guardian angel that had watched over Manka for thirty years may have lost patience. Perhaps by the law of averages there was bound to come a day of destiny for Manka.

That he had managed to survive for so long a time was wonderful, for he was doubly handicapped by the fact of his white plumage. How strange it is that man should desire to kill a creature just because it is rare!

If we could have drawn a chart of Manka's life and compared it with one of Foxy's, how different they would have been! Manka had seen so much and had travelled widely; Foxy had never been farther afield than Boston. He had never even given a thought to that far land across the sea, to the snow-clad hills of Scotland, to the wonders of a wild bird's life. He was content to remain in his own little well-trodden locality, as content as a cow chewing the cud in a field. His life had been the meaner, full of cruelty and selfishness, blind even to the beauties of the marshes and the glory of dawn or sunset. With all his wonderful superiority of brain (I will not say intellect) he had never exercised his intelligence, his only delight was to destroy, to eat, to drink, to sleep.

As he spread out the sack which he carried in his bag (warm now from the hare's body) a break slowly appeared in the snow clouds over Boston, and the sun burst through, sending down long silver bars that lit the water and transformed the muds. It shone full upon him and threw a shadow on the tangled sea-lavender, where the tide had begun to turn back on its ageless journey to the sea. Foxy idly looked at the water. The 'old man' was going out again. Foxy had had many escapes from the 'old man'. A slimy, merciless enemy, who slipped up behind one on the marshes and was always scheming to trap the unwary. Well it had never trapped Foxy, and it wouldn't get the chance. Sometimes when he was alone at night, far out on the outmarsh, he had been gripped by a feeling of panic and had run back to the bank. In foggy weather too, before he had come to know these marshes, that now he could walk blindfold, he had some narrow squeaks.

A redshank came up the creek. It did not see Foxy crouching under the rim of the bank. It lit on the edge of the mud and bobbed its head, making a plaintive, piping noise. Then it began to run daintily along, its bright orange legs twinkling as it probed the muds.

Foxy wondered where Manka had got to. He knew the geese were in the district, for that morning he had seen them on Leader's Drove, appearing on the snow like enormous wood-pigeons. Manka had been right on the far side of the field, he had seen him through his glasses.

Damn the bird! He almost wished some shore-popper would shoot him. Since the episode of the fish-hooks, the tale had gone all over the district and he was a laughing-stock. He'd show 'em. He'd shoot Manka one of these days and walk into the Black Swan and throw the white body on the floor and affect great boredom and superiority.

He looked landwards. A tiny figure was passing along the bank. It was Billy going to visit the lambing-fold beyond the main drain bank. There was a collection of hurdles there thatched with straw, and it had been a big 'fall' this year, the pens were full of unsteady-legged, bleating lambs.

He watched the pygmy figure moving ever so slowly along the ridge of the sea wall till it disappeared over the bank. Billy had changed, he was not friendly as he used to be. Well... damn them all, Foxy would live his own life and they could live theirs, the whole boiling of them. Foxy spat into the drain and watched, with his single eye, the little spot of white, as big as a sixpence, slowly drift away towards the sea.

Glug! glug! gulped the mud walls of the creek. He could see the tide dropping and hear the tiny channels that fed the main drain begin to gush water.

There was a big cloud near the sinking sun. It was edged with a lace of bright burning gold. Flocks of waders passed up the shore like smoke; 'little buds' as Foxy called them.

Come to-morrow and the season would be over. No more shooting for six months. It would be difficult to get work this summer with the farmers, he'd set their backs up with his poaching and stealing, and now, with this last affair, he'd have to go farther afield to earn a few shillings. Well, he didn't care, he'd saved a bit, quite a tidy bit, and his wife worked for the Shardwaners now, she'd be getting something extra for the spring cleaning.

And then Foxy squatted like a partridge, for he suddenly heard the clamouring of the geese, that lovely song that is the voice of the land where no man comes.

Yes... there they were, and my God, they were coming low from the fields! Yes... and there was Manka right in the lead! Foxy rolled up tight, one eye watering with excitement, mouth open. Would they change their line, was there another gun somewhere up a creek who would fire and scare them off? 'Damn!' swore Foxy, they were going too much to the right. But no, he saw Manka swerve and turn. Billy was there with his sheep. Yes, they were heading now straight for Horse-shoe gully. Foxy's big scarred thumb went up and the hammer of his big eight-bore clicked back, click! for safety, click! again for full-cock.

Here they came, wavering a little up and down, not forty yards high. Thought they were safe, did they? That white — in front was going to make his last mistake. Foxy remembered his eye, the fish-hooks, the soaking clothes, the muddy crawls he had had after Manka. Let him come on, that's all; let him come on. He'd get drunk to-night. God! supposing he missed! The last day, too; might be his last chance. If he missed now there was all that weary waiting, the gibes of his enemies, the long days of summer.

Manka held straight, straight as a die, for the big banks. He was taking a chance and he knew it. To-morrow they would be off! Spitz-bergen, the Esker bluffs! The never-setting sun!

Did Manka think of those things? Or did he only seek rest on the sandbanks? The pain to be gone was strong, he sensed the coming thaw.

'Anka!' he called, and his mate answered. She was flying close behind....

Manka did not see Foxy until the latter rose from the gully, not hastily, but with deadly calm. He saw the sudden movement of the gun barrel, and flung himself up with quick-beating wing, crying the alarm.

For a second he climbed. In that short time he drove up eight feet with his broad white wings.

The recoil from Foxy's gun was terrific. The cartridge had been damp and it was a very old one, bought in Boston six years before.

He staggered and nearly fell into the drain, in his nostrils was the keen reek of the powder.

He swore a dreadful oath, for Manka did not fall. Foxy stood, with

The white goose in the lead

smoking gun in his hands, then with a violent spasm of anger hurled it down on the crab grass.

All the geese had ceased to call to one another when they saw Foxy, for exertion had been concentrated in climbing. Now they broke out again, a great clamour.

Manka was higher than the rest and still climbing, and Foxy shaded his eye with a grimy claw.

'By God! He's 'it!' said Foxy. "Es towerin' like a partridge. I've got 'im at last!'

Manka continued to climb, straight up and up like a lark. For a moment or two he was against a dark snow-cloud, and still he rose. The rest of the skein went on towards the sea, already they were out of sight. Foxy's eye was on the white form that still climbed heavenwards. Quickly he bent and felt for his gun, his eye still on the goose.

Higher still, off the dark snow-cloud now, and grey against the thin-washed blue of clear sky, the sunset shining on him until he was as pink as a flamingo. Like Icarus he rose into the burning gold so that Foxy's eye was dazzled.

And then he saw a spot of white, falling as a stone falls.

'HE'S DOWN!'...

The man ran, and the spaniel ran, the former stumbling into gullies and once falling headlong on his face.

The dog went on ahead and disappeared over the edge of a creek. When Foxy came up he realised two things. One, that Manka had fallen in the outlet of a deep dyke; secondly, that from his lower level, the dog could not see the white body drifting slowly down the middle of the drain. The spaniel was splattering about on the margin of the mud, trying up creek instead of down. There was not a moment to lose.

Foxy knew this creek well. Thirty yards farther on it hooked to the left, almost in a hairpin bend, and then went straight out into the Wash. It was at all points too deep to wade, even at low water. His only hope was to run beyond the outmarsh on to the muds, and try and get Manka as he drifted past the sand-bar, or to trust that the dog would see the goose and fetch it in. The wayward little beast was a long way up the creek, and Foxy roared with rage until a dribble ran out of his mouth

and glistened among the stubbly red hairs of his chin. But the dog was too far away to hear him. Always a wild creature and unbiddable, it had spied a dead curlew that was lying on the far side of the creek. Foxy saw it plunge in and swim across. It picked up the curlew and came back, bringing the bird to Foxy in triumph, with wagging stump.

Meanwhile, the white, motionless body drifted away round the bend, straight for the open sea.

Then Foxy lost control of himself. His face flushed red with passion. He raised the gun and shot his dog. It slithered down the bank and rolled into the drain.

Foxy turned about and ran for the outmuds. As he ran he gasped and groaned. Damn the dog, served him right, never had been any good. He'd get the white goose if he had to swim for it. Now, with hard running, he was almost abreast of Manka's body. All he could see was the half-submerged breast and two wings sticking like sails out of the water. The stream was sliding out fast, but Foxy could run faster and he was at the bar, waiting, when Manka's body came round the bend.

Foxy saw it would pass within five yards of where he stood and he plunged in. The water was deeper than he thought. In five steps it was over his waders, and he felt its icy chill. With luck he could just reach Manka with his gun-barrel. He stretched out and touched one white wing. The inert body swung round, paused a moment and then… the current gently wheeled it outwards. Foxy reached out farther, took a step forward and lost his balance. The gun slipped from his hand, and with a gasp, the marshes, the setting sun, the distant finger of Boston Stump, vanished in a yellow choking darkness, that filled eye, ears, and lungs. Foxy bubbled like a bottle, a frightened crab scuttled.

The 'old man' had got him at last and was not going to let him go. The tide tucked him under its arm and took him out towards the sea that is the mother of all the waters of the world.…

Billy, having finished his work with the sheep, came up the bank and started to walk home.

The sun had gone and had left the marshes grey, a little breeze was thrumming in the telegraph wires overhead.

Out over the sea night was coming and far away, beyond the tide-line, a cloud of white gulls was stooping and calling at something in the water. They were making such a clamour that Billy stopped. What could it be, a shoal of fish?… a porpoise, perhaps?

On the little bent apple tree in his garden he heard a song thrush singing, and from the bottom of a tarred rail of the stile a line of drops like pearls were hung all a-row. Yes, the thaw was coming right enough, it would be grand for the lambing. Once again he looked seawards and saw the gulls were scattering. From Boston a line of stars winked and jumped against the clouds of coming night.

The tide was still running out… Foxy and Manka went out on the tide.

Goose Shooting

15.

DARK ESTUARY

A NIGHT TO REMEMBER

I am writing this chapter in the quiet of my studio. It is an autumn night, humid and still, and now and again a moth comes in and flies aimlessly round the light.

When I put my dogs to bed in the garage a few minutes ago, before coming up here to the top of the house, I noticed the last remaining swallow, the feeble one of the brood, which roosts on the cross-beam close to its old nest.

This was one of a second brood, and its parents, brothers and sisters started on their long journey three days ago. Soon this little chap will also depart, and he is wisely gathering strength for that great adventure which he may have to face alone.

Seeing him roosting there reminded me that in another week or so the grey geese will be likewise setting out for these shores. And thinking of the geese leads to other memories.

Something in the utter quiet of this room (with the only sound a far-off intermittent hooting of tawny owls in the woods of the park) turns my mind to those nights spent far out on the lonely tideways when I have had no companion, not even a dog, to keep me company. And there passes before me a succession of pictures. The moonlit sloblands of Fenham Slakes on the Northumberland Coast, the frost sending blue lights from the frozen sea-wrack, the cheeping of little knot, busy at their feed… that time when Charles and I lay out on the frozen mud on a night of intense frost. Even the warmth of our bodies failed to soften the frozen mud beneath us and over all rode a proud, full moon, and all was silence, and stars.

That other night away on a hill pasture, when we waited for the

161

geese to come. Again it was frosty and snow was on the ground; again it was bitter cold, with a full moon.

There have been similar nights on the marshes of the Wash, so silent and still that even the moonbeams seemed frozen.

There is an overwhelming sense of peace at such a time which only those who have experienced it can comprehend. The lust to shoot and kill is present in the background, I suppose. That is the reason why you are there, stretched out under the 'brew' of the merse, staring up at the stars.

Yet you almost forget the wildfowl in the majesty and peace of night and moonlight. Even the little waders seem to be absent, for the tide is barely on the turn and is somewhere far out there across that greenish plain which is the playground of wind and wave.

Though it is a night of frost you do not feel chilled, for your leather, wool-lined jacket defies all wind and weather. It is an airman's jacket and belonged (so the faded ink letters tell me) to a certain Flight Sergeant Ames, RAF. I wonder where he is now and if he survived those dark years of war? Are you there, Flight Sergeant? Perhaps this jacket has been over Berlin with the flak bursting and the groping searchlights swinging.... Quite an adventurous jacket....

This question of the right clothing is all-important, especially when you have passed the forties. Youngsters don't seem to mind how they dress for fowling and they suffer extreme discomfort at times. I can't enjoy myself if I'm really cold and it spoils half the fun.

It has been a long tramp over rough ground to reach this hiding-place of mine under the 'brew'. I sweated profusely even though I'd undone the zip of the jacket. When I took off my hat I could see the steam rising from it in the moonlight.

But now the exertion is over and I lie and watch the shining sands in front. The moon is well up, and across the firth I can see a dim loom of high hills. They look near but they must be six miles or more across the bay. Though there is no wind down here, I can see small, fleecy clouds passing over very gently; they must be three or four thousand feet up. Occasionally they drift across the moon. When this happens the greenish light is dimmed, and if you look closely at the sands you can see the cloud shadow travelling slowly along, just like the shadow of a summer cloud along the side of a fell or a meadow.

All this time the ear is straining and the senses are alert. You are not aware of this at first and then, as it were, you suddenly catch yourself listening intently, and find you are subconsciously holding your breath. Very far away, on the edge of hearing, there is a faint crying. It may be a big, black-backed gull, or more likely, a curlew; it is a second or two before you can identify it.

Yes, it *is* a curlew, passing along the fringe of the tide. The sound, for a second or so, is quite distinct and then passes away eastwards over the lonely flats.

If you turn a little under the miniature cliff of turf (you are lying in its shadow), you can see a line of brilliant, jewel-like harbour lights which appear to be dancing up and down like marionettes. Why they dance like this, I do not know. It is understandable with the stars far up there above you in the black holes in the fleecy clouds. And it is strange, too, how the reflections of these man-made stars are drawn out over the gleaming sands to a point almost within gunshot of your hide.

The shining path of the moon's reflection is almost like the illumination from the headlamp of a car. Studying this for minutes on end you can see, now and again, the small, swift form of a wader pass across it, and sometimes, if you are lucky, the black, flogging silhouettes of silent geese.

On such a night as this when all is so still, greylags will often pass quietly along off-shore. They may be aware of others farther down the estuary, and there is plenty of room here, many miles of moonlit ooze. Maybe somewhere down-river there is a favourite sand-bar where the geese rest. They are making for that.

Again there is that hush, like the hush of death. Now can imagination rove. You think of many things, but mostly the mind just drifts and you don't think of anything: a sort of half-sleep and yet you are very much awake, there is no sense of drowsiness.

If you stare up at the slow-moving clouds and at the dark spaces in between, these spaces appear as ragged black holes. And if you look long enough you find you are falling into them and the brain becomes quite dizzy. It is not a very pleasant feeling.

Those sinister ebony lakes remind one of those other black depths we read about far under the sea where no light can penetrate. The only living creatures there have a sponge-like texture because of the enormous pressures; some carry with them mysterious lights to guide them through those dreadful abysses.

The inky darkness of outer space and the deepest seas is to me truly terrifying and does not bear thinking about.

It is more pleasant and restful to let the eyes rove over the shining sands and to enjoy the silence of this magical night. The cold air is spiced with the scent of salt and sea-wrack, mingled with a certain moorland smell. This heathery, piney smell must come from the wooded hills around, but to the keen nose it is only just discoverable. The smell of the sea itself is predominant. Mixed with it there is the sharp accent of frost. A foggy night smells quite differently; so does a night of wind, and storm.

Somehow, when watching this tranquil, moonlit scene, the memories of other nights along this coast cannot be recaptured, nights when the great winds were up and out and there was sleety rain or driving snow.

There is no sense of peace then, all is war, turmoil, and clamour. The wildfowl hate a night of gales, for they are buffeted unmercifully. One must remember that a big bird like a goose, indeed any bird, must try to keep its head to wind. To have a full nor'easter or a westerly gale blowing up your backside must be acutely uncomfortable. Your tail (even a short one) is blown backwards and every feather turned inside out. Remember, too, that flying into a gale for a big bird like a goose, which has a wing-spread of several feet, must be a most exhausting process. They can't just go with the wind like a sailing-boat, for an off-shore gale will whirl them far out to sea.

But it is no time to talk of strife and noise. This is a calm night of frost and moon, with the tide at the ebb. But we have been sitting here talking like this, and now the tide has turned.

All at once you are aware of it. At first you guessed that faint murmur was a train passing along the opposite shore. Then you realise that it is the oncoming tide. And at once the picture changes. Even a little breeze comes from nowhere and moves the grass on top of the brew. And there are sounds now in plenty, faint as yet but growing. The first you notice

Then for a fleeting moment you see them

is the very musical yodelling of the curlew packs. They are overjoyed at the prospect of food, and as the thin silken film of sea water swills gently over the firm sand, shrimps and other minute sand creatures stir and come to life. They are at it now all down the tide, and mingled with the ceaseless 'courlees' are the shrill pipes of the oyster-catchers. These black and white magpies of the tidal wastes are more excitable than the long-nosed curlews.

They are absurdly gay with their brilliant orange beaks and legs and their vivid black and white attire. Silvery clouds of knot and dunlin, redshanks with them, are now moving hither and thither along the edge of the incoming water.

All this advancing bustle and noise rouses you from your reverie. You sit up and realise for the first time you feel chilled.

The next thing you notice is that what a moment ago was firm sand, out there in front, is now crinkling water which reflects the moon. Ripple on ripple come washing in sideways and across, breaking with a gentle swilling hiss and minute bubbles.

Every shallow pan and gutter of the sands is filling and brimming. It's amazing how stealthily the tide creeps in, cutting in behind you if you are out from the land, brimming, flooding, and spilling over to continue that onward glide. And after this first filmy skin of water which comes washing in over the flat sands there follows the tide proper, a miniature Severn Bore it seems, sizeable waves curving and breaking in one continuous, murmuring roar.

I could watch for ever the coming of the tide on a quiet winter's night of moon and stars. It is a scene which must be dear to the heart of every wildfowler.

Soon there is water sucking and gulping obscenely among the hollows of the 'brew'. It comes washing in round your waders and retreats again, gathering itself for another onslaught.

And everywhere are birds, birds – the night is full of wings and cryings. Curlews, redshanks, dunlins, 'oysters' – they are all in the air at once. It is amazing where they have all come from. The answer, of course, is that they were out on the tide edge and have retreated before it to the shore.

And then comes the moment you have been waiting for. Above the bustle and roar of the breaking tide, above the yodelling and the pipes, the reedy cheeps, and harsh alarm notes of the 'shank, there comes the yelping of the barnacle geese.

I do not think that the cackling of greylags or the chorus of the pinks is quite so moving as the sound of a barnacle pack in full cry. It is unearthly. Phantom hounds most certainly and Herne the Hunter should be riding after!

Wildly you look to left, to right: to the moon's path now rocking and tossing: to the dark solemn edge of the brew. You cannot tell where they are coming or if, indeed, they will come at all.

And then for a fleeting moment you see them, or rather half-see them. They pass, not along the tide edge where you expected them to pass, but well inshore behind you, not five feet above the close-cropped merse, a moving, nebulous cloud, dim and speeding. Had you been forty yards back from the brew in that gully you jumped over on your way out, you would have had the whole pack over you!

A moment – and they have gone, and the ear follows them as they pass along the lonely marshes away to the river's mouth.

For you the spell is broken. This land of the Sleeping Beauty is no more, you somehow feel this is the end of the act. Your gun-barrels may be as clean as when you got out of the car and no warm bulge is felt in the goose-bag which hangs on your left hip.

But that does not matter, not one little bit. If you are a true fowler and lover of that magic land 'between the tides', it has been a night to remember.

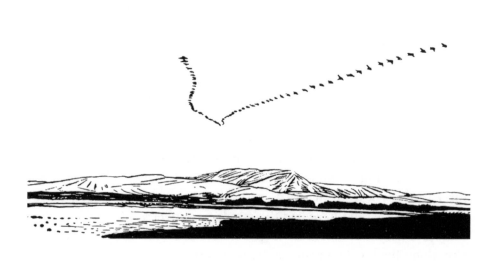

THE MILL O'MONTEAGLE

Those sky gypsies, the pinkfeet, are a restless tribe, even in a land where they have found secure pasturage. They may feed for a few days (usually three of four) on some chosen field and nobody molests them. But a change of weather, perhaps, or simply a love of wandering and exploration, makes them go elsewhere to seek fresh fields.

One morning the tide may be musical with their battalions and the watcher in the dyke sees the long, weaving skeins go in, the next dawn the estuary is vacant and silent save for a few greylags and the resident wader flocks.

These wanderings may take them to another seaboard, the Wash, the Severn, or some lonely loch among the hills where man seldom goes. I believe they have certain remote Highland lochs to which they repair when they need a complete rest – possibly when they have been much harried by gunners – though they can never long be absent from the salty muds and the sound and movement of the tideways.

At times they still use the estuary as a dormitory, but change their pasturage ashore, coming back to the sea once in the twenty-four hours for salt and grit and a smell of the sea, without which they cannot live.

These secret feeding grounds may be in the most unlooked-for places, and it takes a good deal of scouting and inquiry from the 'locals' to find where the birds are going.

This was so during one winter just after the war when the old gang – David, myself and my cousin Tony – were working one of the northern firths. An account of this may be of interest.

When we arrived, there were a lot of pinks on the bay and they were using a stubble about four miles from the shore. According to the locals they had been coming to this field at night for over a week and we hoped for great things. We built hides in the dyke bordering the stubble and went next evening (it was almost the full-moon period) but not a goose showed up. All we shot was a mallard which fell to David.

But as the moon rose we heard some big lots passing in on our right, heading for the mountains. The following morning we went to the shore and saw the pinks come back in force. That evening they again made away to the northwards over the mountains. They had evidently found fresh pasturage. It was up to us to find exactly where.

David spread out the map on the table of our fowling HQ and together we tried to locate the most likely spots.

Beyond that mountain range were several lochs, some of considerable size and some set far from any road. Any of these might be their goal, though I had the idea that they were using some stubble in the wide strath of arable land which lay on the far side of the range.

The moon was nearly full and the geese would be feeding at night, and I argued that the lochs were not the attraction: it was food they were after. At the period of the full moon, night is the most favoured time for feeding. One must remember that they are large birds and need a considerable amount of food to keep them going. A large gaggle of pinkfeet will eat as much as a small flock of sheep. Actually they are beneficial to grass pasture as they manure the ground, and the farmers do not mind them. It is only when they start on springing crops that the damage is done, but this does not occur until the end of the winter.

David pointed with his pencil-stub to a narrow road which wound away through a pass in the mountains some six miles to the east of where the geese went over that morning.

'That's our road; let's go and see. We'll have a look at the loch nearest the road; the others we can't explore; but we'll just hope they aren't there.'

Soon after breakfast we climbed into the shooting-brake and were soon on our way, steadily climbing the winding road which led to the top of the pass. There was a mild mist over the river valley behind us, but as we climbed the air became so cold we had to shut the windows and set the defroster going.

There was ice on the road too, and soon – snow. It was amazing how quickly scenery and mood seemed to change. We left behind the warm fir woods with their red-bracken floors and glimpses of tumbling burns, and soon there were no trees, nothing but barren, high tops of rich-toned heather patched with frozen snow. The road was treacherous too, and now and again we felt the stern of the van slide and wag.

At last we reached the top and, pulling in to the side of the track, we got out of the van with the spy-glass. On all sides the heather stretched away. On our right was a yet higher ridge, topped by a small, thick wood of hardy firs which stood out boldly against the skyline. Below us on the left the ground fell away into the misty strath shrouded in wintry vapour.

Somewhere in this direction the geese must have their pasturage, but whether this was near the lochs we had seen on the map or on the flat lands, how could we know? We might be within a couple of miles of their ground or might well be a dozen miles or more distant. The only point in our favour was that a gaggle of two hundred or so pinkfeet are not easily concealed, especially if they are feeding on the arables, and inspection of the stubbles would give us a clue.

Of course, should they be on the remote lochs we had seen on the map, that was another matter; there was no way of getting at them save by interception on the shore. Even in the Highlands you can't go 'brassing about' wherever you like. Some of the remote lochs are well keepered by local lairds who are not so easily persuaded as the farmers.

Scotch farmers are a truly grand race, and very rarely have I been refused permission to try for geese. It is the cad who pretends he is after geese when he is in reality out for a full day's shooting at anything he can see which spoils the game for honest fowlers. I have often been told by Highland farmers I may shoot grouse, pheasants, and partridges, when after geese, but I never do so. Even a grouse is scorned if geese are in the offing.

After scanning the ridge on both sides, we went on down towards the strath. Then a bend in the road revealed an old grey-stone building set in the hollow of a burn. Very old sycamore trees crowded it in and a lively little burn chattered merrily under a disused and crumbling mill-wheel. Close by, too, there were the remains of the mill-pond, choked now with willow and coarse rush. On our map this building was marked 'Mill of Monteagle'.

We found the farmer busy in his yard loading manure which steamed in the frosty air. Here was a useful man who, living on the spot, might have some news of the grey legions which we had seen these last few days heading in this direction.

'Aie, aie, the geese' (Scotchmen pronounce 'geese' in quite a different way from the Sassenach but it cannot be spelt, it is just the way they say it), 'the geese are aboot and were over here the nicht. They'll be using the top stubble. I pute them off these yesterday morning... aie.'

He raised his finger and pointed to the ragged firs on the skyline. 'Yon's the field, on the ither side of yon firs. It's a barley stubble and the ducks are workin' it at nicht too. Aie, ye can have a goo at the geese... Sairtenly! Sairtenly!'

His daughter, a fine buxom girl, was helping him load the manure, and we could not help wondering what chances she had of a gay time in that remote spot. The Mill o'Monteagle might be entrancing enough to the nature-lover and sportsman, but hardly the sort of place where an attractive, full-blooded young lassie would find all that was her due.

These Highland water-mills lack the homely, sleepy air of our own water-mills of the south. I always associate the latter with high June, flies weaving over the pond, the faintly-heard hiss of the mill-leat among willows, and that fruity exciting aroma of swamp and river water, and of course the lusty fish which cruise around the mossy piles.

These Highland mills are grey and weather-beaten, crouching under the lee of the hills and with boulders in place of reed beds. It must have been many a long year since the broken wheel revolved in the current of the tumbling burn, large now with the winter rains, rushing and roaring among its stones. There was frozen snow a little way up the hillside and icicles hung from the mill-wheel like a castle's portcullis.

Thanking the farmer, we went back up the track a little way and following his directions left the van in a gateway. Then we set off to climb the hill. Here and there we ploughed through snow and our feet sank in the heather. We put up some grouse near the skyline and a curlew rose from the heather to go crying over the misty valley.

It took us almost an hour to reach the stone wall below the fir wood beyond which was the stubble, and by that time the afternoon was beginning to grey. From our vantage point we could see right away to the firth, which shone faintly in the wintry evening light to the south.

As our sole mission was to scout the ground, we had not prepared to stay. In any case, a moonlight foray needs a little preparation in the matter of a well-filled flask of rum and so forth. But if we could find abundant goose 'sign', it would be worth our while to come on the following night.

We clambered over the wall and soon gained the fir wood. There

Geese circling the field

was a lot of snow up there, but on the bare stubble beyond, the wind had blown it fairly bare on the ridges.

It was a largish field, so we separated. I took the north side, David the centre, and Tony the south section. It was not long before we found abundant evidence of midnight visitations. There was goose 'sign' everywhere, and the snow-powdered stubbles were criss-crossed with a maze of large webbed footprints. Geese had evidently been using the field for a considerable time, for my experienced eye noted much old goose sign as well as fresh. Here and there a bird had sat down and had a nap. There was the hollow in the snow made by its breast and a little pile of droppings at one end.

All three of us made the same report, that there was most 'sign' at the south end near the stone wall.

By the time we got back to the car it was almost dark and an owl was hooting in the fir wood. It must have made him a draughty bedroom.

That night, when David went out of our fowling quarters to rug up the van (it had to be parked in the open inn yard), he came back with the report that thick cloud was coming up from the north and it was beginning to snow. Any secret schemes we had for going back to the field that same night were accordingly squashed, and we only hoped the fall would not be too heavy to make the passage of the hills impossible on the following evening.

Next morning dawned clear and frosty, and there had been only a light fall which would not be enough to stop us, at least so we hoped, though it was difficult to judge what depth had fallen on the high ground.

At about four o'clock that afternoon, we set out again fully prepared to stay out the night on the hill. As we began the long climb to the pass, we looked back to see a huge, rose-red sun going down over the firth. Flocks of pigeons were going to roost in the thick fir woods of Fusshie Priory.

As we gained altitude, the snow became deeper. I began to doubt whether we should get the van on to the high ground by the Mill o'Monteagle, but we did, after getting stuck twice on the frozen road,

174

a contingency we had provided for with spade and chains.

The van was parked in the gateway and well rugged up, and we set off once more to climb to the wood. This was more exhausting than on the previous day, but we at last reached the top and rested in the shadow of the firs.

A lot of pigeons went out as we reached the trees and, as we did not expect the geese until the moon rose, we had twenty minutes' good shooting at them as they came back. When the flight was over we went out on the stubble after drawing for places. David was the centre gun, Tony was to the south, and I was to the north, choosing a spot where the goose droppings were thick.

I spread out my lying-sheet and, making my labrador sit close beside me, I settled down to wait. All over the field there were relatively bare places which had been cleared of snow by the wind, so that we had a tolerable background. To ambush geese on virgin snow without a white covering is inadvisable on a moonlight night; the dark form of a man can be very conspicuous. Luckily there was no wind on this high field, or it would have made our long wait an uncomfortable one, despite the fact we were warmly clad. Even so, the old dog was shivering and was glad to creep close beside me.

For a long time after sunset I could see the dark form of David very clearly as he sat in the centre of the field about a hundred and fifty yards to my right, and beyond him the fainter darker smudge of Tony. But gradually, as the light faded, those dim forms melted into their background and soon the only visible thing was the black mass of the fir wood showing over the white rim of the hill.

From my high vantage point I could just see a single, bright light from the Mill o'Monteagle down in the glen, where the farmer and his family were cosily sitting down to supper (no doubt listening to the 6 o'clock news on the wireless).

The stars shone frostily high above and I heard the owl hooting in the firs. He had had a noisy awakening when we were shooting at the pigeons (we had bagged seven birds) and I hoped that he was also in for a noisy night as well!

Before the moon rose I heard mallard quacking and once or twice the wicker of wings and glimpsed a dark shape passing swiftly over with

175

that peculiar thin whistling. We had arranged not to fire at anything but geese, or I should have had a smack at them. One duck actually pitched on the snow within thirty yards of me but immediately sprang up again and was lost against the stars.

The cold clamped down with great ferocity. It came as stealthily as the tide, worming its way inside my clothing, and Judy cuddled ever closer, grumbling a little under her breath. Now and again waves of shuddering passed through her (and me, as she was pressed tightly up against my side), but I suspect it was excitement as much as a sense of chill.

Just as the moon rose out of the misty vapour I heard the distant yelp of a single pinkfoot to the north, but saw nothing. Half an hour passed without any other promise.

Waiting for geese is rather like waiting for a coarse fish to bite. You are full of eagerness at first and sit as still as a rock watching, hoping, and waiting. And then one's enthusiasm begins to ebb away and your feet begin to tingle. The cold of the gun-barrels in the crook of my arm was felt through my leather sleeve and the moonlight began to glisten on the small corn-stalks which showed above the snow. I felt horribly conspicuous, and now I could see David again quite clearly, and even Tony behind him. There was a defined shadow now on the snow behind me.

Something came over the white rim of the hill on my left, a cautious, halting spectre. I thought at first it was a fox setting out for his night's hunting, but soon saw it was a hare. It passed across between David and myself and vanished in the direction of the fir wood.

I was just on the point of rising to my feet and having a 'cabman's' warm as my finger tips had no feeling in them, when I distinctly heard the sound of geese approaching from my left. This was rather unexpected as I thought they would be sure to come in from the firth and so over Tony and David.

By the sound, it was a big skein and as the seconds passed the babel of cries came ever nearer, which was exciting. They were evidently circling the field, for the next moment I heard them over the fir wood, swinging round. Were they going to lower or had they seen us in the moonlight and were passing on to the lower lands of the strath?

I pivoted round, staring into the greenish, moonlit sky, my eyes full of stars. The crying loudened, and a moment later I heard Tony fire both barrels. There was a moment's silence as the geese climbed, and then they came baying right over my head. I could see them fairly well. I stood up and fired both barrels at one bird which was directly overhead outlined against the thin, fleecy cloud. Immediately it seemed to swell in size and, with a whistling rush, hit the snow with a tremendous thump not ten yards behind me. Judy went out and brought it back.

After that there was a pause of about ten minutes. I called out to David to know whether Tony had a bird down but received no reply, so concluded he hadn't heard me. Then I saw a dim figure walking about at the far end of the field, so I imagined Tony was gathering his goose. I hoped so, anyway, for I had heard no thump after his shot.

Then I heard the geese again, this time coming in from the firth. They circled as before, but they were high and none of us (very wisely) attempted to fire, though they came over us in a gliding, scattered mass. They all alighted at the far end of the field and remained quite silent, so much so that I thought they must have gone. But on peering into the half-darkness I thought I could see a black shadow on the snow. They must have been about 100 yards from me and were probably a little nearer to David. Anyway, it was wise to let them stay, for others were coming and those on the field would act as decoys.

This lot, a party of thirty or more 'pinks', came sailing in with paddles down almost on top of David. I heard him fire twice and also heard at least one goose hit the snow. The next moment they all came over me in a frantic hurry and climbing. I had an easy one on my right and hit a second bird which fell slanting, some way off on the edge of the stubble. I was afraid it was a runner and might get into the heather, so I sent the dog for it and she brought it back in about seven minutes.

After this episode there was a long lull during which time we all got up and stretched our legs and tried to get some warmth back into our limbs by pulls at the flask. Tony had had a goose, and David two, which made our bag six, and still another four or five hours to go to daylight, so we weren't doing too badly.

Soon after midnight a very large skein came in. David missed with both shots. I also distinguished myself by missing, unaccountably, as they came past me on my left within thirty yards. Perhaps they were farther than they seemed, but we should have had one, if not two, out of this lot.

This concluded our night's foray at the Mill o'Monteagle, for though we waited another two killing hours on that frozen hilltop, no other geese were heard or seen, and it was three very cold and weary men who stumbled down the snow-clad hill to the warmth of the waiting van. But our bag of six geese was ample reward for frozen hands and toes, and it will be a long while before any of us forget that wonderful moonlight vigil at the Mill o'Monteagle.

16.

RECOLLECTIONS OF A 'LONGSHORE GUNNER

Tomorrow at dawn we will come, but first we must pick positions for our hides, and if possible, construct them should cover be scanty. This is most important; nothing is more foolish than to leave the making of hides to the darkness of dawn, when the geese may arrive any moment.

I select a rather uncomfortable position between two small thorns which grow close to the river. There is plenty of driftwood lying about, flotsam of the last big spate. In a very short time a rough breastwork is constructed, and stakes planted to which I can attach my camouflage netting which is so invaluable.

The spreading branches of the thorn will no doubt serve as an additional screen, though it will be awkward to shoot through. If possible the shot must be taken by stepping out from under the tree; one so often misses if one has to fire through twigs.

Whilst I have been busy with my hide, Mick sits watching me, a comical expression on his wise old face. He knows very well that later we shall be here again, and maybe he will have a cold douche in the swiftly flowing river close by.

Meanwhile Tom and Mike have chosen their positions, Tom farther along the river, where he constructs a solid-looking 'igloo' in a niche of the bank wall, and Mike about a quarter of a mile on, near a line of thorn bushes and a fence, so as to intercept any geese which may cut across the loop of land and do not follow the river's course. After about an hour's work the job is done. We quickly leave the field for the geese will be coming back before sundown and may pitch again on their favourite pasture.

179

Back then, up the ridged frozen mud of the lane. We meet Mr Macpherson in the yard, a massive Scots yeoman who has, in fact, no love for the geese. They foul his pasture, and he is a big sheep farmer.

'We shall be early tomorrow, hope we shan't wake you!'

Macpherson smiles a slow smile. 'You'll nae do that, I'm thinking, we're up and aboot by five with the coos!'

As we drive away down the narrow twisting road under the hanging fir woods we see the strath spread out below. A pearly mist is quickly gathering, veiling the distant mountains. High in the western sky there is a smudge of shadow which changes shape. Now it is strung out in a twisting thong, now it bunches to a cloud. It is the geese coming back!

It seems to take a tremendous time for them to come up to the field below the farm. But at last they are clearly visible, wheeling and turning, spiralling down beyond the Drum. Will they be there at dawn? That is the question which will be answered for us in sixteen hours from now!

As so often happens when an ambush has been laid on, we all slept badly. Again and again one goes over in one's mind a host of possibilities. Will the geese come up river, or will they come over the hills opposite? Is my hide in the best position? I don't fancy those overhanging branches. Will Tom and Mike get all the first shots and turn the geese before they are within range of me?

Just beyond my hide there was a deep dyke and a stout wire fence; a devil to get over if one was in a hurry. If Mick leapt it for a retrieve he might tear himself on the barbed wire, I must watch that. I had a spaniel once who disembowelled herself jumping barbed wire. I pushed her entrails back and got her to the vet to be sewn up and she was none the worse. But it taught me a lesson. Perhaps the geese wouldn't come at all! For, as every fowler knows, plans 'gang agley'; very often, what promises to be a grand morning, turns out a complete dud, for some reason, change in the weather, or set of tide, not a single bird shows up.

It was soon after six when we reached the lane down to the farm. Lights showed in the house windows, men were going to and fro in the lighted barns. Their day had begun long since. The life of a farm moves with a rhythm akin to a steady heart beat; there is a naturalness about it, the tending of flocks and herds, the sowing and planting of crops, that gentle unhurried rhythm which is part of life itself, of the seasons, of the good earth.

Soon we were clumping down the lane burdened with our rolls of camouflage netting and six stuffed decoys (which we thought might help to draw the geese). These, together with our guns, three Thermos flasks and sandwiches, and heavy gear, were enough to make us all puff and blow. At the foot of the Drum we separated, Tom and Mike going off to the right where I noticed the first keen flush of dawn growing beyond the hills. I struck off through the rushy end. Snipe rose up 'scaaaping' continually, the queer tearing sound growing fainter and fainter as they arrowed away into the dark.

I was soon settled in my hide with the netting hooked in place. Mick sat beside me with ears cocked. The low murmur of the river hard by was continuous. Just below me was a deep pool fringed with ice. Fragments of stick and reed revolved on its ebony icy face. Somewhere a peewit was calling, that keen, lonely sound which belongs to the twilit world of dusk and dawn.

These moments of waiting are always the very best of the day. Each little sound means so much, the 'wheeo' of a wigeon, the far off 'frank frank' of a heron, going back to his roosting wood after a night's fishing, and the human-like call of a wandering black-backed gull, always early risers.

Every moment now the light was growing, promising a day of sun and hard frost. Not a cloud anywhere and overhead the stars shining. I could smell the river's own personal smell, a sort of peaty aroma, and as I idly watched it swirling onwards, I thought of the clean silver torpedoes of the salmon who, with fluttering tail, held themselves head upstream as though tethered by the nose, and the fat golden-hued trout with their leopard spots, likewise poised behind river-bed stones.

If the geese *did* come I must try and drop them on the sward, for Mick would have a mighty cold swim and the river ran with power.

181

Now in the growing light the fence was visible ten yards away with its double strands of wire. That is where the drainage ditch joined the river. All along the fence hung tattered strands of reed measuring the height and force of the last big spate. The whole of these goose grounds must go under in a big spate and maybe there lies the secret of their popularity with the geese. At last, unmistakably, I heard a faint croak which set the pulses leaping. It came somewhere from the east, beyond the big clump of willows which grew right on the river bank. Seconds passed, the goose noises became louder.

Then I saw them, a small bunch of seven. They came, not from down-river as we had expected, *but from over the hill opposite!* They came flying round (Mick and I crouched low, watching them), dim half-seen flapping shapes almost lost against the loom of the hill. To my astonishment, they all pitched on the grass over the river, about three hundred yards distant. As soon as they alighted I lost sight of them. Geese will always do surprising things like that!

Never mind, thought I, they will act nicely as decoys. Any geese beating up from the south will see them and cross right over me. But this was not the way things turned out. After sitting on the grass quite silently for about twenty minutes the little lot got up, again quite silently, and flew over the hill, the way they had come. Then there was a lull, with nothing but the river's voice and a single curlew calling. Mick was shivering quietly, partly with cold, partly with excitement. Then... more goose voices! This time there was no mistaking their purpose. A skein of about fifteen greylags came flogging over the tall willow, right overhead. At my single shot a bird fell plummetwise. It landed in the little stream beyond the fence, sending up a plume of spray quite eight feet high which was visible over the bank top.

The current bore it swiftly out into the bosom of the river but Mick was sent. He hesitated a moment, then plunged manfully in. The current was rapid, and Mick had to swim hard to overtake it. He grabbed the goose a hundred yards below and brought it back in triumph, his curly coat already white with freezing drops.

He had hardly regained the hide when I heard a loud clamour from over the field. There was a big lot beating up for us now. I could see them lowering their wings as though they meant to come down on the

At my single shot a bird fell plummetwise

grass. Some did so, but a small outlying party picked up again just as planes, about to land, give a burst to their engines, and came beating low directly for my may trees.

I fired. The leading bird struck the opposite bank where it rolled into a hollow. I sent Mick over, the current was strong and he landed fifty yards below me. There I saw him galloping about trying to wind the fallen bird.

He came up opposite to me, disappeared in the hollow, and reappeared with the goose in the mouth. He then plunged in and started swimming across. The goose was a big one and heavy, the current strong. Now and again Mick's head went under, but he held on and landed below the willow and came back with head high and stern swinging, proud as a grenadier.

A shot or two went off down-river and I saw parties of distant geese crossing and recrossing. Then came a lull.

The sun was up now and with its coming multitudes of wigeon, golden eye, and mallard flew past, all heading down-river. Had we been duck shooting we should have had great sport, but as always happens when after the geese, it was the larger, more elusive fowl which were our set quarry.

In clear light of day the mystery of hill and river melted. I could see the Drum, and the chimneys of the farm, and some cattle with steaming breath, standing in a motionless frieze beside an old yard wall. Pigeons wheeled, white and shining, round some black bean stacks, and from over the river a pheasant called. I saw it strutting about under some oaks, shining like metal in the early sun. Then happened a pretty thing. About twenty yards away down-river from my hide were some small thickets of alder, young trees with dead coarse grass around their bases. I saw a minute bird moving there, far smaller than a blue tit. On going gently closer I saw it was a golden-crested wren. Never for a moment was it still, a minute fluffy ball puffed against the cold, searching diligently among the dead withered grass. I came within a foot of it but it ignored me – it thought I was a tree, for a moment later there was a faint fluttering and fairy fanning in my face and it landed on my shoulder! It flew off again immediately, but returned to the alder saplings where it was soon joined by its mate. These delightful diminutive creatures were busy there for quite five minutes before moving on to the willows. They are as fearless of man as phalaropes.

Soon after this episode a bunch of geese came over the hill opposite and I dropped one exactly in the centre of the river where it landed with a tremendous splash. Poor old Mick had another cold swim. It was his last, for the flight was now over, and beyond a few distant travelling skeins we saw no more geese.

17.

LEPUS THE BROWN HARE

THE FIRST DAYS

In the first four weeks of his life Lepus had many lessons to learn, and there was nobody to teach him. But the leveret is a self-reliant animal, well equipped by nature to fend for itself. Now, at five weeks, he felt no need for his mother's milk. All about him his dinner table was spread, the half-grown clover leaves he loved so dearly, the tender grasses, the minty flavoured herbs.

Already he was a solitary animal, quite content to be so. In fact he preferred to be alone, so different from the rabbit which must have companionship of its own kind. After the first day his mother had separated her babies, carrying them in her mouth, as a cat does her kittens, depositing them in different 'forms', a long distance apart, but in the same field.

It is rather difficult for us to imagine how the life of so small and helpless a wild creature is threatened. There was the white owl in the belfry, whom we have met already, sitting up there in the cobwebby gloom with such a 'pi' expression. If he chanced to spy Lepus as he swept over the dew-damp mowing grass in the gloaming, he would have dropped upon the leveret in a moment and sunk his talons into his body. There was the red stoat with a black tip to his brush and eyes which were without mercy, a mighty hunter, who lived under the old ash root in the corner of the vicarage garden. He would have dearly loved to catch a leveret unawares, though he preferred rabbits, which were easier to catch because they crouched and screamed when he was on their trail. There were the vixen and her mate who had an earth in Coldharbour Wood on the edge of the down. They were perhaps the most dangerous enemies of all. Even the rascally carrion crows would have had a go at him with their terrible pick-axe bills, if they had the chance. Their eyes were as sharp as needles. They sought out the nestlings in hedge and spinney, they quartered the reeds around the lake in the hills looking for the eggs of moorhens, coots, and wild duck, but Lepus was growing so fast he would soon be too large a morsel for the crows.

There was Tom, the village poacher, and his white whippet Nailem, and the parson himself dearly loved the gun and would sometimes take a walk around his glebe on a still evening, though most of his serious shooting came later in the year. There was the parson's dog Honey, a big-boned yellow labrador, who often went hunting on her own account. With her long legs she could have run Lepus down with ease.

But Lepus was not easily to be found. All day he lay secure in his 'form', the thick forest of the mowing grass, which was like an intricate jungle, screening him from the eyes of enemies. The grasses grew about him like a mould, which is why a hare's resting place is called a form.

He did not always sleep. There was always something to smell, see, or listen to. He watched by the hour the antics of the strange green angular grasshoppers which shrilled their vibrating songs to him and flipped, prodigiously, from stem to stem, sometimes misjudging their distance and landing on his head and back. Field mice, too, rustled about him, darting with sudden incredible speed between the close-woven grass stems.

With the fat fare Lepus grew rapidly. By the end of the month his legs were long and powerful, his senses keener than ever. He was a self-reliant creature in full possession of himself.

The night dew did not bother him nor did the rain, for his coat was so thick and fine. On his nightly wanderings he sometimes met his brother and sister but they passed each other as though they were strangers. He left the hayfield when dusk stole over the fields and went into the vicar's glebe where the young wheat was sweet and tender. How delightful it was to run under the stars, to be unhampered by the mowing grass through which he had to tread his way. The wheat was not yet high enough to cover his back, it grew in straight rows with spaces in between, forming interminable corridors down which he raced with wild abandon like a child let out of school.

Other hares visited the vicar's fields and several times Lepus met a

Dozing in the early summer sun

grizzled old Jack hare who pursued him savagely, hitting out at him with his powerful kangaroo-like pads. Though Lepus did not know it, this Jack hare was his own father!

Each night was different. Sometimes it was still, with the deep velvety sky above him pricked with the pin points of the stars, and the serene moon riding slowly over, giving him more light than he needed for his foraging. Sometimes a soft rain fell, whispering down, wetting the outside of his fur coat.

THE PRIZE CARNATIONS

It might truly be said that the only dangerous enemy who remained, apart from the beagles, was old Tom Tollard. Tom had many scores to pay. Lepus had raided his 'garden field' as he called his allotment, again and again, in the dead of winter; he had even been into Tom's little garden and eaten his greens and carnation roots.

These carnations were Tom's great pride. They lined the path up to his cottage and made such a show and scented the summer airs so sweetly that passers-by stopped to admire them as they passed the gate. They were originally cuttings from the vicar's plants, and Tom tended them with the greatest care. So whenever Lepus visited the little garden he was truly entering the den of the lion. As he chose the early hours of night the old man did not find the damage until the morning. Then the language was terrible!

The village flower show was due in a week's time. Tom was nursing his finest blooms for the great day. He fenced them about with cotton, he stood a scarecrow among the hollyhocks close by, he set snares in the most likely places where a hare could enter.

As the date of the flower show grew nearer, Tom did all he could to see that his precious blooms were in perfect condition. He took to getting up at night when the moon was shining, to see that all was well.

Four days before the great day, Lepus crept through the hedge and went lippity loppity down the brick-tiled path, as bold as brass and looking as big as a well-grown springer dog. There was a half moon up in the quiet sky and the night was wondrously still, full of the scent of Tom's flowers, sweet williams, the syringa, the old-fashioned roses, and the carnations.

The old man lay awake on his little iron bed in the corner of the front parlour, for he now no longer went upstairs to sleep. His legs would not work properly, he had worn them out. That night he was restless. As he lay upon his bed the oppressiveness of the atmosphere lay like lead in the darkened humble little room.

'Coo! Must be thunder about,' thought Tom. 'Very like the rain'll come and flatten them carnations to the ground so that they won't be no good for the flower show next Saturday. Drat it.'

Somewhere a young tawny owl was uttering its monotonous hunger call *kiswick, kiswick*. It sounded like a pair of rusty garden shears.

Tom threw aside the single grubby blanket which covered him and lowered his old legs to the floor. He had only to slip on his unlaced boots and coat and he was dressed. He rarely took off his clothes.

Unsteadily he went to the door and opened it a little way, peering out. There, looking as big as a dog, was Lepus sitting on his back pads surveying the carnations!

Tom was just about to roar 'geerchur' when the old poacher instinct suggested a better plan. In the corner of the room was the old single-barrel gun which he so rarely used these days. Up in the 'chimbley corner' was a cartridge, old but serviceable, loaded with number four shot, specially for dealing with hares. With shaking fingers, the old man loaded his gun and stole back to the door, which he had left ajar. But when he peered out the path lay empty. White moths blundered among the dim flowers. Lepus had heard a movement in the cottage, he had gone back through the hedge. Tom's lips moved in a soundless oath.

He thought of going down the path to the end of the garden, for the hare must be very close, possibly in the meadow over the hedge, but he decided to wait quietly by the half-open door. So he pulled up a kitchen chair, with his gun across his knees he waited, peering out through the crack. He had wonderful long sight for a man of eighty-five, though he had to wear glasses for reading.

'I'll give 'er carnations,' he muttered to himself. 'She'll come back, sure as 'arvest, so 'er will.'

But nothing moved on the brick-tiled path save a large black rat which ran across like a clockwork toy. A chill breeze puffed over which set the hollyhocks nodding and the coat on Tom's scarecrow flapped once. In the village the cockerels began to crow, others untucked their heads and answered. The white owl flew back to the tower. Over the sleeping village three solemn notes reverberated as the clock struck three in the morning.

Tom, with his natural poacher's caution, was right, Lepus hadn't gone away. He was, at that identical moment, sitting in the meadow just over the hedge, his large ears cocked looking towards the thatched cottage. He hadn't really been scared, there had only been one suspicious sound, and the smell of those carnations was to him like the smell of roast beef to a hungry man! So after a wait of twenty minutes he crept back through the hedge and entered the garden once again.

Tom Tollard saw the dim figure of the hare as it came loppiting cautiously round a clump of Michaelmas daisies. His old heart began to knock in the base of his skull, how it did thump, just as it always did when he was about to shoot game, the old hunter's excitement!

In search of the carnations

At last, *at last*, Lepus was his! Never again would his greens be stripped on his garden field. He'd give her carnations!

Dump, er dump, went the old man's heart. It beat so loudly it was like a great hammer, thud thudding there, in his skull. He began to raise his gun... Then his world revolved giddily, he fell backwards to the floor. Just that extra excitement had been too much for that old pumping engine, his heart. It had faltered to a stop like a worn-out clock.

Tom wasn't missed in the village until the day before the flower show. They found him lying on his back just inside the door with the gun cocked and loaded beside him. They first thought he had had an accident. The carnations destined for the flower show were made up into a wreath and everyone marvelled at the magnificent blooms.

Look! There's a white owl sitting on the tombstone with the cherub's head on it. He gives a prodigious gurk and brings up a beetle casting which falls down into the Herb Robert at the foot of the stone.

Close by is a mound of freshly-turned earth. It covers old Tom's worn-out body which is now of no use to anyone but the earth itself and is laid beside his ancestors. A magnificent wreath of carnations, lying on the mound, shines palely in the scented darkness.

The white owl bobs up and down, peering at something which is coming along between the grassy hummocks. He utters a wild skirling screech and flies away over the yew, peering downwards with his huge black eyes at the hare which is lippiting loppiting over the grass. Lepus smells the carnations and pulls at a flower, a magnificent pale pink bloom which alone would have won Tom the prize. His mouth works like a little grass cutter bar, his big ears are in a V, his prominent eyes staring at the solemn tower and the tombstones. He can hear the sheep bleating up on Tontem Down, the faint, far away 'tink tonk' of a sheep bell. Behind the square tower with its leaning curved gargoyles the sky is a sort of ice grey. Dawn is coming, the dawn of a new day.

18.

THE SHOOTING MAN'S BEDSIDE BOOK

One golden and hazy afternoon, in the first week of November, I set out with my spaniel to shoot over Barrett's Farm. I had never shot there before, but had always cherished a desire to do so, and a lucky encounter with the old farmer himself, over the matter of a load of manure for our garden, led to a hearty invitation. 'You'm welcome to have a walk a-round,' he said, 'you won't get much, but you may pick up a pheasant or two in the Ma'sh Spinney, and they're plenty o' rabbits; you can shoot as many as you like o' they.'

There is an added interest in shooting over unknown ground, and I looked forward to my 'walk a-round' with keen anticipation. I could not have been more fortunate in the choice of a day. It was one of those peerless afternoons we sometimes get in the English autumn, still, and tranquil, the sun shining from a cloudless sky, but with a gentle warmth. There were wasps and big flies busy round the ivy bush on the farmhouse cartshed wall and, late as it was, some red admirals were sidling on the Michaelmas daisies that peeped over the garden fence. They seemed to me perfect specimens, lately hatched, without tear or blemish. Yet these insects, bees, wasps, and flies, seemed to me a little lethargic, they moved from flower to flower with a certain hesitation; the red admirals did not quit their feast when my shadow fell upon them. Despite the sun they sensed the coming of winter, they were not deceived.

I thought it strange, though, to hear no twitter of swallows over the barn roof. I searched the sky but saw none, only countless starlings which glided about over my head, clumsily fly-catching. They do this in the first warm days of spring; it is a sign, as sure as the opening of

195

flower and leaf, of coming summer, as it was now a token of approaching winter.

Leaving my cycle by the farm I went down the muddy lane which led to the fields and spinneys. Major, the liver-and-white spaniel, was beside himself with joy, frisking about before me, grinning up into my face, scampering before and behind, throwing himself full length on the wayside grass, panting with out-flopped tongue.

But as soon as we reached the head of the lane and passed through the gate he came to heel. He sensed my will by looking at my face, he knew his place.

I stopped a moment, when through the gate, to take a look at the boundaries which had been pointed out to me a day or two before by old Mr Barrett himself.

The pastures sloped away from the farm quite steeply, and the field I was in was rough with tussocky grass. Below was a fine old double hedge, some ten or twelve feet high, ablaze with the clear yellow of the dying maples and pink and rose with the hawthorn leaves. There were, I remember, many crab-apple trees in this hedge, and that year they bore a heavy harvest. The yellow apples shone from a distance on the bare branches (they had mostly dropped their leaves) and many lay below on the hard caked earth, for it had been a dry autumn. You could have gathered many bushels of the bitter fruit. Some appeared as red and rosy as orchard apples, some showed a faint maiden's blush on their mellow-yellow cheeks.

This double hedge (always a good place to 'hunt out' with a gun) led over two fields to melt into a maze of other hedges, well timbered with oak and elm, with here and there a scattered spinney of oak and ash poles. A faint pearly mist hung over the distances and in the hollows in the hills. Many of the stubbles had not yet been ploughed in, and over them I could clearly see flocks of rooks and grey wood-pigeons, all busy at their gleaning.

We first of all tried the double hedge. I sent the spaniel in the middle while I walked on the sunlit side, wishing I had a second gun to guard my flank. Major was a good dog at hedge-hunting, he never worked out of gunshot and, if at times, when for instance he got on the trail of a rabbit and excitement and keenness made him forget my rule, he would

196

poke his head out at the limit of gunshot range, waiting for me to come up with him. There are not many spaniels who will do this and only months of hedgerow hunting had made him wise. He had found that if he put up the game too far away all his efforts (and mine too) were useless. It had taken him two years to learn this.

For some time nothing happened. I heard Major scuffling along among the crab-apples and the dying nettles and occasionally caught a glimpse of his busy stern wagging in a gap in the bushes.

With a loud clatter a few wood-pigeons left the oak trees which grew between the hedges but, pigeon-like, every bird left the far side of the tree where I could not see them, and offered no chance of a shot.

All at once something moved in the nettles in the ditch about twenty yards in front of me. At first I thought it was a rabbit; the next moment I saw it was a hen pheasant. She was running for all she was worth down the ditch. I only caught quick glimpses of her, head down, back hunched, and long tail stuck out behind her. An instant later Major darted through, standing for a moment in an opening under a rail, looking with a puzzled and very excited expression up and down the ditch in each direction. It was laughable to see his tense face, the ears cocked forward almost hiding his white muzzle, and he gave two little jumps so as to see over the dead 'gix' in the hedge bottom.

I ran, with my gun at the ready, and Major, turning round and at last using his nose, ran too, down the ditch, and getting a little too far in front, I had to call him back with a whistle. He stopped at once and waited for me to come level with him.

The pheasant had evidently darted back through the hedge again. At any rate there was no sign of it. I told Major to 'follow on', and he vanished again. I was afraid that the bird would break cover the far side, so I shouted to the dog to go right through, at the same time hurrying on down my side. I had now come to another hedge which joined the tall one at right angles and the only place where I could get through was at a gap and two rails. I was on the top of the rails, with the sun almost in my eyes, when I heard the sound of the bird rising with a great bustle of wings.

She rose out of the ditch, rocketing right up, evidently making for a small spinney which lay across the stubble field in front of me.

Somehow or other the gun came to shoulder and at the report I saw a cloud of feathers burst outwards and glimpsed the pheasant falling to the stubble thirty-five yards away. Major was out in a moment and racing away and by the time I had climbed down from the top rail of the fence he was trotting back, head held high, the bird in his mouth.

This was a good beginning, so good that I sat down under the hedge and, giving the dog a biscuit which I always carry with me as a reward for good work, I filled and lit a pipe.

On every twig the spiders' webs glistened in the sun, the filmy threads shone in the pale sunlight very clearly and I saw that they were laced, even from the tips of the stubbles, so that, looking into the sun, it appeared as if there was a pathway of shining webs stretching right across the meadow. Redwings were clucking in the oaks.

Some rooks, disturbed by my shot, wheeled and cawed over a far field. Some alighted in the trees of the little spinney. After smoking for a little while (the dog lying panting beside me and trying to bite some burrs out of his long ears by pulling them downwards with his paws over his nose) I got to my feet and continued along the hedge. Where there is one pheasant there is often another, perhaps the whole brood, and the bird I shot had evidently been hunting for the acorns which lay about in the stubble under the oak trees. These trees were still in full leaf, indeed they showed little sign of decay, only an upper branch, here and there, had turned to that soft buff yellow which is the tint of undressed leather.

Major went in again and we had nearly got to the end when I heard him give a muffled excited bark (a thing he very seldom did). I thought he had another pheasant. But the next moment a rabbit rushed out within fifteen yards of me.

It ran out into the stubble and stopped, its eye wide with fear, not knowing what to do. Perhaps I was between it and its hole. Just as I was raising my gun it bolted off down the hedge, offering an easy going-away shot which a schoolboy could have made a showing of. But for some inexplicable reason both my shots went wide, the rabbit rushed on with bobbing white scut, and dived into the hedge again some ninety yards away.

Major then emerged, looking at me with the most laughable expres-

Hedge hunting

sion on his face and then gazed pathetically in the direction the rabbit had run. I shook my head at him and he came to heel. This little failure had sobered me down.

We next went across to the little spinney. I felt sure I should find another pheasant or two there; it looked just the place for them, quiet, lonely, and with several large oaks growing among the ash poles. We cut across the stubble and entered it. The hawthorns which formed its underwood were lovely, every tint of yellow and rose, some leaves were almost scarlet. But the field maples were the loveliest, their black slender twigs showing through the veils of incandescent yellow.

As I pushed through them these leaves fell in showers. Major had only to gently knock against one of the bushes to send a flurry of them on to his back.

We went slowly and with caution. The spinney smelt deliciously of damp, wet leaves and rich earth, a wintry smell. There was a little boggy ditch in the middle and long coarse grass and a holly or two. I had just passed the bole of an oak when a bird flew up. (I thought it was a partridge by the way it rose, though I should have known no partridge, save a wounded one, would be found in the middle of a spinney.) It went straight up with great swiftness, Major standing beside me, rooted to the spot.

And then I saw what it was. A woodcock! Never before, in all my wanderings about these midland pastures, had I ever seen a woodcock, yet there was no mistaking it, the long bill carried downwards, the large but rather snipe-like wings.

It soared over the yellow maples and the rose-red thorns and turned left. I glimpsed it in a gap, straightening out, and at that instant I 'followed through' and fired. By that time the bird was out of sight, for a spray of maple came across my gun, but I thought I heard him drop, and Major darted off.

I stood among the trees, waiting for him to return, hardly daring to look in his direction. It would be awful to have missed, yet it was a difficult shot. Imagine my joy when he reappeared with the woodcock in his mouth! He trotted up to me, but instead of giving it into my hand, as he did the pheasant, he put it down at my feet and licked it. He was not used to woodcock, it was the first one he had ever retrieved.

I was beside myself with bliss. I could have danced. When we get older we lose this surge of inner joy at the successful accomplishment of a shot. What a pity that is!

I took the warm bird up and held it in my hand, looking at it intently. It was only the second woodcock I had ever shot, and it was the first I had ever held in my hand. The stout and stumpy body, the fine full eye as full of expression as a gazelle's, the exquisite tints of its barred plumage, what a miraculous treasure it was! I could not bring myself to put him with my pheasant in the game-bag for fear his delicate plumage might be soiled. I wrapped a handkerchief round him and put him in my pocket. I would never forget this moment. I would have him stuffed, I would have him mounted in a case with dead oak leaves about his feet, I would look at him for years after and remember this golden autumn afternoon!

And now, as I write, I seem to be standing once more in that little tinted spinney with the weak sunlight filtering through the half-bare branches; I smell again the rare aroma of the leaves, the earth, and hear, as I stand in a trance, the sweet trickle of a robin's song somewhere in the thickets and the faint 'caw caw' of rooks.

I cannot remember anything more of that afternoon; it is strange that I should recollect so clearly the events which led up to that moment.

Major is now no longer by my fireside; Barrett's Farm is far away, many, many leagues; old Mr Barrett, like Major, is dead (God rest their souls), and I am almost middle-aged. Is it not strange I can still live again that experience so vividly when other far more weighty and important occasions have been forgotten and passed out of mind?

Part Four

A WANDERING MAN

In the boathouse

From *A Child Alone*

Then my thoughts would fly – over the ha-ha wall, down the slope where dense clumps of nettles grew into which the baby rabbits scuttled, apparently immune from stings, to the iron gate which clanged, and the winding footpath which led under the whitebeams and whispering poplars.

There would be dank rich smells on hot mornings from the dock leaf bog, glittering dragonflies darting under the oaks. I had once found a tree creeper's nest in one of these oaks, behind a piece of loose bark. Then came the boathouse – nobody there but questing moorhens and the roach lying idly about like grey bars just under the top of the water, revelling in the sun, basking like cats, occasionally dimpling the surface in a lazy way. Then, in spirit, I would step gingerly out on to the Long Log and let down a wriggly worm between the lily pads. All this was far better than lessons!

The great outdoors drew me with a powerful magnetism as great as the laws of gravitation. I felt in those hours of sunlit glory that my life was being wasted. Here I was, in a shadowed room, wrestling with stupid figures! We don't remember the grey days of our childhood, only the sunlight ones, the happy ones, and mostly those to do with summer.

19.

THE WAYFARING TREE

There was mist in the high valleys about Ettrick Pen, mist at sunrise and no wind. It meant one thing, a fine day, or, should I say, 'a feen dee?' 'Feen dees' are rare among these hills (which must surely be some of the wettest in Britain) and they are not to be squandered. Not that the climate matters very much in this part of the world, every day is 'feen' to me, loving this country as I do. Perhaps I am so fond of it because I have Scotch blood in my veins, my grandfather was a Border man.

When, as I was shaving, I looked out of the window of the Lodge, and saw afar those spacious, broad-browed valleys wreathed in silvery vapour, I thought, 'Ah, a day for the hills and no mistake!' With a packet of sandwiches in my pocket and a handful of cartridges I would be away, as soon as that breakfast of brown trout, caught but yester eve in the Byreburn, was disposed of, and I would go alone, to walk the limits of the March.

I could smell those frying trout as I was shaving, the merry 'snop, clop' of my razor strop mingled with the cooings of wood-pigeons in the beech trees on the lawn. I felt absurdly like a boy on the first morning of the holidays, and tried to forget it was my last. It was not until the clock 'chapped' eleven that I could get away, however, as I had to wait for the post and Postie was late. Soon, however, I saw him cycling over the stone 'brig' half a mile away and after glancing through my mail I set forth.

I had never been to the limit of the March. Hitherto all my shooting had been done nearer home. But those distant ranges lifting one behind the other to the sky always beckoned. In my mind I pictured them peopled with packs of grouse and multitudes of hares.

I met the grieve by the sheep pen and asked him exactly how far I

206

could go, for I was a little hazy as to boundaries.

'To the skyline,' said he, 'as far as ye can see, mon!'

To the skyline! That was the sort of answer I had wanted!

The track I followed wound up the side of a brae, rutted by wheels and pocked with hoof stamps. The peat we burn at the Lodge comes by this track right from the uttermost limit of the March, which was my destination.

Heather was in full bloom on either side of my way, soft and springy it was, with big cushions of brilliant moss, like full breasts, here and there, over which the crane flies danced. Below me chuckled a little burn, beer brown, winding this way and that with waterfalls and rapids. Had we such a stream near home it would be the Mecca of many people; here it was just an ordinary burn.

From the fir plantation beside the track a red-flanked sparrow hawk made off with a lifeless pipit clasped below his tail. The sun, slowly rising on my left, shone warm and golden upon the fir tips, and a wood-pigeon with a white collar was visible, perching among the thick green tassels. I stalked him up the burn bed, preceded by a flock of darting troutlings but he saw my shadow and departed. So I left the wood and returned to the track climbing, climbing, all the way.

Soon I heard a thin, pipit-like whistle and a crowd of frightened sheep came jostling into view along the narrow track. Behind them was the shepherd whom I had seen yesterday making his way towards the flooded river. Now he was coatless and had a staff in his hand. On his head was a small round deerstalker, his feet were encased in thick wooden-soled boots; blue-grey woollen stockings clothed his stout calves. He was a square man, sturdy as a stunted rowan, and as hardy.

I stood awhile and talked, for he was in no hurry, seemingly, despite the busy time, for the sheep sales were in full swing at Lockerbie and all the flocks were being brought down from the hills.

For some days past I had seen strings of sheep, like maggots, wending their ancient tracks along the high hillsides and round them circled the untiring collies.

From him I gathered two most interesting things. One concerned eels. He told me that one day, when he was up on the high tops, he noticed his dog setting at clumps of grass. He went to investigate and saw multitudes of eels wriggling along through the coarse wet growth. I had heard of eels migrating in the lowlands but never over the high hills!

Yet it is well to remember that in this country the grass is always thick and wet. I had noticed that eels caught in the river below, if dropped from the hook, soon vanished in the matted herbage; they were gone in an instant as swiftly as a snake or a burrowing mole.

The other thing he told me was particularly interesting. It concerned a robin's nest which was built – where do you think? – *in the shoulder of a sheep!*

It was right amongst the wool and, what is more, that robin, travelling with its strange companion over the sheepwalks, reared its brood in safety!

I can vouch for this story because, still an unbeliever, I asked the shepherd's master, and he said:

'Oh, yes, Angus was not spinning you a yarn. I saw the nest myself with the hen sitting on her eggs!'

I would have given much for a photograph of that nest.

At last I said good-bye to Angus and continued on my way. I noticed the sheepdog (which all the time I had been talking to his lord had been crouched in the grass on the other side of the burn) leap to life, and away went the stupid sheep until the hill hid them from view.

The skyline was now marked by a rise in the ground, which was covered with clumps of rush. The burn still kept me company on my left, but soon it became a mere trickle which glittered like quicksilver in the sun. The track petered out at last, and I was wading through long coarse grass which reached to my knees. It was rough walking. Little drab pipits kept rising before me, sending my finger to the trigger by their sudden burstings forth. The sweat began to gather on my eyebrows and trickle down into my eyes, so I took off my cap and put it in my game bag.

I saw no game, no hares, no grouse. The grieve had told me there was little on the hills. A May snow had killed off the poults, and hares were scarce; he never remembered seeing so few.

Now the burn divided, by a rough greystone sheep pen, and coming to a little knoll I saw the skyline once again.

It still seemed a long way off. Gentle slopes, bleached to bone colour, rising tier on tier to the sky.

Looking back I could not recognise any well-known landmark save Ettrick Pen, away to the north, patched with sun and shadow. Fat larks rose from the grass, many of them tail-less; they seemed as big as snipe. The lark is a 'gamey' bird and setters and pointers will 'wind' them.

This did not look a good place for grouse; indeed all my energies were taken up with my climb, and my gun was now on shoulder.

I still had a little burn for company, very busy with its bays and waterfalls, and in its slower reaches darting arrows of troutlets fled over the spotted stones. At last even the burn forsook me, and then there was nothing but grass, toil and sweat. I felt my shirt grow clammy on my body. I passed several steep gullies – 'haughs,' as they are termed in Cumberland – and sheep were grouped along the sides scratching themselves. These sheep scratches were visible on all the steeper parts, showing the bare earth.

An empty valley, reddish with thistles and white with cotton grass, opened out on my left, and away in the distance black peat stacks and a tumbledown sheep pen, full of stinging nettles.

It was up that valley I saw the first game of the day. Five blackgame rose, appearing as big as capers, and swept away on curved wings round the shoulder of a knoll. Should I follow them or climb on? Climb on!

And so I climbed until, soaked with perspiration and with hammering heart, I gained that distant ridge which had for so long mocked me. I was at the limit of the March.

I threw myself down on the heather and lit a pipe. What a view! On every side hills and yet more hills, silvery and unreal. Only once have I seen this country painted with truth.

In the last century there lived a rather obscure water-colourist named James Orrock. He portrayed these hills with great fidelity. Old 'Ettrick Pen' I could see, and beyond him, at the uttermost range of vision, other blue hills which might have been cloud.

And the eye, sweeping the horizon north, south, east and west, saw nothing but fold on fold of silvery ranges. Over the Lake District sulked a dark storm cloud, but elsewhere all was sun and flying shadows.

Overhead the sky was a deep cobalt, on the horizon it was washed

Dogging on the moors

down to faintest Prussian blue, and across it drifted billowy white clouds. My eye travelled downwards to seek the Lodge, but it was invisible. I lay on my back and drank in the sweet air, spicy air, full of the scent of peat, heather and grass.

After a while the loneliness of the place crept about me, until I began to feel almost light-headed. Looking up at the travelling clouds made the head reel, my fingers felt the grass to prevent myself falling out into the sky.

A speck of white appeared against the red-brown moor below. It moved and came jigging my way – a Large White butterfly. It was flying due south in the teeth of the breeze and passed not five yards from where I lay. I watched it out of sight. Soon came another, and yet another, all flying in the same direction. Strange little travellers these, each very set upon its purpose. Some magnetism was drawing those atoms, what, no man could tell. They, like me, fitted into the scheme of things, their hold on existence as sure as mine – no less. And like a familiar acquaintance from another country, a homely bumble bee boomed by, his treasure bags stuffed with heather nectar, I have no doubt.

I had been hot climbing to this place, now I felt almost chilled. I got up, gathered my game bag, empty still, and slung my gun across my arm. For some time I followed along the spine of the ridge. The grass was quite white here, and there was no sound but the 'swissssh' of the bennets.

Then faintly I heard the lamenting cries of sheep. There is no sadder sound in Nature than the bleat of the flocks in the high places. 'Where? Where? Where?' they seemed to cry, as though they were lost souls searching the wide moors over, it is a sound inseparable from the lofty sheepwalks. This is the country of Robert Louis Stevenson, 'standing stones on the vacant, wide-red moor.' There are standing stones in plenty about here, no man knows their age or purpose. Below, in the valley, are strange circles of stone, older than Stonehenge.

Those who raised them, where are they? The Romans, who had their encampments hereabouts, where are they? Gone! Gone! All gone! The wind blows the dead yellow grass and another white butterfly plods by, and there comes again the age-old plaint of sheep, softened by distance. Not very many men come here, a shepherd maybe once in a while, we do not belong to this pure place. The grouse are glad when we are gone, the pipits and hares are glad and are at peace.

Coming to a tiny burnlet I threw myself down full length and drank from a fairy pool on which black and white fiddlers skated in all directions, horrified at the sudden descent of a shadowy giant sucking at the sweet, ice-cold water.

Three grouse were bagged 'ere I turned for home, the only game I saw within range. And as I at last reached the sheep pen by the peat stacks a ragged hare started forth and went away unsaluted by my double tubes of death.

The sun had set, a few pink tresses of cloud, like a child's blown hair, waved about Thunderbolt Knowe. It had been a rare day. My legs ached with weariness but it had been a memorable tramp. I was almost drunk with happiness.

How loud the burn sounded in the quiet of evening! How good it was to hear its friendly chatter once again!

20.
A SUMMER ON THE NENE

We left Fotheringhay with regret and steered safely through the middle arch which has proved disastrous for some incautious voyagers. It has a knack of carrying away one's windscreen; indeed, we met a fellow traveller later near Peterborough, whose shattered screen presented a sorry sight. It must have made erecting the hood at night a most inconvenient task for the canvas buttons down on to it. He was, I could see, a feckless sailor, and even whilst we watched them from afar, a child fell off the front of his cruiser, and finally he went aground.

We went on down-river from the old bridge and the lantern tower sank slowly astern, silhouetted against the soft sunset sky. We found an admirable pitch, about a mile from the village, under some very ancient willows. All had been pollarded and were full of holes and crannies. A little owl flew out of one of them, which, no doubt, had its nest there. This was a Lilford or Pygmy owl, introduced into this country by Lord Lilford. I often wonder why he chose this particular bird. At one time they were under a cloud of suspicion and they will certainly take the young of game birds. But they also devour an enormous number of harmful beetles and, of course, mice and moles.

They are handsome little fellows with richly spotted coats. Their mating call in the spring is a low musical 'hoo hoo' all on the same note, and uttered during the day, for they are not always active at night like the tawny and white owl. They have taken a beating, along with other members of the owl family, mostly from pesticides and some severe winters. A long frosty winter is especially hard on this species.

There was a vast hatch of fly under the drooping willows and soon the whole river boiled with dace and bleak. I speedily caught a fine fry for supper, and made a most satisfactory ending to a pleasant travelling day, for well-flavoured and cooked in oil, they are indistinguishable from whitebait.

The sunset had seemed to suggest good weather on the morrow, but it was cheerless and grey when I drew aside the cabin curtains next morning. A brisk wind was bustling the ripples under our keel with quite a slap and rattle. It formed miniature rollers in mid-river, puny grey wavelets, which broke over each other and toppled in silvery bubbles; a big sea in miniature.

Soon we saw the guillotine of Warmington lock swim into view. We found this a brute to raise. The first few turns were almost beyond the strength of my ladies, and because I was under doctor's orders I could not lend a hand. But we got through at last and made a mental note to enlist aid on the return voyage.

We found the stretch between Warmington lock and Elton one of the most attractive of our voyage. The Elton woods march down to the water's edge on the starboard side, and there are large plantings of aromatic poplars which stand in regiments along the bank; their newly-opened golden leaves limp and sticky, rustling softly in the grey wind.

We went on down to Elton to do some shopping, but decided to return up-river to sleep, for nightingales were singing in the leafy woodlands and there was snug anchorage beside the bank out of the wintry wind.

We found Elton delightful, straggling up a hill, and along the main road at the top. Here we found a wonderfully provisioned post office furnished with a deep freeze and all manner of good things for the nomadic life. It is a great place for dogs; I have never seen so many in a small village. They ranged from pekes to alsatians, with some 'varminty' little terriers for full measure.

The old mill appeared derelict, with gaping timbers and roof slates missing, but I was told in the village that it still grinds beans and corn for the estate – by electricity, not water power. One day it was working, for from the dim interior came grunts, groans, and shudderings. A bicycle propped against the wall suggested the 'miller' was at home. But I could find nobody and all I saw was a great black rat busy about a bag of split beans, half-seen in the cellar-like darkness of one of the lower rooms. These mill rats must lead a jolly life, as all rats like water, and with plenty to eat, and little disturbance save on occasional days when the machinery is active, they have nothing to disrupt the even tenor of their days.

Perhaps they have become immune to such things as rat poison, Warfarin, and the rest of man's machinations.

We had some drinks in the cool bar parlour of the Black Horse up in the village, which was once kept by the State executioner, who still, I believe, lives in the village.

The landlord, a genial, pleasant host, with the cut of an ex- Sergeant-Major of the Guards, told us that Elton is a dying village, that there are few children nowadays and that all the young people leave for the towns. This must be so in many hamlets today. He himself was shortly leaving for another inn not far distant, but said that he would be sorry to go because Elton is such a peaceful place. Its old houses are still presided over by the dignified mansion – the home of the Proby family – which is open to the public on Thursdays and Saturdays. We did not inspect this ancestral pile for I have an abhorrence of conducted tours around the dwellings of the aristocracy.

We finished our shopping at the excellent village stores and returned to the river. The sky was now sulky and it began to spit with rain. Moreover, the wind was rising and it began to blow hard from the south. So we untied and turned about, making away up-river for the shelter of the Elton woods.

This proved to be a very different berth from that of the previous evening, when we had looked across to the calm pink sunset beyond the lantern tower of Fotheringhay.

Now, the wind blew with boisterous breath in the wood top, but not a ripple, not a puff, disturbed us under the bank. Nor were there any fish rising. No birds sang to us; the nightingale had fallen silent, for who would feel like singing on such a cheerless evening?

All I had to interest me were the under-water, cabbage-like plants which I could dimly see, waving and wagging like the ears of elephants below our keel. These plants, whatever species they may be, do not seem to venture to the surface, but live a sort of drowned life in the deeps of the river bed. The silver roach and dace thread the mysterious labyrinths, and barred pike hang like moored airships. With their cruel shovel mouths, and soulless eyes set upwards in their bony craniums, they wait in ambush for their unwary prey in the gloomy, drowned thickets. If I peered long enough into that twilit world I could see, occasionally, a flitting slender shape as a dace was brought up against the current, or a water flea scooted about.

Sometimes those huge leaves seemed to sleep, but then would come an unseen river current to set them swinging and stirring like trees in a sudden night breeze.

The rain was now falling in earnest, fairly drumming on our roof and I knew if it continued the doors of Elton lock would be chained against us and we should be held prisoners once more. But this was not such an alarming prospect now for we were in a beautiful reach of the river and were better off than we would be farther on. Between Elton and Wansford there are no sheltering woods, only open water meadows.

As we had so often found sanctuary in our wanderings with a caravan over the length and breadth of Britain, so here, in this little boat, we had a sense of cosiness in face of the inclement weather and approaching night. The lowering evening and pouring rain, the uneasy agitated leaves and the multitude of water rings in the river made us feel as snug as the river bank voles which amused us by their antics. One repeatedly swam across, just astern of us, from one side of the river to the other, appearing exactly like a diminutive, blunt-nosed beaver. I think he had some business with house moving for at times he carried pieces of weed. As he voyaged across, propelled as if by an outboard engine, he left quite a furling wake astern. These industrious and pretty little creatures had their holes all along the river bank. Some were high, so as to be above flood level, others well below the water line. These creatures are sometimes called water 'rats', but they are not in the least rat-like, having the blunt faces of pygmy guinea pigs.

Before dark a boat passed us in the pouring rain and gathering dusk, towing a crippled cruiser which had got into difficulties down-river. The helmsman was hooded against the rain and they went churning away into the distance, the wash lapping our keel. We were glad that we had not to face the task of 'locking' up-river on such a night, it is a tedious, slow job at the best of times.

Fotheringhay Church

Despite the lashing rain and the low fret of the wind in the poplars over our heads, there was a wonderful quietness all around; the same quietness which lay over all country districts half a century ago, before the coming of the car.

Lying in my bunk looking out at the now darkling sky I thought of that long-lost peace in far-off summers. I pictured myself once more as a boy of six or seven, lying on top of our old rectory wall at home, watching the sun-drenched village street on a boiling hot July afternoon. And how, at intervals of half an hour, and sometimes longer, there would come the very distant sound of horses' hooves, 'clip clop' on the dusty road. Soon in the distance appeared a fat old horse drawing a cart loaded with farm produce, or with sacks bound for the country station a mile away. Gradually horse and cart would draw nearer with the man sitting sideways on the shaft. They would pass by, the man quite unaware he was being watched by a small boy lying hidden in the shiny ivy leaves. I would watch those huge barrelled wheel hubs (black with 'lovely grease') turning, their metal tyres grinding on the dusty road. I would admire the faded pinks and blues of the shafts and waggon sides with the name of the farmer and farm painted in scroll-like letters. Gradually the sounds would die away and then there was nothing but the empty street, white and glaring, with the dust, and perhaps a sparrow or two brawling, hopping, and chirping in the gutter.

No bumbling planes then, or cars, or motor cycles; no sounds but country ones. And that is what we had here in our peaceful anchorage in the lee of the Elton woods. We slumbered well in those surroundings, in spite of the fret of rain.

21.

THE WHITE ROAD WESTWARDS

IN CUCKOO GROVE

Our wanderings began again on the morning of the third of June. Brazen was the sun on the Salisbury road, and we thought regretfully of the cool green glades of Savernake we were leaving behind us. Before us was unknown country; where should we find ourselves by evening?

Now I had long promised myself a visit to Selborne, to pay homage to Gilbert White, to see for myself the famous hanger where the honey buzzard built its nest, and to see the last resting-place of this good old man.

So instead of heading away westwards, we travelled south, by the lush green valleys of Test and Itchen, where crouching anglers stalked the lusty trout. The mayfly was 'up' under the glowing June sun, which shone from a brassy sky; over the water meadows the heat rippled and slow-moving cows, like black-and-white barges, were belly-deep in the meadow flowers.

What better place on a June morning than beside the clear crinkling stream, a rod in your hand and a creel on your back? But these magnificent trout streams are only for the rich: the humble man must look upon them from afar.

Traffic was beginning to thicken on the main Salisbury road, the road which we had to take for a while before diving into Hampshire's muffled hills. The noise of the passing cars, the dust, the heat, jarred upon us, and we had to travel with the hood of Winston brailed up because of the power of the sun. By devious ways, through Winchester and Alton, we came at last to the Selborne country, with its hop gardens

219

and pinkish-grey earth in the fields, and saw before us the wooded heights above the village.

A mile or so before Selborne itself we stopped at a fine, prosperous-looking farm surrounded by hop fields and flowery meadows where massive cattle grazed contentedly.

Mr Peter Butler, the owner, graciously gave us permission to pitch camp. When we pleaded for a shady place, he piloted us up a narrow lane which led to a tree-girt hilltop. There, in a meadow, was a diminutive church, with a steeple spire, and to the west of it a shady grove of sycamore, copper beech, lime and oak. This we came to know as Cuckoo Grove for a cuckoo called lustily to us on arrival, and later each morning serenaded us from the tallest lime tree, rousing us from sleep. Blue-backed swallows were forever coursing about the grove all through the hours of daylight.

Down in the valley the heat had been insupportable; here, on the high ground, blew a cool, delicious summer breeze – a true hay-harvest wind, which stirred the fresh green leaves of the limes and sycamores and set the tall soft grasses bending. It looked a delectable site indeed, and I blessed our kind host.

We jolted across the field, Heron swaying behind us, to reach at last that welcome shade. There was peace for us here, with no sounds but the rush of the wind in the trees and grasses, and the constant warblings of blackbirds from an old tangled hedge on the fringe of the meadow.

The little lost church of Hartley Mauditt was close by, and the site of an ancient manor house. This must have been of considerable size, judging by the hollows and low ramparts, now overgrown with stinging nettles, where the whitethroats bubbled incessantly their sweet summer song, and wove frail nests of hay.

How strange that a great mansion such as this could vanish away so completely, leaving only green mounds and hollows! Did the family die out? Did the plague wipe out the village which once stood nearby, to the north of the church?

All over Britain one finds the remains of lost villages and great houses which, for no apparent reason, have crumbled to dust.

Beyond the church I found a large pond. Cattle were knee-deep along its margin trying to keep cool. Two small boys were fishing from the far bank. I talked to the elder of them, an attractive lad with a freckled face, a Huckleberry Finn type. I asked them what they were fishing for. 'Carp,' he said, and the evening before he had caught eight, all over a pound weight.

He and his friend told me they had stocked the pond themselves, transporting small carp from another pond in a 'cricket bag'. Certainly they had been successful, judging from the numbers I saw moving in the pool, some of them good-sized fish, in the five-pound class, and others busy spawning. I am fond of carp fishing myself. I had of course brought fishing tackle with me, and promised myself a quiet hour when the sun was down.

We had provisions to get before the Whitsun holiday, so, after making camp in cool Cuckoo Grove, we descended the dusty lane once more to the main road and found, in Selborne village, a most obliging butcher, Mr Gallop, who sold us a fat juicy steak, such as I had not seen or tasted for many a long day. Mr Gallop was one of many in Selborne who showed us every courtesy and kindness, unusual in these modern days.

The heat in the main street of Selborne was very great, so after making our various purchases we were thankful to regain Cuckoo Grove and its cool breezes.

Whilst Cecily and Angela went to look at the little church, which was lovingly and beautifully kept, even though it had a summer-season service only once a fortnight, I sat writing in the van with the soft rush of the wind in the grasses, admiring the efforts of a particularly full-voiced blackbird which was singing from a mound of white hawthorn on the fringe of the meadow. His roundelays pleased me as much as those of the Savernake nightingale. W.H. Hudson rated the blackbird a finer songster than the nightingale, but I cannot agree with him. The nightingale has more variety of repertoire.

After an excellent supper (of Mr Gallop's steak, and onions) I set off for the carp pond. 'Huckleberry Finn' had landed four fish in my absence, all common all-scaled carp, and the largest weighed one-and-a-half pounds.

Beyond the church and its dark clustering trees the sun sank in a mellow sky, our cuckoo was still calling, and now and again a carp

Hartley Mauditt from across the carp pond

would leap out in the centre of the pond, sending ever-widening rings wheeling outwards. Soon among the distant dark trees the caravan windows lighted up, and the light grew so dim I could not see my float. I left 'Huckleberry' still fishing. I found myself in complete accord with his keenness. Fishing is almost entirely a masculine occupation and here was a boy who fished all day from dawn to dark, and even after sunset was loath to come away.

A few yards from our camp was an ancient mulberry tree which must have stood in the garden of the old manor house. It was full of bloom and loud with bees. The original tree had fallen – its main trunk lay horizontally in the nettles – but from it sprang this one small trunk which still possessed abundant life. No doubt it is good for another half-century.

I could well picture the lady of the manor, one of the de Mauditts, five hundred years ago, gathering fruit from this very tree, and her children playing in its shade on many a summer's evening. Perhaps it was the thoughts of times past which made me wakeful that night and unable to drop asleep, despite the peace of Cuckoo Grove. The trees were black against the sky, and no breeze now moved their leaves above us; the little church stood in the moonlight with the pallid rays shining on the few standing gravestones in the well-tended churchyard.

I thought of the generations of men and women who had passed their lives in this remote spot, when the only means of travel was on horseback; of the inexorable procession of seasons, summer, winter, spring and autumn, up to the time when Gilbert White lived down in the valley below and wrote about the small birds and animals which peopled the woods and fields about the village. For him, too, life must have flowed peacefully, with its hay-time and harvest. He must have listened to the same sweet warblings of the velvet blackbirds from the hawthorns in the 'hollow lanes'. These steep-banked 'hollow lanes', which are such a feature of this part of Hampshire, must have been almost impassable, even to a horse, in the depths of winter.

I will not say there was a sense of sadness and melancholy at this shadowed grove yet, all the time, I felt it heavy with history. From time to time, in the sweet silences of the summer night, mysterious raps smote the roof and sides of our little van. These nocturnal rappings awoke me time and time again, just when I had dozed off. When at last I sank to sleep it was to dream of the people who had lived and moved upon this very plot of ground, the ladies in their medieval costume and steeple hats, the lusty men in doublet and hose with daggers in their belts, and the leather-coated serving men, coming and going.

HARTLEY MAUDITT

We returned to Cuckoo Grove by way of the wild and lovely Woolmer Forest, and there I spied a large black pond, set among birch scrub and heath wherein I was told a man had caught a twenty-pound carp the Sunday before, when fishing in the early morning. This pond must be the one described by Gilbert White as Bean's Pond near Oakhanger. The fringes of it were carpeted with an attractive pond weed I had not seen before. It had a small blue flower, resembling a water forget-me-not, but its foliage was dense and of a neat pattern, not unlike that of diminutive bog bean. As the day wore on the heat became more oppressive. Even on our hilltop at Hartley Mauditt the cool wind ceased to move. It was too hot to do anything but lie on our bunks and read. Naturally I took up my Gilbert White. By chance I came upon the following entry:

On June 5 1784, the thermometer in the morning being 64, and at noon 70, and the wind North, I observed a blue mist, smelling strongly of sulphur, hanging along our sloping woods and seeming to indicate thunder at hand. I was called in about two in the afternoon and so missed seeing the gathering of the clouds, in the north, which they who were abroad, assured me had something uncommon in their appearance. At about a quarter after two, the storm began in the parish of Hartley Mauditt, moving slowly from north to south, from thence it came over Norton farm and so to Grange farm, both in this parish. It began with vast drops of rain which were soon succeeded by round hail, and then by convex pieces of ice, which measured three inches in girth. In the parish of Hartley Mauditt it did some damage to one farm.

This storm mentioned by White took place exactly one hundred and seventy-six years before, and as I read those lines the far rumble of thunder reached me, and the sky to the north of our camp grew an ugly brick-red, flanked by black cloud. Though a few drops rapped the grove, the storm passed westwards, melting away in the mysterious manner peculiar to thunder.

The late afternoon sun made Heron uncomfortably hot, so we moved the van right into the centre of the grove so that we were shaded on all sides throughout the daylight hours. We berthed the van close beside a large lime tree in whose trunk there was a small crevice within a yard of our back window. In this crevice a pair of blue tits had their nest and were continuously in and out, feeding young. Though our sudden appearance so near at first dismayed them, they soon became accustomed to our presence and continued feeding as busily as ever.

It was fun to watch the parents at such close quarters. When father and mother arrived at the crevice at the same moment (and this happened frequently) father politely waited whilst his wife went inside. When she emerged she would take the grub or caterpillar from him and go in again, whilst he flew off to get fresh supplies. All the tits feed their young at very short intervals, sometimes every two minutes, and they kept this up all through the daylight hours.

Having nothing else to do I explored the old tangled hedgerow across the heated field. I found it to be a 'hollow lane' in miniature, the ditch some ten feet deep and seven feet wide, the roots of the hawthorns and oaks protruding from the sides, forming a dark, dank burrow. The bottom of the ditch was stony, green with moss, and a very small trickle of water showed there – overflow from the carp pond across the lane. Chaffinches spinked at me from the bushes, and from the thick-leaved oaks numerous pigeons bustled away: they were resting there in the cool shadow, digesting their morning meal. In the ditch I found the remains of a hedgehog; only the skin was left, the inside having been neatly removed, no doubt the work of fox or badger. Seeing these pitiful remains of skin and pale-tipped spines, I was reminded of an unusual story told me a few weeks before by a man in the village at home, a keen and trustworthy naturalist who has lived all his life in the depths of the country.

He told me that one summer's evening he was walking up the side of an old unkempt hedgerow when the hay had been cut. He heard what he took to be the murmuring of rustic lovers from the far side of the hedge. They were conversing in low and affectionate tones. Not liking to eavesdrop, or be labelled as a Peeping Tom, he went on his way until he reached a stile over which he climbed. He glanced back along the hedgeside but was astonished to see nobody there. Greatly mystified, and feeling perhaps a little uncomfortable, he was determined to get at the root of the mystery. So he walked back along the hedge to the spot where he thought he had heard the voices.

On drawing near, sure enough, the murmuring endearments were heard once more, but he was unable to see anyone at all! On peering through the tangle of the hedge he saw two hedgehogs, a male and a female, in the marital act. They were standing up on their back legs, facing each other with their little front arms twined around each other and were talking 'like real people', so my informant told me.

W.H. Hudson visited Hartley Mauditt for he describes it in *Hampshire Days*. I could well imagine his tall tweed-clad figure walking up the path to the little church in the hot sunshine of those far-off summers in the early part of the century, his dark, hawk-like eyes noting the grove of trees where we were now encamped, hearing perhaps the rich warblings of the blackbird singing from the same hawthorn hedge across the golden meadow, hearing, too, the goldfinches, twittering their loud liquid song from the lime trees in the grove, just as they sang for us.

On the sixth of June the weather was a little cooler. We awoke to see soft grey skies which were strangely restful after the continuous glare of the past few days.

We walked again, for the last time, along the 'hollow lanes' about Selborne, we visited the hanger where the silver hay lay in swathes at its foot, making sweet fragrance in the air. We found it hard to drag ourselves away from this quiet green country, which looked so gay and bright in its bridal dress of high summer. But on the morrow we must be on our way, for we had many miles to go, and many adventures lay before us.

It seemed a fitting moment to pay our last visit to the little church, and after supper that evening, I read in the porch some lines by the vicar, which I give here.

To the Wayfarer

Here is a place where prayers are said
Or, if you'd rather sit instead, pray do!
And as you sit, and think and rest,
Your further journey shall be blest
For by the King of Kings
You shall lose all pain and fear,
In quietness God is very near.

I hoped, too, that *our* further journey would be blest. We had, indeed, found peace and quietness at Cuckoo Grove.

22.
SUMMER ROAD TO WALES

THE VALLEY OF THE KITES

Just as the golden eagle might be said to be the national bird of Scotland, so the kite should be for Wales. I feel the Welsh have never made the most of this rare and beautiful bird, nor honoured it as a priceless heritage, for it is a species far rarer than the golden eagle; indeed, it might be said to be our rarest British breeding bird with the exception of the osprey, for not more than a dozen pairs remain in these islands. Even with the stringent protection afforded it – and I feel that this protection is still not vigilant enough – it teeters on the verge of extinction. Every reference to the kite tells how it was once the commonest bird in the streets of London at the time of the Black Death. This of course is true. Today it is a most useful scavenger for many cities in the Far East.

I had never seen one, save stuffed specimens. One of my primary objects in making this spring journey into Wales was to see it, but I felt I had little chance.

On the sixth of May we left Heron beside the banks of the rattling stream and took the Land-Rover northwards up a wild river valley. To those who have never seen the more majestic glens of the Highlands of Scotland, this beautiful twisting valley road, with its crags and woods, would have seemed impressive. The morning was exactly right, cloud shadows, strong gleams of sun, the woods just putting on their first tender tints.

There is a time in May when trees *en masse*, poplars, oaks, ashes, and elms, have an almost autumn flush of colour. One grove of poplars we passed was an incandescent tawny gold. Here and there on the hillsides sycamores and beeches showed up a fresh silvery green, but the great mass of trees was glazed with warm pinks and buffs, the colours of opening buds.

The road grew narrow and steep, houses less plentiful, only odd whitewashed farms on the hillsides. I had the choice of two valleys: both appeared equally wild and inviting. First, I took the right-hand one, for several miles, climbing all the time until the trees were few. We passed a streamside meadow which had a wide gateway where I would have dearly loved to park our van, for then I should be in the heart of the kite country, and if I stayed long enough would be sure to see one. In passing I made a mental note of it. Each wandering speck, soaring above the mountains, might be the bird I had come to see. Again and again I cried out to Cecily to stop the Land-Rover whilst, with beating heart, I focused my glasses. But those far-up soaring specks always turned out to be either ravens (we saw scores of those) or buzzards; there was scarce a moment when one of these broad-winged noble creatures was not in sight, wheeling and turning over the high tops.

Drawing a blank up the first wild valley, we took the other which led westwards between mountains whose crests were crowned with crags and towers of rock and stunted trees with naked windswept boughs. Leaving the Land-Rover on a grassy verge, we took our sticks and walked. Now and again I stopped to search the jagged ridges hard against the blue sky and massed white clouds. We came to a turn in the little narrow road. On our right towered a tremendous crag around whose pinnacles seven ravens dived and swung, 'cronking' in their guttural voices. Here, if anywhere, I should surely see the kite!

A moment later, with dramatic suddenness, a bird came sailing over a saw-edged rock upon which grew a single twisted tree. I had my glasses on it and could have shouted with delight. Its wings were slender and curved, its long tail was forked. Here, at last, was the very creature, seen for the first time in my nearly sixty years of life! Only the student of birds can know how much the drama of that moment meant to me. As if to give me the best possible view it soared right over, swinging sideways, its head turning from right to left. Then, with one grand sweep, it passed along before the hanging woods showing its yellowish-

Kites fighting

red back plumage. All along the wooded crest it flew, or rather glided, with only an occasional movement of its slender wings, much as a man dips an oar as he floats upon a slowly moving current. Then, with a twist and curve, it vanished over the crags.

Later, as we neared the Land-Rover, I focused on two more. They were at a vast height above the earth, twisting and turning and making passes at each other. I was witnessing a truly regal battle of kings. They feinted, twisted, dived and swung until at last they broke away, and dwindled into the distance. My binoculars are extremely powerful and as these two kites flew higher and higher they became mere specks in the lenses, two thousand feet above the valley. I was so excited at seeing them that my thoughts went back to that little green meadow in the other valley. How I wished our camp was there! I was greedy for another view of them before going on towards the sea, and despite protestations from the ladies I was determined to take the van there on the following day.

We returned from the valley of the kites in rain; the brilliant promise of the day was gone but no amount of cloud could dull my sense of triumph and satisfaction.

On that last evening by the stream I fished down the pool at the bend and caught two more tasty little trout which we had for breakfast on the following morning. The rain lifted at evening and the sun shone brightly on the bend of the stream, breaking up the water with splinters of light. But dark rainclouds were massing in the west which made me doubtful of the morrow.

23.

SEPTEMBER ROAD
TO CAITHNESS

THE ULTIMATE LAND

The first of October, and what a beautiful, *beautiful*, day!

Occasionally the Highlands of Scotland present us with these pearls, when, from dawn to dark, no cloud is visible anywhere not even pluming from the highest mountain peak. It came as a greater surprise, for, listening to the weather men as we sipped our tea among the Dunnet dunes the previous night, there had been no mention of a fine spell.

In the early light the sea caressed the sand, breaking in miniature wavelets with barely a murmur, yet during the night I had heard it roaring. To the westwards a faint mist, like a veil, hung over Thurso. In the effulgent light of morning white gulls soared on effortless wings and I was surprised to see many wheatears flitting among the dunes, all on migration I have no doubt. Occasional stonechats, too, perched on the tops of the stunted bushes of furze, and all along the tideline the curlews fluted joyously.

As we journeyed west beyond Thurso I saw many more flocks of hoodie crows perched on the stooks, stuffing themselves with grain. The fields were deserted because of the Sabbath. How different to my own part of England, where one sees work going on in the fields like any other day, a sign of the times which bodes ill for us all.

I say this not because of religious conviction, but because man needs to rest from his labours. A day of leisure helps along the rhythm of life and of the seasons, too, and our enjoyment of them. Far too much time is taken up with the sole purpose of amassing money. There is much truth in the well-worn cliché that 'money is the root of all evil'. In this far northern land there might be some excuse to work on Sundays for the weather is so fickle, and harvests so hard to win, but down in the south this does not apply, especially with mechanised farming.

Soon we saw upon the far horizon what appeared to be the dome of a silver mosque or a gigantic captive balloon. In the haze of that lovely morning that ethereal bubble seemed dreamlike and quite extraordinary in the wild, flat, desolate landscape.

This was, of course, the atomic plant at Dounreay, or Doomsday as it might well be called. That far silvery globe appeared harmless enough in the clear morning sunlight, with its buildings and masts about it, but I was glad when we had passed and left it behind, for it reminded one of the awful potentialities of man's latest discovery.

At last the road, which hitherto had been wide and well-metalled, grew narrow, though it still retained its good surface with passing places at intervals.

At one point beside the way was a little meadow. A red deer hind was feeding there with two calves, not an unusual sight in this part of the world for the deer calves are found out on the moors and brought home and domesticated.

A calf, newly dropped, has no fear of man whatsoever, indeed it will get up and follow anyone, as those who wander the hills can testify. There is a passage in an enchanting book by Seton Gordon describing how he once had this experience when walking the hills south of Loch Vrodin in Atholl. He had been photographing a bird, and was sitting quietly beside his camera when he felt a soft warm pressure against his side. On looking round he was amazed to see a red deer calf which had snuggled up beside him!

He had some difficulty in giving it the slip for it followed him for half a mile, at last lying down in the heather.

Before us as we journeyed on, we could see the blue massif of the Western Highlands which seemed all the more impressive after the flat wastes of Caithness.

Nearer they came, steeper became the hills on either hand, until at last we came to Bettyhill with its brilliant blue sea and white rollers creaming on its pale sands as peaceful and tranquil as in June.

Beyond this place we took a narrow side road which led us away south-westwards. The road twisted and turned and in places grass grew down the centre, which showed how little it was used. But the surface was excellent and I was amazed to find that now, in even the most remote parts, the roads are well-metalled. Once done by modern methods they last far longer than roads in the south as there is not such wear and tear.

All through that glorious morning we followed it, past lochs, rivers and miniature waterfalls. We drove with the windows of Winston lowered and it was hard to believe that we were not at the height of summer.

Then we turned a bend in the road and saw before us the vivid blue of Loch Naver, that same intense blue we had noticed before. For some frustrating miles we followed its banks. I was determined to make camp somewhere along its shores but not a single space could we find until, on nearing a corner, we came to a quarry on the right of the road. It seemed to me the only possible spot and after some violent manoeuvring we got the van off the road and backed up into the quarry, which had a good hard bottom. But we were right on the edge of the road and close to a sharp corner. I had great difficulty in parking Winston and did not manage it until we had put all hands to moving several large rocks.

The sun was shining with considerable power, we were hot and exhausted with our exertions, and after all was in place I still had an uneasy feeling about this site. It is never pleasant to be within a few feet of a highway, even a little-used one like this, so after a snack lunch we walked on round the corner and down the winding road to spy the land. Within a hundred yards we came upon the loveliest site imaginable. Had we gone on round the corner instead of dropping anchor in the quarry we would have saved ourselves a lot of unnecessary toil.

On the right of the road was a wide-open space with a hard bottom well away from the highway itself. Behind rose a huge hill clothed with bracken and birch, which climbed to the vivid blue sky, whilst opposite was a fairy wood of birch and beyond that, the blue waters of Loch

Naver, winking and clashing on the shore.

We rushed back to our corner, backed up Winston, and with some difficulty wormed our way out of the quarry and on to the road. Within twenty minutes we were settled into our new site with gas connected, gas burners fixed, and legs wound down. This was something like a site!

Later I climbed the hill behind us. It looked easy and I went up hand over hand until, gasping for breath, I reached the base of a vertical crag on the top of which grew scarlet-berried rowans. The view spread out below was breathtaking. I could see the whole expanse of Loch Naver to the north − a vivid blue lake in a golden setting. The stems of birches far below me looked like silver threads and the van no bigger than a matchbox.

It is far easier to climb up than down, and I have no head for heights. I found I could not return by the way I had come for I could find no foothold. So I worked my way gingerly along the face of the rock to where the slope eased off. By the time I regained the road half a mile below our camp the sun was setting.

Peaceful lay the waters of Loch Naver as evening came, and the light died off the crests of the far hills. The water became glassy calm, broken here and there by the widening rings of a rising trout.

From across the loch came the grunting roar of stags, the first we had heard. Through the glass I could see a herd of hinds and the master stag with them. Now and again his muzzle would go up and horns would be laid back and some seconds after came the roar. Twilight deepened, the stars came out.

Just behind our camp were two enormous blocks of rock which had fallen from the precipice above, possibly many hundreds of years ago. They were as big as cottages and had fallen almost touching each other. In an angle formed by these massive chunks, a wren had built her cosy nest.

It was made entirely of scarlet sphagnum moss and was sheltered from every wind that blew. Had the occupants safely flown? I wondered. No doubt the family would be glad to return here when winter came to the glen, and snow sheeted the world. Wrens use their old nests for roosting in; indeed they will build nests solely for this purpose.

The lone sentinel

It was a pleasure for me to hear in this magical place the merry 'spink! spink!' of cock chaffinches, and see the flash of their white shoulder bars. At home they have all been killed by the farmer's sprays.

I set a night line in the loch baited with a fat worm which I had brought from my garden lawn at home. Going down later to the shore in the darkness, picking my way along a winding mossy path through the birch wood, I hauled it in and found I had caught a writhing eel.

At the best of times, and in broad daylight, an active eel on the end of a line is a handful; in the darkness it soon writhed itself into an intricate tangle and ball, line, hook and all.

So I carried this active worm through the birch wood intending to dispatch and disentangle it by the light of the van. But when I reached the road, my eel, which I had hoped to have for supper, was not there. I was left holding a bunch of slimy cast and line! He had managed to wriggle off in transit and it was hopeless to try and find him. An eel on land can make itself invisible as quickly as a snake.

I stood on the shore last thing before turning in, drinking in the magic of the place. The loch lay absolutely silent, aloft the stars burned brightly, and over the crag was a wonderful display of Northern Lights, the best I have seen for a long while. The sky seemed to be a moving curtain to the north, now glowing bright with rays shooting upwards, silvery and mysterious, the next moment dying away.

The only sound I could hear was the far roaring of the stags from over the water. Such an ancient sound and most moving when heard in the silences of the hills on an autumn evening.

24.

THE AUTUMN ROAD TO THE ISLES

HALLOWE'EN IN FAR GLEN GARRY

On Hallowe'en I took my stick and binoculars and climbed away among the bracken, following a winding sheep track. The light was going fast. Below me through the dark oaks the waters of Garry gleamed wanly, echoing the light of a wild, pale sunset sky in the west. The bracken smelled divinely, a sort of herby peaty smell. Now and then I pushed through bog myrtle whose delightful scent is such a stranger to the Midland plain. Very soon I had left the caravan behind and was in as wild a wood as one could wish for. It stretched away upwards, giving glimpses between silver-stemmed birches of corridors of tawny red rush and bracken, their furthest corners cloaked in dusk; more birch and yet more bracken, and many a knoll, and flat, and dell, threaded with silver black-banded stems.

There were no blueberry bushes here as in Glen Affric, and the woods seemed quite devoid of life. I was reminded of those unending forests of Labrador where, I have read, one may walk for many days and see no living thing. Very soon I was lost in a maze of brackeny dells and hummocks with the light growing ever more dim. By one knoll there was a hollow full of brilliant green moss; it was, I suppose, about twice the size of a washing bowl. I found it to be a miniature bog, quite a deep one, for my walking-stick thrust down never found bottom.

The sheep track I was following twisted here and there, as clear-cut as a gamekeeper's woodland path. When it came to a barrier of fallen birch (and there were many in this glen) it wound about, always tending up hill. I suppose the heavy-fleeced, black-faced sheep come down from the high tops to the cosy glens at the onset of winter. I had expected to see no living wild creature save sheep, but I was soon to find I was mistaken.

At one point (when I was passing a brake of fallen birch and tall red bracken, whose tiers of branching fronds rose one above the other in serrated layers) there was a sudden rustle. There regarding me, twenty yards distant and no more, was a red deer hind. Her great dark eyes were wide with suspicion and fear, her ears spread. Then she leapt gracefully away down the dell, crossing an open spot in front of me. She was followed by two much smaller beasts. All their coats were rough and dark, matching very well the russet tones of the bracken. What sanctuary they must find in Glen Garry! For I would call parts of it, at any rate, a cosy winter-defying glen, with plenty of warm bedding and fodder for the wild things of the hills.

By the time I regained the road which led me back to camp the light had nearly gone. Wild and fine it was; looking back up the glen to the head of Garry, with the last gleams of day reflected in the heaving waters, for a shrewd wind bustled the waters of the loch.

How cosy it was to see the shining orange light in the window of the caravan, down over the brae among the branching fern and guardian oaks! What a sight for an autumn evening and a returning traveller! Perhaps it was the trees I had missed most in far away Durness. Give me the wooded glens where wind and winter can be kept at bay!

As I walked that night among the gathering shadows up Glen Garry I thought how easy it would be for a hunted man to hide there. If he had a gun and a rod he would come to no harm. There is many a cosy shelter he could find in those wild hills.

After supper, a very good one of mutton chops, cabbage and potato, followed by cheese and biscuits, and coffee, I lit a 'yog' (gypsy term for fire) close by the van. I gathered together birch twigs and oak logs and soon had a scented fire glowing. By the light of it I played my pipe, mournful tunes of my own composition and various renderings of Highland airs which I considered were in accord with my surroundings. The fire was greatly assisted by an old nightdress of Cecily's which

BB's caravan at Loch Venachar in the Trossachs

was brought out for cremation. By then the wind had died, and it was a fine still night with the moon shining on the calm loch below us.

We sat side by side on a log by the fire playing our mournful tunes which sounded well in that wild place. The scent of the wood smoke and the gleaming flames reflected on the oak trees overhead were greatly to my taste, for what is life in the open air without the scent of wood smoke, and a dancing flame to sit by?

As every Scotsman knows it is on this night of all the year that 'ghoulies and ghosties' are abroad.

As we sat there with the firelight on our faces, ruddy and warm, watching the little sparks fly upwards among the birch leaves, Ping's ears pricked and she gave a low growl. A man was going by on the highroad. He had a pack on his back and a stick in his hand, and his face was set up the glen. He looked neither to the right nor left. Where was he going at this late hour and in this wild place? Lone travellers at night always intrigue me.

At an early period of my life I was forced by circumstances to live in London, shut away from the grass, and the trees, and the scents and sounds of the sweet winds. Often at a late hour when I heard the double beat of feet passing along the pavement under the pools of gaslight, I would lie and wonder how life was using that unknown man or woman. Faint at first, growing near, then dying away into the distance. As a child I was fearful of the sound of footsteps heard from a long way off and gradually coming close. It was, I think, a sort of primitive fear, which I experience even now.

We heard the steady beat of this stranger's feet a long while after he had passed; the sound increased our sense of loneliness and our satisfaction, too, for the fire was warm, and our home was close at hand among the bracken.

I recounted all the most creepy ghost stories I had ever heard and we decided that footsteps in the night are perhaps the most hair-raising tales of all. There is something fearful in the thought of the restless dead.

It would have been better if our midnight traveller in Glen Garry had sung, as Robert Louis Stevenson's traveller had sung, 'lit internally with wine' as he went by his fir wood in the Lozère.

Goodnight to the Isles

'Play me a Highland lament,' said Cecily, putting another log on the fire. But I could think of nothing but the hymn *To Be a Pilgrim*. Anyway, it was the only tune I could coax from my tin pipe which was recognisable.

Then from the north we heard a music far superior to mine. At first it was on the edge of hearing but growing all the time. It was the double musical note of wild whooper swans.

What better time or in what more suitable place could we have had this experience? The birds were, of course, invisible, and they were passing westwards for the sea, probably for the Kyle of Lochalsh where their fellows gather each winter. No doubt these were migrants, they might easily have just arrived from some far tundra, from some 'steel grey lagoon that no man knows'. Those musical notes, which have more poetry in them than even the cry of the wild pinkfooted geese we had heard at Braco, were signal cries, telling each member to keep station as they drove on through the dark.

No man quite knows how wild birds steer their way, it may well be some sort of radar. We know that fog confuses them and that then they are utterly lost, which to the layman, suggests they navigate by well-known landmarks. That could well have been so on that Hallowe'en in Garry. The stars were shining; below the birds would lie the familiar pattern of pale loch and river, a pattern handed down from one generation to another back into the mists of time. No doubt they saw the pin-point spark of our fire, and wonder stirred in their delicate craniums.

James Fisher and R.M. Lockley in their book *Sea Birds* have this to say: 'Sun or astronomical navigation seems to be the most satisfactory explanation so far; and more research into night migration might reveal that the migrant is guided by moon, stars, pre-glow and after-glow, which may assist it to keep on a course already begun before the sun or its glow has left the sky.'

At last the music, like the footsteps, sank to silence; there was nothing but the snicks and rustles of our dying fire. It was time for bed.

THE WATERFALL

Across the road from our camp the bracken was almost twice the height of a well-grown man, while up among the woods in the sheltered hollows it was still green.

When I looked out of the window one morning, three little roe deer stood in a clearing hedged round with the delicate gold and red fronds. They were the first I had seen in Scotland. One, a trim little buck, lifted a back leg as I watched him, a leg as slender and graceful as that of a greyhound, and scratched his rump lazily with his little horn. They grazed for a while, showing their white 'flags' as they turned, these white hinder-ends which must serve so well as beacons to their calves. Then something scared them. They melted into the fronds which completely covered them.

When later that day I took my stick and glass, and climbed up the glen, I found their runs, like those of rabbits, which wound in and out of the branching bracken stems. It must be well past Christmas before these tall bracken forests are felled by the keen frost and the roe, and red deer too, must winter here on the steep hillsides.

It was a glorious frosty afternoon when I began my walk, but a mist lay over the loch and veiled the lower slopes of the mountains to the south. By following sheep paths and deer tracks I climbed away up the side of the glen, taking my time, and filling my lungs with the glorious air, the scent of which was beyond description.

Soon I heard a distant murmuring rush, yet perhaps it could be better described as some distant bulldozer at work. Surely they were not felling the trees? The sound seemed to get louder and then fade away, and for a long time I was puzzled as to what caused it. Soon I knew. It was the sound of falling water. I turned to my left and climbed up among the silver birches, whose trunks were a dazzling white in the sunlight, and the bracken, the colour of which was something no artist's brush and palette could ever capture.

In front of me the hill rose steeply with huge granite rocks protruding from the bracken, and over the top of a massive boulder I saw the fall at last. A tenuous veil of white water pouring over the top, to tumble into a deep brown pool at the foot.

Green ferns grew round it, the bracken arched it over, and, at one end, caught in an angle of a rock (a sort of miniature cliff) a raft of yellow birch leaves, like a tessellated table-top, gravely revolved. At the tail of the pool the water slipped away, a fulvous brown, shot with golden darts and coloured bubbles, to fall in another series of waterfalls down the steep slope towards the loch. The rush and roar of the water cascading down the smooth dome of rock filled the ears; underlying the main turbulence of sound were musical notes like kelpies piping on flutes of reeds.

To complete this perfect picture a scarlet-berried rowan leaned over and the bright fruit was reflected in the water. I looked back behind me to where the sun was westering, its lower half turning to a soft rose. Mist covered the loch, which lay, a lake of whiteness, of milk perhaps, from shore to shore.

I left the fall at last and climbed onwards to the crest where the bracken became shorter and the trees fewer. Then I was out on the open moor with its deep tones of madder, ochre, sienna, and buff. Few artists have painted the high tops at this time of year. Sir D.Y. Cameron's superb etchings and drawings give, I think, a truer picture of these hills than his paintings. The trouble is that the colours of the winter high tops are sometimes so rich and varied that they are almost gaudy, and people who have never seen them would never believe that they could be so full of brilliance.

Once out of the glen it was piercingly cold, even though there was no wind. I walked for some miles over the peat hags, passing several ugly-looking green bogs here and there, until I came to a low ridge strewn with boulders. I lay down among them and took out my glass. Ahead of me the ground climbed away to rugged peaks. In the middle distance was another waterfall whose voice I could just hear at intervals when a puff of lightest breeze brought me the sound. The white twisting rope of water fell from some considerable height down a mass of tumbled rock, and birch trees grew up the steep sides. Through the glasses it appeared to be a delightfully remote spot.

At first I saw no deer anywhere, though I searched all along the flanks of the mountains to right and left. I brought the glass back to the waterfall and systematically searched down the little glen below, where thickets of birch and uneven ground might hold deer.

As I was looking through the lens I saw the horns of a stag emerge quite slowly from the little corrie – first the pale tips, then his handsome head and shoulders came into view. He walked across a little flat beside what was obviously a burn, and stood there looking towards me. He was soon followed by seven hinds of various sizes and colours (it is amazing how they vary in colouring). They grazed peaceably, all save one, the last to appear, who was constantly on the watch, turning her head first one way then another. It is the hind who is the sentry, the old stag leaves that duty to her.

It was fascinating to watch these lovely wild creatures in their natural home enjoying the afternoon sun. It was wonderful also to be able to project myself, through the magic of my powerful stalking glass, to within a hundred yards or so of them. I could even see some field-fares busy among the rowans by the fall, and a red grouse erect on top of a stone to the right of the deer. I felt almost ashamed to pry on their private lives, like a Peeping Tom.

The stag was not in restless mood, though once I saw him stretch his neck and his big mouth opened to emit a soundless steam (he was so far distant I could not hear his call). After grazing in a desultory fashion he at last lay down in the sun under a heathery brae and swung his great head into his flank.

Not a bad life, I thought, short but vivid; better than many a human one, dragged out in some factory or slum, shut away from the air of heaven.

I closed the glass at last and began to walk across the moor towards the waterfall. As I did so the sun withdrew and a chilly mist came down. I thought nothing of this at the time, but walked on. The corrie with the deer in it was now hidden from me by dead ground. Three red grouse burst from the heather right in front of me 'back, backing' hysterically. They went curling away to my left and were lost in the veils of mist.

It is amazing how deceptive distances can be. Through the telescope the glen and waterfall had seemed so close, but it seemed to get no nearer as I walked on and the mist was thickening all the time. I came over the ridge at last and there was my objective, in front of me, and the sound of the fall was considerably louder than the one back in the glen. Soon I was walking among the birches where I had seen the deer but to my great disappointment they had gone; only some 'sign' was steaming gently on the short grass by the rippling burn. I thought of climbing this last ridge by the fall to see what lay beyond, but now the time factor had to be considered. I wanted to be back in camp in time for supper at least (tea was now out of the question).

When I glanced back across the moors the way I had come I was brought up short with a sense of uneasiness. A thick white mist had quietly shut down behind me like a sinister wall. Only the very top of the ridge in front of me was visible now, glowing a most rare mother-of-pearl as it caught the last of the sun.

I was annoyed at not being able to explore the little glen and more annoyed, perhaps, that the deer had gone for I had hoped to see them at close quarters. But there was nothing for it, I must get back to camp. So I turned around, and keeping the sound of the fall behind me, I set out over the moors.

Within, I should say, another five minutes, the mist had shut down, forming walls of white before and behind me. I could smell it, too, a musty peaty smell.

Now I pride myself on a good bump of locality. I have been lost before on the Solway marshes (which was a most unpleasant experience). Here at least there was no menacing tide creeping in to cut me off, filling the hidden gutters and brimming over as a full wine glass spills.

What was a little disturbing was the fact that the setting sun was now barely a guide; soon I did not know exactly where it was for the white wall wrapped me like a shroud. The only guide was the sound of the fall. I kept it behind me as well as I could, with its voice growing even fainter, until I could hear it no more. I looked at my watch. It was ten past four, in another half an hour it would be dark and there was no early moonrise.

I walked on, I skirted soft ground – once I went in over my knees, suddenly, and felt that curious warm dart of fear in one's vitals which one gets in an emergency. Of course I was in no danger, it was just stupid, natural reaction, I suppose. All the same, I did not fancy a night on the moor for it promised to be a hard frost. As is always the case at such times, my imagination began to paint the most exciting pictures. Cecily in the warm van, pretending not to be anxious, Ping on her cushion, the lamps lit, fog and darkness outside; the frequent going to the door to look and listen, only to see the white wall of vapour, in the gaslight. I thought of what she would do during the hours' slow passage from midnight on to dawn, the fear, the panic, and then (let's go the whole hog!) search parties from Invergarry – sturdy men, used to the hill mists and the corries, ghillies, and stalkers, shepherds, and perhaps even a rangy Laird or two! Then the police, with their chequered peaked caps, stretchers, tracking dogs, and finally to the last grim scene; the discovery of the inert body lying among the heather, with the dew-like hoar frost on the jacket, something which had to be lifted on to the stretcher, no longer a 'him', but an 'it'. Perhaps they wouldn't find me until the spring and the melting of the snow!

I walked on. The light was now diffused all over, not dark, not light. I seemed shut in a white room. Visibility must have been about two feet, possibly even less. I knew after walking through endless peat hags and heather, with here and there a rock, that I was well and truly lost. I literally hadn't the foggiest notion where I was!

* * * * *

I looked again at my watch. It was now ten minutes to five. I had been walking for forty minutes. All at once a splash! A loud grunt, rather like a boxer hit by a low blow! I jumped like a kangaroo.

A huge, misty shape dashed past my front – either a stag or a hind, I couldn't tell which, and I wasn't particularly interested in natural history at that moment! For some moments I heard its splashing bustle through the mosses, then silence.

I stood still, at my wits' end. Perhaps this wretched fog would clear, but there was no sign of it doing so. It might last all night, all tomorrow, even the next day! Anyway, keep walking, I told myself, keep walking and listening. Curiously enough, though it was now past five o'clock, the mist about me made the night quite luminous. But it was most uncomfortable walking, really most trying! I kept stubbing my toes on hidden boulders, and once I ran full tilt into a rock as big as a pantechnicon; and I wasn't too keen to go head first into a bog. I'd rather meet death on the tideway than in a bog, which suffocates you at leisure, like a fat boa constrictor.

Now and again I would stop and listen, but there just wasn't a sound, not the call of a bird or the bleat of a sheep, nothing! Thick fog seems to make all things dumb. After I'd been going for another quarter of an hour I heard in the distance a whispering rumble. I stood and listened carefully because I wanted to make for that sound, it was the only movement in a white tomb. I began to edge towards it, cupping my ears. Once I thought it was to my right, the next moment, surely, it was on my left, then it was behind me. But after another five minutes I knew I was going to get there. This must be the waterfall I had seen earlier in the afternoon, at the top of the glen, when the sun shone on the birches and the red–golden bracken.

Louder came the sound through the fog. It struck me as rather an awful noise coming like that out of the wall of white. Louder still, *too loud!* It sounded uncommonly like the waterfall of the deer. IT WAS! I was back to where I started.

I sat down on a stone, not because I particularly wanted to but because I sort of fell over one, backwards, and finished up with a bruised coccyx, which, to those who are shaky in their knowledge of anatomy, is our rudimentary tail. And I was aware that I was very, very thirsty,

Loch a'Chroisg in Wester Ross

horribly hungry, and fairly steaming with my exertions.

I found a burnlet trickling through the mosses and threw myself headlong on the soft ground and drank the ice-cold stream. I felt in my pockets for a possible half-packet of chocolate which I had meant to take along and hadn't. I remembered now I had left it on the caravan table. Ping had probably eaten it by now, for she is a little pig for chocolate.

I began to wonder then whether I'd better stay where I was, light a fire, and get some shelter. There was fallen wood handy by the birch trees, enough to keep a fire going all night. If it hadn't been for Cecily I might have done just that, but I must confess too (and this without shame), that I sensed something uncanny in my surroundings. There flitted through my mind the story of the terrible Fear Liath Mor, the Big Grey Man, which haunts the summit of Ben Mac Dhiu and has been seen and heard by several level-headed, educated people such as the late Professor J.N. Collie, a former president of the Alpine Club.

It is easy to imagine ghostly apparitions and inexplicable sounds, especially in misty weather, in these wild high places, and no doubt my nerves were in a strained condition. But I was aware that from time to time, above the ceaseless tumbling of the fall, I clearly heard a curious sharp 'clack', as of one large rock being struck against another, or of a stone being hit repeatedly with a hammer. The sounds were not regular, sometimes there was a minute's or so pause before I heard it again. I must confess I soon abandoned all idea of staying the night there alone, even with the company of a fire.

I rested there, from sheer exhaustion, for about twenty minutes and then set out again. I knew that if only I could keep a straight line the glen wasn't more than a couple of hours walking to the south. Then I hit upon the idea which I should have done before, of following the stream. I knew it must find its way somehow down to the glen as long as it didn't go underground as they often do, and as long as it was the right glen (I just dared not think of the alternative).

I found the burn without much trouble. I couldn't miss it because the fall guided me to it, and I began following it. This wasn't all that easy because of the rocks and soft ground. Once I thought I was bogged for I went in up to my knees. After some hours' walking, just when I was beginning to feel all in, I heard a sound which cheered me a good deal, another waterfall! Then a birch tree loomed up in front of me, then two more, then the bracken. I was on the edge of the glen; the ground fell steeply below me. Here the fog had thinned considerably and I found my bearings. Even so, it was some time before I hit the hard road. I got stuck in seemingly impenetrable thickets of bracken higher than my head, and once I fell into a boggy hollow and went up to my armpits in black mire.

I can only say the road felt very good under my feet when I eventually reached it, and a faint radiance, shining through the gloom, which was the caravan window, was even better. Very soon I heard Ping giving tongue, and a sudden glow showed as Cecily flung open the door. It was ten minutes past two in the morning.

After all, I think Cecily had had the worst of it.

25.

RAMBLINGS OF A SPORTSMAN-NATURALIST

There are but few areas left today in any agricultural county where sprays are not used on crops or pasture. But the disused railway cuttings are completely free and here the wild flowers still bloom profusely – the knap weeds, thistles, poppies, the beautiful delicate grasses, the moon daisies.

Who would have ever guessed half a century ago that the day would come when the railway was to become obsolete in many parts of the countryside! Now there must be hundreds of miles of disused railway tracks in Britain, both north and south, all remaining exactly as they were since the rails and sleepers were lifted, except for the encroaching bushes. The boundary hedges grow downwards on the embankments until they meet at the bottom, and there are acres and acres of wild hawthorns and tangled grass, ideal nesting places for partridge and pheasant and for hosts of the smaller birds like finches and warblers.

Agricultural sprays have destroyed so much. Gone are the golden fields of buttercups. What child today can say he has seen these glimmering yellow fields? Richard Jefferies described them beautifully as 'gold nails driven into a green ground'.

It was down in these golden forests of the waving grass that, as a boy, I heard (but never saw) the skulking corncrake whose voice, as surely as that of the cuckoo, told that summer had really 'I-cum in'. What a true sound of summer that monotonous and mysterious 'crake crake' was, an almost mechanical sound which could be heard both by night and by day. The last corncrake I actually saw was shot by the gun next to me during a partridge shoot in about 1934, near Brixworth in Northamptonshire.

But to return to disused railways, not long ago I took a walk down one. It was one of those mornings in spring when the buds are fat and yellow on the hawthorns, and the plovers weep over the river fields.

It cannot be more than fifteen years or so that the very last train came puffing down that line, its white smoke billowing low over the wayside fields, making the sheep bustle and run, with their newborn lambs following after in a panic. The new grass was just beginning to pierce the old dead herbage, and new teazel leaves were showing down among the old brown stems. The teazel heads were still intact even after the winter rains and snows, though they had been stripped of their seeds by wind and goldfinches. Here and there in the hedgerow were

A cautious peek at the nest

very dead-looking field elms – smitten by the hateful elm disease, that myxomatosis of the tree world – and these will still be winter trees when all else is burgeoning into fresh leaf.

Now and again I caught the faint sweet perfume of wild violets. On the sunny side of the embankment, they looked like a sprinkling of snow for they were the white variety whose scent outmatches that of the purple.

Down in the cutting there was no breeze for the high banks and bushes gave shelter. In the windless air, I could smell that faint sweet scent of spring – of growing grass and opening leaves. It is a delicious heady scent which belongs only to spring. Surely it is this which sets the lambs running races, and makes the birds sing as they fly, the children to shout and skip!

Out in the fields above the bank I could hear the April sound of diving peewits as they hurled themselves in gay abandon up into the sky, there, with twisting motion, diving downwards almost to the ground. A wild 'wheet a-wheet! two bullocks a-wheet!' again and again.

There was an old hawthorn tree half way up the bank which must have been often veiled in white smoke from passing trains. Its trunk was creased and sturdy, lichen-covered, its branches spread wide, each twig crammed with buds. In another month it would be a snowy splendid thing, perfuming the air. The peak time of the flowering hawthorn is very brief – only four or five days at the most, but what a glorious scent it is!

In the top of this tree I spied the untidy stick fortress of a magpie's nest. The cunning bird had left before I came close – very rarely will you see a magpie leave its nest. But up there in the grass-lined cup, under the protective roof of thorns, the handsome green and blue eggs would still be warm. Why is it that the magpie chooses to protect its eggs in this way? The jay, an equal rascal, does not do so, nor rook nor carrion crow. It must be its guilty conscience for magpies are great nest robbers. There is only a small entrance at the side – perhaps that is to fence her youngsters in when they get their first quills.

A little way past this hawthorn tree a brimstone hove into view, plodding along, its yellow wings the exact colour of the primroses in the woods. I stood quite still and it went leisurely by, turning now and then to inspect some bush or leaf – no doubt, it was looking for the buckthorn on which to lay its eggs. It settled briefly on a leaf, its wings fanned – beautifully-shaped wings quite different from any other British butterfly. All winter it would have been sleeping in the ivy on some oak tree.

Somewhere up in the green thickets on the bank I heard the faint 'falling' scale of my first willow warbler of the year. Soon I saw it hopping about among some sallow wands whose silver buds were powdered with gold – a goat willow. I stood so long listening to and watching this beautiful little bird, so delicate and with the colouring of the opening buds, that the magpie came back to perch in an ash tree some eighty yards away. It flirted its tail and chackered the alarm note, sounding exactly like a football fan's rattle. It hardly stayed a moment but dipped away over the bank; they have a dread of the human figure.

A hundred yards on, I came to a real spring scene, four grass snakes curled round one another in a knot, half-screened by a bramble. They were intent on love making. I was thankful no ignorant passer-by had come upon them and broken them with a stick. They lay in a tangled knot, gently stirring – sometimes showing the vivid under-belly marking of palest yellow with black bands. The grass snake has its

The grass snake with its distinct patterning

Hunting hedgehog

distinct patterning on the belly and not on the back like the adder.

I passed on, treading gently so as not to disturb them, and just as I reached the end of the cutting I heard the first cuckoo of the year – calling afar off from the old duck decoy a field away.

This decoy was in use up to sixty years ago and Lord Lilford, the owner, took a great interest in it, and no doubt enjoyed many a succulent mallard from it. Round the actual pond, tall elms grew; now most were dead from the foul disease, but the herons still had their nests in the tops of them and through my glasses I could see grey hunched shapes standing around among the bare twigs.

Herons are early nesters, laying their eggs in March but the incubation period is protracted. It must be a long uncomfortable period of incubation for these stilt-legged birds. Because of their size, they are forced to build high in the trees like rooks, but they find it an awkward business landing and walking about among the tree tops and must be thankful when the breeding season is over.

As so often happens on a day in spring, the sun gradually withdrew and I almost felt winter coming again as a sudden chill wind rocked the sallows. The snakes had gone, their lovemaking done; and the willow warbler had passed on elsewhere. But the scent of violets remained, to remind me it was still the sweet spring, and I wondered where the brimstone was now – perhaps curled up under a leaf now the sun had gone.

26.
LETTERS FROM COMPTON DEVERELL

THE OCTOBER LETTERS

Compton Deverell Priory

My Dear John,

I have a friend, a bachelor parson of the old school, a type which is fast dying out, who is a very keen naturalist (he is a sort of twentieth-century Gilbert White) and with him I frequently go for long country walks, not along the well-known highways and country roads, but down remote and hidden pathways which he alone knows. He lives in a rambling old rectory beneath the shadow of his church, a good shepherd of his rustic flock and much beloved by his charges.

He and I have just had a delightful adventure and before the memory of it fades I hasten to write and tell you of it.

The afternoon was serene, windless, the sun warm and shining with a mellow golden light which gilded the dying leaves of wayside oaks and beeches and made a glory of the chestnut trees, shining through the transparent palmated foliage so that it seemed to add yet a fiercer and more glowing fire to the already radiant boughs.

Our way led first down a little winding lane beside the rectory and from thence across a field or two, tussocky and harbouring 'lying out' rabbits, to the crest of a hill which overlooked a splendid vale. Along the spine of this hill was a straggling wood of beech, chestnut and oak, which stretched for half-a-mile or more along the very crest; a more attractive place it would be hard to imagine.

A delicious languor lay upon the ripened scene, the distances were veiled in luminous vapours, yet each field, copse, stubble, and fallow,

261

was clearly defined with enamel-like transparency. There seemed no activity going on, no tractors at work or signs of labour in the landscape, the distant spires and towers of churches in the vale could be picked out and identified one by one by my companion as we stood awhile on the verge of the wood. Rooks were busy about their nests, as they often are in autumn, perching beside them, some even flying to and fro with sticks in their bills making believe at housewarming. Their voices, however, had not the urgent timbre of spring, they were sleepy and full-fed voices, they might almost be said to be purring with content as cats do before a warming fire.

Already the tops of the elms and oaks were partly naked so that the black nests were clear and plain to view and the ebony birds perching among the glowing autumn leaves made a fine contrast.

We entered the wood through a hunting gate. Out of the sunlight, in the shadow of the trees, the air struck cold and slightly damp, there was an aromatic smell of damp leaves and earth. The long grass of summer, growing beside the riding, was now dead or dying, weighty and grey with silver dew, and the woodland path inside the gate was soft underfoot. We walked along this path, which was poached by the hoof marks of the local pony club, until we came to the smooth silvery pillars of the beech boles, and the pale sunlight patterned the copper-coloured leaves which rustled about our feet. Bride who was with us started a rabbit from a rose-red bramble brake. It went bobbing away among the underwood flirting its white scut and Bride stood like a statue with one front paw drawn back, her enquiring ears cocked forward, puzzled and a little disappointed that her master had not fired a gun.

My old friend began to hunt about the bases of the trees, digging in the loamy soil with a spud stick for the chrysalids of the moth which he has frequently found in this particular wood. These chrysalids apparently are most often found on the northern side of the trunk, possibly the reason being that they are not awakened too early from their long winter sleep when spring returns. But he found none and soon we went on beneath other trees, beeches, elms, and oaks, until the path rose steeply to a little clearing.

Bride who was running in front busy with numerous gamey smells of rabbit and pheasant, all at once stopped in her tracks and stared

The path through the beech woods

straight in front of her as though she had seen something which was not visible to us. We stopped, too, watching her, and I saw her eyes following something which appeared to be coming towards us though we could see nothing whatever on the sunlit chequered path. She backed a little and I suddenly sensed a little creep of the spine. Evidently she was watching something which was clear enough to her but which we could not see. I spoke to her, asked her what was the matter, and she turned her face and looked at me in a puzzled and half-scared manner. Then she gave herself a shake and went on as though nothing had happened. Perhaps, who knows, she had seen the spirit of some old forgotten squire taking his stroll on this serene autumn afternoon, his flintlock under arm and shadowy hound at heel. Or perhaps it was the ghost of some long-departed gamekeeper, clad in velveteens, who for a moment or two was clearly visible to her as he came towards us along the path. I sometimes think that dogs can see such Spirits and are more sensitive in these matters. As far as is known dogs are creatures of little or no imagination and I have noticed that those of the humankind who claim to have seen ghosts are unimaginative men, plain matter-of-fact people, often with a limited intelligence.

Soon pheasants began to crow ahead of us, the underwood thinned, and we came out of the wood upon a warm and sunny bank where the grass had been eaten close and fine by rabbits. Below us was a dense gorse cover and a tangle of elder trees. The elder seems to thrive among the gorse the reason being that the seeds are carried thither in the autumn nights by the blackbirds and thrushes who resort to furze for roosting.

How the sun's rays flooded this sheltered bank! Bride began to busy about with waving stern for obviously but a few minutes before pheasants had been dusting and basking there. We found the 'scrapes' and saw the barred feathers. Drunken bees and flies were sidling on the bare sandy patches, a wasp or two hummed past.

On our left, peeping above a tangle of elder trees and hawthorn which were glowing with rose and amber leaves, I saw a chimney. A step or two and we came upon a house, a plaster-walled dwelling with wide eaves facing west.

It was once a keeper's house. No glass was in the windows, the door was gaping and when we entered in we found plaster lying on the stone floor, and broken glass. Someone, a tramp or poacher perhaps, had lit a fire in the rusty grate some long time back, the charred and blackened sticks lay among a heap of grey ash.

Pinned to a shutter was a pencilled notice written on a tattered notebook page. It read: 'Unless the spades and netts left here are returned by next week the perlice will be enformed.'

Behind the hanging door I spied a black leaf-like pyramid half-hidden by a flake of plaster. It was a hibernating peacock butterfly which had chosen this snug place to pass the winter. And hard by we found two more, one close to the window, the other behind a hanging shutter. We left them to their sleep and wished them well. The warm sun without was not tempting them forth with any false promises, they were already deep in their winter sleep. Not until some prying wren or tit came that way one pale winter's day or the delicate chiff-chaff's voice called them forth would their long sleep be done.

Fourteen weeks or so lay ahead of them, the leaves would fall from the trees, the snow would come and the nights of frost, they would sleep through it all.

It was chill and a little melancholy within the old forsaken house and I was glad to come out once more into the sunlight.

There, in what was once the vegetable garden now choked with weeds, dead nettle stalks, and the decorative brown heads of withered teazel was a gorgeous riot of blackberries shining like beads of glistening jet in the warm rays. I have never seen such luscious blackberries, not even in Norfolk which is famed for them, nor have I ever tasted such sweet and delectable wild fruit. We moved along the bushes pecking like hungry birds until we could eat no more. A tawny butterfly went past and settled on a spray in the full sun where it laid flat its serrated wings. It was a comma butterfly, a lovely specimen. He, unlike the peacocks sleeping in the chill, already wintry gloom of the ruined cottage, was making the most of these last warm days at summer's end before retiring for his winter rest. He seemed as lively as in summer, flitting and gliding about us, we watched him for a long while, as we sat on the bank smoking our pipes and feeling the grateful warmth penetrating our bodies through and through.

265

These are moments which are worth relishing to the full, it was an ideal hour for a lazy man. In the mellow light the cottage seemed very cheerful and homely, glad to see us, almost, and content with our company. I could imagine myself very happy living in such a place if I had no family ties, if I were a lonely man whose interests lay (as did my own) with birds and wild creatures and the peace of woods. It would not be difficult to make the cottage habitable, to put the glass back in the windows, to rehang the door, to bring the little garden back into cultivation. It was the sort of place which would, no doubt, have delighted Thoreau, Richard Jefferies or W.H. Hudson. One would have to bake one's own bread perhaps (no hardship in normal times), and a journey twice a week to the village would have to be made as no grocer or butcher would deliver supplies. There would be rabbits to shoot, and pigeon and woodcock, pheasant, maybe hares now and then, all would help to fill the larder. A delightful life indeed!

And I thought of the moonlit winter nights when snow lay between the trees (it must have drifted here last winter!) and how I should lie alone in a little bed upstairs seeing the pattern of the diamonded panes upon the floor, while the owls hooted outside and hungry foxes barked. Perhaps it would be lonesome without human company but I should have my dog or dogs to keep me from feeling creepy. For this forsaken place must be full of ghosts, ghosts of bygone gamekeepers who must have slept for generations in the upper room. I thought also of the wild stormy nights when the wind boomed in the beechen wood and the fitful moonlight gleamed on the pale smooth pillars of the massive boles, striped with branch shadows; of the deep warm midsummer nights when the fern grew high and green and badgers grunted on the garden patch. There are many badgers in this wood, we saw their setts, huge cavernous pits driven into the steep sandy slope. At that time the nightingales would be singing and the nightjars churring in the fern, and later, in July, an all-embracing silence broken only by the small secret noises of the sultry night.

My reverie was disturbed by the loud crowing of a cock pheasant in the furze. That bold and armoured warrior, spurred like a knight, with gleaming neck of green and purple mail and breast-plate of burnished copper, had sensed that trespassers were upon his ground. His brazen shout of 'Karkoff!' that single klaxon-like call was full of indignation and a challenge. I wished that I had my gun to answer that challenge, that I could go down among the yellowing elder trees (whose boughs still bore plates of purple berries) to seek him out. But the sun was setting in a misty bank of vapour, already the glow and warmth was fading, the distant vale beginning to dim. It was time we left this magic place to its rightful owners, the badgers and foxes, and the wild birds. I suppose that man will never dwell there again, that the walls will crumble, and that in one hundred Octobers from now, when I shall no longer be able to feel the warming rays of autumn suns, nor hear the caw of rooks, nor see the golden glory in the beechen trees, nothing will remain to show that a house was here, save for a few mossy stones half buried in the yellow fern.

I am not sure that this need be so disturbing a reflection. It is only when one is in the prime of life that one has the sombre thought that one day these beauties will no longer be for you to enjoy. As age creeps on I suppose we mercifully feel less keenly about such matters, though I can only say this from my talk with others and from my own observations. But it seems to me that anything which is natural and obeying nature's laws is good. The plant must spring up, flower, and wither away, for without this arrangement we cannot have that refreshment each year, that strong tide which makes all things new. What I do regret is that we do not live long enough. I would wish for at least two hundred years of youth and health to enjoy the things I do. For whatever the wise men say, whatever they have written, those old philosophers, I know that the things I prize most in the world, the woods and fields, rivers and streams, the procession of the season from minute to minute and month to month and year to year, with all the changes that they bring to the land I love so much, these things, I say, are among the best experiences in the world, if we couple with them a happy home life and children of one's body.

But how easy it is not to realise the worth of the simple things, the things that really matter. I dare to say that not one man in five hundred or even a thousand leads a really happy life, nor gets from it the highest pleasure. Nobody who lives in a town can do so, though they may think otherwise. In the country you are close to the warm and throbbing body of the earth from which you sprang, you cannot feel the stirring if you are enclosed in an artificial box of stone, stone beneath your feet and stone walls about you and an almost constant covering which prevents you from seeing the sky.

Yours
James

Part Five

A HAPPY COUNTRYMAN

The harvest of flowers

From *Indian Summer*

I have noticed one thing about myself – now that I am well past the allotted span – that one becomes much more aware of the passage of time. This is especially so at night when I go to bed and turn out the light. For a minute or so the room is in darkness, then, as my eyes become accustomed to the shadows, the dim shape of the uncurtained window appears. This is, to me, as emphatic as the striking of a clock and has slightly sinister overtones. Also, as I grow older, I sense the rhythm of my days more acutely and at times I seem to be like a leaf carried inexorably onwards on the breast of a great river. Yet as I journey thus, I can observe the landscape as it passes by with unflagging interest. It gives a sense of comfort and stability. Everything is so gradual – the passing seasons which so echo one's life span, the advent of spring, the coming of summer when the natural world is bursting with youth and beauty; then midsummer, middle age; autumn; and finally winter which can hold beauty too outdoors, for nature is rarely ugly.

27.

THE IDLE COUNTRYMAN

SPRING

May 29th, 1941

Coming home late tonight from a walk round my shoot I surprised a family of wild ducklings with their mother. They were in a little brooklet and when the duck saw me she crawled up the bank close by and hid under a root, calling her babies to her. They obeyed at once, burrowing into her feathers, and I stood within three feet of them watching them out of the corner of my eye. The duck was watching me and I had to pretend I had not seen her.

One chubby-faced youngster poked its little striped head out from under her scapulars. Before the summer is over carrion crow and other vermin will have taken heavy toll of that happy family and I doubt whether five ducklings out of the eleven I saw would survive.

As it grew dusk a heron croaked as he winged his way up the darkling valley, his huge wings with their cupped vanes seemed to move slowly, yet in actual fact the bird was travelling at a good pace. Speaking of herons reminds me that I once had a very interesting experience with one of these strange plumed birds. I was on a holiday in Scotland and towards dusk one night we began to cast about for some place to camp. At last we came to a little meadow close to a burn. It was a wild spot far from any house and sheltered on both sides by high bracken-covered hills. We pitched our tent close to an old stone bridge and while Jock, my companion, cooked the supper, I went for a stroll up the burn to gather firing.

Before very long I came to a bend in the bank where there was a low mound which overhung the water in a steep bluff. On looking over I immediately saw a heron standing with his back to me in the shallow water just below. His head was sunk in his shoulders and he seemed asleep, or unusually intent on his fishing. As a general rule the heron is both quick of sight and hearing and it is very seldom one can get so close.

To my complete astonishment this bird never moved but continued to gaze into the stream. I climbed down the bank as quietly as I could and stole up behind him over the short grass. Then very gently I stretched out my hand and actually stroked his back! My gentle caress did not at first rouse him, but after I had passed my hand down his back several times, he suddenly sensed something was happening. His neck shot up, his round fierce eye glared into mine with an expression of utter astonishment and horror. Then with a loud 'squawrk' he spread his huge wings and sailed away.

He must, I think, have been digesting an exceptionally heavy meal and was possibly asleep. I can safely say that never again shall I have the experience of stroking a truly wild heron in its natural surroundings. I can never overcome the feeling that somehow this bird appears strangely out of place in the English countryside, it seems too ornamental and artificial. I do not know why I should feel like this, but the heron, to my mind, seems to belong to tropical rivers, along with spoonbills and pelicans. Not long ago a village woman told me in an excited voice that she had seen a tame stork standing by the brook below the hamlet. I soon found, of course, that she had seen a heron.

When I told her what it was she was astonished that such a distinguished-looking bird could be really 'wild'. She must have seen herons scores of times, but never before had seen one close at hand. Another instance of rustic ignorance occurs to me. Not long ago I visited a particularly charming village in the valley of the Ouse. I was after butterflies and had in my pocket a small book which gave accurately coloured plates of all the British butterflies. As I walked beside the river (it was a hot afternoon in June) I met an old man with a rake over his shoulder. We got into conversation and as he seemed intelligent I began to ask him whether he had seen any unusually beautiful butterflies along the river. I particularly described the Swallow Tail, a specimen of this insect having been captured by a friend of mine near this very spot many years before.

I showed him the coloured plate and after glancing at it he said 'Why yes, scores on 'em! Them things are common along the reeds, I see one or two every day when the sun's out. I got him to describe the insect to me. True, he seemed somewhat vague, but he insisted that the butterfly he had seen had long pointed wings with tails, yellow and black, and with beautiful eyes on each hind wing. He was so positive I naturally became very excited. 'We calls 'em Devil's Needles round 'ere, they sting an' all, you maun 'andle 'em.'

And then I knew to what insect he was referring. Devil's Needle is the country name for a dragonfly. Yet he had seen the picture in the book and was quite indignant when I suggested that what he had described were only dragonflies.

'I can see ye don't believe me,' he said, looking intently at my face, 'but ask any o' the village children, they 'ave lots o' Devil's Needles set up proper in the school.'

It is amazing that people who have lived all their lives in the country, who have played as children in the fields and woods, should be so ignorant of natural history. Yet it is really true that this ignorance arises from being unobservant. Most small boys are shockingly unobservant, and I remember it was so in my own case. I have often wondered whether the average villager loves the country; I believe they would be much happier in a town where they could go to the 'pictures' and see more bustle and life. Perhaps one reason for this lack of observation is that they have no time to 'stand and stare', as my old friend W.H. Davies has it, their eyes are on the ground guiding the plough or digging the soil. Perhaps it is only idle countrymen like myself who can study and appreciate nature. Yet some village characters I have met have shown great intelligence and appreciation of natural history and have shown profound learning. Keepers, of course, whose job it is to watch their masters' policies, automatically acquire a store of natural history knowledge, yet some keepers are ignorant of some of the most simple facts. Such men can never make good keepers because they *are* unobservant. The man who is a good naturalist will serve his master better.

SUMMER

August 21st

Beyond the may tree the meadow sloped up into a steep round knoll which marked the duck pond, a square green pond flanked by willows and elms, all ivy clad, in which the wood pigeons built their nests. From behind that green knoll I have sniped many an unsuspicious moorhen as it jerked about among the green weed. At the far end of the pond was another warren and I there have shot many a rabbit too, as it sat outside its burrow, sunning itself. The knoll was a deadly ambush.

From behind the green mound I saw the trickle of water from the pond winding down towards me, to lose itself in the long bright green grass which grew in the 'quaggy' ground about the foot of the oak. Usually at this time of year the pond is low and the stream dried up, but now, with the wet summer, it was full.

I think I knew every blade of grass in this meadow. On that green knoll the first celandines came into flower and lower down, in the moist green bog, the first cuckoo-flowers bloom. Looking up into the hawthorn above my head I saw the frail platform of a dove's nest. The green trunk close to my cheek was twisted and had a hollow about five feet from the ground. I once found a dead stoat in this hollow, years ago. No doubt it had crawled inside to die.

Standing there, I listened intently to all the quiet sounds of a summer's evening. A pigeon was cooing up in the willows, swallows kept passing and repassing over the meadow grass close beside me, and I saw five young ones perched on a telegraph wire at the far end of the paddock. I noticed that each young one was fed in turn, the parent birds hovering delicately in front of them as they proferred them flies.

Soon a pigeon wheeled past. It did not see me until I stepped out from the shadow of the hawthorn and at my shot it fell out in the field, bursting its crop and scattering grain broadcast. It had been feeding on a stooked field on the far side of the valley.

Aeroplanes passed over occasionally, some high, others low, of all types, from the old-fashioned trainer 'crates' to the latest heavy bombers. This was a new note. Twenty-five years ago there were no aeroplanes to disturb the country peace. But otherwise the scene would not be much altered. Yet on looking more closely I realised that the countryside *had* altered. True, the oak would be no smaller twenty-five years ago; the may trees and willows would be growing, though the latter would be half their present height. But at the foot of the tennis lawn were three new trees, an oak, a walnut, and a sweet willow. And then I began to piece together the old scene, as I remembered it, and I realised that in those days there were many more trees which had now completely disappeared and which I had quite forgotten. For instance, half way up the meadow there used to be a fine apple tree in which a starling built every year, and over against the paddock hedge, a gigantic oak of which little now remains but a stump half hidden in the grass. Another new feature was a five-barred gate in the hedge yonder. And then I remembered a fence which used to run right across the meadow close to 'Peter Pan'. This has now gone and the meadow is all one piece.

So gradually the country is changing, or rather the face of the country is altering. Trees grow up, others fall, fences and gates alter their position, ponds are choked up, others appear.

And then I looked onwards in time and visualised the trees, the oak, and walnut, and the sweet willow, grown to their full height. Perhaps 'Peter Pan' would not be growing then, only a stump sticking out of the red sandy bank.

One thing will always remain, the contour of the ground. There will always be the gentle slope of the field, and the little knoll at the head of the pond. And perhaps the first celandines will always bloom in their ancient haunt. One day perhaps the old house will go, and another be built in its place.

Three fine hairies came trooping down the mead and went splashing and blowing into the pond's edge, their velvet muzzles feeling and sucking at the water. When they had drunk their fill they slowly lifted their handsome heads, and the water dribbled down in shining drops. Then, one after the other, they left the water and grazed away up the slope, whisking their long tails and tossing their heads, their coats shining with health. It is now holiday time for the farm horses, a respite from the daily toil of winter. They have well deserved this rest. In the quiet of the evening I could hear them cropping the grass.

AUTUMN

October 29th

Many things seemed to happen this afternoon which brought home the nearness of winter.

I took the twelve bore and the retriever (Sparkie having been sent to the vet's), and motored to Tanglewood after tea.

All day the wind had blown a gale from the north, and as I started out, the sky grew dark and the first snowflakes whirled, blotting out the landscape. From under the tall beeches on top of the hill flocks of finches flew up from the beech-mast. A great many had white rumps and rich chestnut markings. Bramblings! The first bramblings of winter! I saw at least forty of these richly-coloured finches and they did not seem shy. They hopped about in the lower branches of a hedge waiting impatiently for me to pass on and leave them to their feast. No doubt they were very hungry after their long journey.

And when I dropped over the five-barred gate on to the stubble a flock of fieldfares arose and flew away 'chuck chucking' as they went. They soon settled again out in the stubble, rising before me like larks as I advanced, the rear birds 'jumping' the main flock and settling in front.

And then, when I reached the lee of the wood, I saw one small bird hawking up and down. It was the last swallow of summer! It is not often one sees swallows, bramblings, and fieldfares in October, and snowflakes falling at the same time.

Why did this swallow linger here on this wild autumn night, what were its chances of ever reaching a sunnier, more kindly, land? He swung up and down, back and forth, in the calm air of the woodside, never venturing out into the open where the wind raved and the snow whirled. This wind, which was now tearing at the shabby outworn oaks had brought the fieldfares and bramblings. Perhaps this lone fugitive was waiting for a favourable wind to bear *him* away.

As I walked slowly along, a host of pigeons swept overhead, taking me completely unawares, but a hurried shot took effect and Busy bounced out into the kale to bring a bird back to me. It was not a foreigner but a plump English-bred pigeon. The big 'foreign' flocks will be arriving nearer Christmas time. These are much smaller and not so 'blue' as the English-bred birds.

I hurried on because I knew that with the wind in the North any other pigeon which came would go to the southern end. I reached the far end of the wood at last. The yellow glare of the setting sun was in my eyes (the snow clouds had temporarily passed) and those level blinding rays seemed unreal. Once within the trees it was more calm and quiet though overhead the tops of the oaks were threshing and rocking. Despite the lateness of the season their leaves were thick and few showed the buff leather colour of dying leaves. The wet summer is responsible.

As the sun dipped down beyond the lake, party after party of duck arose and headed inland in the teeth of the wind, but all were high and out of gunshot. Soon some more pigeons came over and a snap shot taken between the gaps in the trees proved successful, Busy again returning in triumph with another bird.

As I waited under the oaks the sky grew bruise-coloured and sombre, the leafy shadows above were gloomy and forbidding. Now and again there came a violent gust of wind which tore some of the leaves from their hold, whirling them far out into the field of kale. The West grew wan and the sheet of water reflected it, glinting through the darkling trees. A lonely spot this, with not a soul within a mile of me! Very soon these oaks will be bare, it will be difficult then to find cover to ambush the pigeon, as the underwood of thorns is too thin for a hide at this spot. Handfuls of leaves went spinning up among the oak tops and eddied about between the boles as if dancing a death dance. More pigeons blundered in, higher up the wood, and very rapidly the light drained from the sky. Snow began to fall once more. So 'that's the way it is'. In these last few hours winter has come. Today corresponds with that first day of spring when the sun shines warm and we hear the tentative notes of a newly arrived willow warbler. Never have so many 'winter things' come on the same day, fieldfares, bramblings, and snow. That poor hunted scrap of a swallow made it all the more poignant. There was something inexpressibly sad and romantic in that lone mite, true bird of summer heats, striving to find some sort of food and shelter in the calm air beside the rusty wood. How sombre was this autumn evening, yet it was beautiful too.

WINTER

December 5th

Whilst ambushing for pigeon in Hodson's I had an interesting experience. At 4 p.m. I reached the wood with a bundle of evergreens, with which I repaired my hide among the blackthorn. This took me some time. It was a perfectly still evening, mild and soft. When I had finished the job I loaded my rifle and settled down to wait. After about twenty minutes, my eyes, roving over the tall ash in front of me, caught a movement near the top of the tree, about forty feet from the ground. It was a small animal and for a moment I took it to be a grey squirrel. But after a little while the beast showed himself my side of the tree, and I was immediately struck by the reddish tint of its fur. I then thought it might be a red squirrel, though they are excessively rare in this part of the country, but the body was too long and slender for a squirrel's. There was a large bracket fungus protruding from the tree bole and on this the animal sat, raising its head and looking about it. I then saw that the chest was sulphur yellow! I raised the rifle, but it must have caught the movement for the next instant it vanished and I did not see it again. Could this beast have been a pine marten? In size it was as large as a grey squirrel. It might have been a stoat, but it is extremely unlikely that a stoat would climb so high, though I have seen them in low thorn bushes.

Last week a friend told me the familiar 'stoat story'. A stoat appeared on the lawn in front of his house and began to whirl about and turn somersaults to attract a pair of wagtails which were feeding nearby. The ruse was successful. One of the wagtails, overcome with curiosity, ventured too near, and the animal seized it. That stoats *do* 'waltz' to attract birds has been proved. I myself have seen this happen. One day I noticed a great commotion among some jackdaws and on going to investigate I saw a ring of them gathered round a stoat which was rolling about in the grass. But the 'jackies' were too wily to be deceived and when at last the stoat made a run at one of them they all flew away. W.H. Hudson also witnessed this same trick.

The ducks are beginning to come to the barley stubbles on some high land behind the village. During the hours of dark I have heard them quacking and flying about, but so far I have not had a chance at them.

February 19th

Seeing a knot of people standing on the canal bridge I stopped my car and joined the spectators. What was the matter? had somebody fallen in? I found the scene was well worth watching. Twenty horses, attached to a barge, were roped together along the tow path. On the barge, standing upright on either side of the centre beam stood ten men, five a side, and as another man urged the straining horses forward the men rocked the craft from side to side. Such shouting and cracking of ice I never heard. But even with all this bustle and turmoil the thick ice on the canal only yielded after much effort, cracking sideways in huge thick panes, like glass. Here indeed was a winter picture, one to remember, the leaden sky, the starved snow-covered fields, the straining line of horses, and the swaying barge. It reminded me of an old Dutch painting. By rights I should have found a coach and pair well stuck in the drifts by Honey Hill. I found instead its modern counterpart, the red mail van, with the driver shovelling sand under the back wheels which buzzed round on the frozen surface.

The bargees had managed to break a jagged path for some way along the canal, but when I passed later I saw that the water was again frozen so that all their labour had been in vain.

Out on the ice of the reservoir the duck are still huddled in a black mass, from a distance they appear like a dark-coloured rug laid on the ice. Despite all this bitter weather I notice across the paddock, two stock-doves flying around the ashes with upraised wings. This is their courting flight. They glide like those paper gliders we used to make at school.

Oak in Salcey Forest

28.
LORD OF THE FOREST

Snow lay in the forest showing the prints of all its four-footed people and three-toed birds, the neat double prints of the deer, the small cloven prints of the bristly boars, and the big pad marks of wolves. Around among the bushes were the fairy-like toemarks of finches and tits and even the smaller spoor of mice, stitching the white surface.

Few human footprints showed, only the hoof marks of horses where the mounted agisters, the forest keepers, had been on patrol. For those were bitterly hard times for many of the poor, and a nice fat boar or stag was a prize indeed, worth the risk of imprisonment.

Under the drifted snow near the mighty oak tree, under the dark soil, was the acorn which Hugh had planted five months before. Through its tough skin it felt the grip of frost, how the frozen ground clamped around it, then the false warmth of snow and thaw, then frost once again.

All through the cold of that, its first winter, Hugh's acorn was like a hibernating animal. Yet even under its covering blanket of leaf mould peril threatened.

A long-tailed field mouse, foraging for food, tunnelled under the brambles close to where the acorn lay. It was a pretty little creature with large eyes like black, wet pebbles, big ears sensitive for every sound, and with a sheen on its guard hairs, those long hairs which cover the under-coat. It could sense the hidden morsel. But, the white barn owl, which lived in a hollow of the father oak, swept down on noiseless wings and plucked it from the snow with one sharp talon leaving a rose pink spot of blood. He carried it back to the oak, to devour at leisure; a welcome meal indeed, for he had to hunt far and wide for a living in those hard times. He was the descendant of a family of owls who had nested and roosted in the father oak for over a hundred years, a real aristocrat of the forest.

Then one day in late March something exciting began to happen inside the acorn. It felt the earth relenting. Soon the grip had relaxed for good. From the base the skin split. A pale root finger thrust out groping with wonderful purpose, feeling the rich mould, and the hard brown skin at the tip split open to thrust a probing determined stalk upwards to the light. It bore upon it two little leaves called seed leaves which remained in the darkness of the earth, and above them the slender stalk, seemingly so tender and brittle, yet so tough, continued to grow until it broke surface like a periscope.

That was a great moment for the acorn, the very first tentative step in its life.

Then it was April. Yellow primroses glowed in fragrant posied clumps among the drifted leaves; it was as if the whole forest was waking from a long sleep, every living thing was up and stirring. Each morning the glad chorus of birds echoed through the quiet glades. Blackbirds warbled as sweetly as oboes, and spotted song thrushes vied with each other to produce the finest repeated phrases. The missel-thrushes had already built a nest in the father oak, unmolested by the white owls who drew the line at doorstep kills, and the cock bird serenaded his wife with wild windblown notes as she warmed her lilac-spotted eggs in the mossy nest built in a fork near the top of the tree.

The adders of the forest awakened from their winter sleep and coiled luxuriously in the pale spring sun. One chose the bramble patch close to the acorn shoot for its sun parlour, coming day after day, when the sun shone, to arrange its handsome patterned body in a neat piled coil on the dead bracken fronds. It did not like full sun, however much it revelled in its comforting embrace. The opening bramble leaves cast little moving shadows on its barred back as the wind stirred the briars, and its wicked nut-shaped head, with its unwinking blazing eye, rested on its top coil. Its sight was not good, its hearing less so, but those dry, neat, scaly coils served it as radar. Any vibration, such as the footfall of a deer or a rabbit, sent it sliding and rustling down its hole close to the acorn shoot.

Full to the brim with succulent wasp grubs

Soon two leaves unfolded from the tip of the stalk on each side of a centre bud, which was the most sensitive and precious point. By the end of May the two leaves were open and perfectly formed, and showing the serrations so typical of the oak leaf. Where before all had been airiness and sun, there was now a filtering of that light as the forest trees came into full fresh green leaf.

One sunny morning the little oak had another visitor – a queen wasp. She was a handsome insect striped in warning colours. She had slept all winter in a crevice of the father oak across the glade, close to where the white owls had their nest, and where the female was now sitting on three big rough white eggs. The queen wasp came humming, a low sinister hum, and the wind from her winnowing gauzy wings stirred the dead leaves by the little oak.

She found the adder's hole (the adder had been eaten by a forest buzzard two days before) and she seemed to take a fancy to it. After humming to and fro across the mouth of it she settled and crawled inside. She came out, then went in once more, as though she was undecided, but she found this hole was just what she had been looking for. She liked the patch of brambles where the sun shone so fitfully. It was warm and dry. Then began, from that moment, an heroic effort of toil on the part of the queen wasp. Hour after hour she laboured with her powerful jaws, excavating a circular chamber. Hour after hour she emerged with particles of earth which she dropped some distance away, like a tiny bombing plane.

After five days she had completed this part of her task. From the roof of the cavity inside the hole she began to build a centre pillar of chewed wood which she attached to the root of one of the briars. Day after day she flew back and forth to the father oak, cutting away with her jaws at the dead wood, pulping this up into a sort of paper which was tough, waterproof, and fine. From this she began to construct the cells for her eggs, working downwards all the time, with the care of a master mason. Her nest grew each day, mathematically exact, the shape of a child's ball, with an outer covering of chewed paper. When some three rows of cells had been finished she began to lay her eggs, which hatched in ten days into grubs. These in turn had to be fed, so she was architect, mother, and breadwinner combined.

Hundreds, thousands of times she flew back and forth to the oak, only crawling, tired out, into the nest at night for rest. No man, no creature, could have worked harder than that queen wasp! And when at last the grubs hatched into wasp children, these were able to help the queen mother to finish the nest and feed the evergrowing population of fat wriggling grubs, each one in its waxy cell.

By midsummer the nest was complete, the population growing larger every day as the wasps hatched, the insects streaming in and out in all directions to get food for yet more grubs. And then, one windy night of storm and darkness, when the warm rain battered the leaves and the father oak groaned and creaked in the force of the wind (its interior was hollow now with age), a hunting badger came through the branching fern. He smelled the hole with his broad black nose and began to dig. His furry grey body bunched with the effort, the dark earth and leaves flew backwards from between his muscular legs and soon he reached the nesting chamber which was now humming with rage and alarm.

The wasps settled on his striped head and fur and tried to sting their foe but he munched noisily on. Succulent wasp grubs are a great delicacy for badgers. Within half an hour there was nothing left of the nest but a few tatters of chewed paper. Where the adder's hole had been was a gaping cavity, and the spoil from it covered the little oak entirely.

By happy fortune, those powerful curved claws and groping mouth with its fierce teeth had not damaged the acorn root – it had been missed by half an inch – but all those weeks of effort and planning by the queen wasp had been brought to nothing!

The perils which beset all living things threatened the little oak; a turn of fortune could mean disaster or triumphant survival. Already in its short life two dangers had been overcome.

White Admiral

29.

THE NATURALIST'S
BEDSIDE BOOK

VANISHING BUTTERFLIES

In the April sunshine, on the southern edge of Bullocks Wood, I watched that first butterfly of spring, a yellow brimstone. In actual fact I saw my first brimstone in March during that delightful spell of weather which brought out the golden crocus in all the parks and gardens. I greatly admire the brimstone, not only for that clear primrose colour of the wings, which matches so well the primrose clumps in the woods, but also for the lyre-shaped wings which no other British butterfly can match.

My particular brimstone by Bullocks Wood was revelling in the gentle warming rays, flitting in and out between the hazel stems where the green dog's mercury was already hiding the bare woodland floor. Eventually it came to rest on a dead stalk of grass and spread its wings, luxuriously as a cat stretches before a fire.

Some years ago I watched the mating flight of two brimstones in my garden on a warm March morning. The female ascended high into the sky with the male in attendance, just as the female purple emperor soars skywards when mating. Then down she came in a steep dive and hid herself in an ivyclad archway. The male followed, and there they mated. The interesting fact is that they remained in coition for four days. This surely must be unusual in a butterfly, though there is one recorded instance of a pair of brimstones being in coition for a fortnight.

Altogether, it's a curious insect. It goes into hibernation soon after emergence from the chrysalis in late summer, July and August, and therefore it has a long sleep until the following March. This accounts for the perfect condition of many of the spring brimstones. They invariably choose ivy for hibernation and their resemblance to the underside of the ivy leaf is one of the miracles of camouflage. The food plant is the alder buckthorn, though the brimstone will also select the purging buckthorn, that hedgerow bush which has large glossy black berries but which the birds will not touch. Neither bush is common, and for that reason one may see the brimstone travelling many miles in spring, plodding along the sides of the hedges and lanes. The caterpillar is a soft velvety green which matches exactly the colour of the buckthorn leaf.

Like the brimstone, the small tortoiseshell is another butterfly of early spring and, like the brimstone, it hibernates, often coming into houses in late summer where it likes to rest on curtains. But many of these spring tortoiseshells are not in the immaculate condition of the brimstones. The very rare large tortoiseshell, which is so seldom seen now, and which is probably counted as one of our rarest British butterflies, is a lovely insect with all the rich browns and reds of an Indian carpet. I have only seen one once in my life and that was down a drove in Wicken fen where there was an avenue of elms. The larvae feed on elm, always at the top of the tree, though sometimes they have been found on sallows and willows.

I remember that fine Norfolk naturalist Ted Ellis telling me he once found a mass of large tortoiseshell larvae on a willow when he was voyaging down a Norfolk creek. Not being a collector he left them there, but I would have been sorely tempted to take them to 'bring them through' for release, as the larvae are the special prey of ichneuman flies. A friend told me last year that he saw a large tortoiseshell in a west-country walled garden where it was feeding on Michaelmas daisies. He was so excited he rushed home some miles distant for his camera and when he returned the butterfly was still there and he took a photo of it.

At one time the tortoiseshell was not at all uncommon around London and the Midlands but it began to disappear about thirty years ago. Why this should be is a mystery, and the same applies to the lovely silver-washed fritillary which is one of our most beautiful butterflies. I have seen the brambles on the rides of Salcey Forest in Northamptonshire absolutely glowing with these golden-winged creatures, but one rarely sees them now. The same may be said for many of our once-common butterflies. Many can remember the waysides of country lanes alive in summertime with the bobbing flight of uncountable thousands of meadow browns. They have gone, along with the lovely little blues and small coppers.

Now that was a little gem which fascinated me as a boy! That small jewelled insect whose outside wings were as attractive as the inside, but which was outshone by the very rare large copper which now only survives in the fens under rigid protection and careful conservation. It was there one lovely summer day that I saw what I thought was a glowing coal in the middle of a bush; when I came close I saw it was a large copper sunning itself. When it flew it was transformed into a blue butterfly for the underside wings are a metallic blue, more noticeable in flight than when at rest. I talked with the warden of the reserve and he told me what a struggle they have to keep this species going as it feeds on water dock and this is often submerged by floods, and although the larva can apparently stay submerged for some time, prolonged floods will kill it.

The gradual disappearance of our native butterflies, as well as some birds and plants, is one of the most worrying things today. Even the red admiral, once so plentiful in our gardens in later summer, seems to be becoming scarce. I saw only four or five last year. Can the cause be that our climate is changing, or that we are polluting the atmosphere and the land? The disappearance of the meadow browns can be explained by the spraying and cutting of roadside verges, and the spraying of crops and woodland trees.

Some thirty years ago I saw as many as ten or a dozen purple emperors on the wing in Salcey Forest but this insect seems to have disappeared entirely from the forest since the oaks were sprayed for tortrix. Yet a friend of mine who went to the south of France last summer told me that it was just like old times. There were butterflies everywhere, and the waysides and woodlands were alive with all the old familiar species.

A certain south country forest I know, where the purple emperor still occurs, is now under threat. When I last journeyed there I found that the sallows bordering the rides were being cut down. I am doing what I can to remedy the situation.

Along with the butterflies, the crickets and grasshoppers have vanished. A walk in a meadow thirty years ago meant grasshoppers jumping in front of you at every step. You do not see them now. All the richness and beauty which I remember is being eroded. This is very sad.

Of course I realise there are many people who could not care one jot if the purple emperor went, together with all the frogs, insects, plants and animals threatened by modern inventions and discoveries. One thing I do know is that the countryside is an infinitely poorer place than it was when I was a boy, and though there is much on the credit side of the balance sheet, such as the advance in medicine and technology, I am fearful for the country-lover and his enjoyment of the natural world. If we could rid ourselves of this dreadful feeling of impotence when we see the destruction caused by modern methods of farming I should have more cause for hope.

EMPEROR AND EMPRESS

There is a certain area of my favourite forest which is never visited from one year's end to another by anyone save myself; it is my own secret haunt. Only in the stark winter days may hounds pass through in pursuit of a fox, but they will be unaccompanied by horsemen. How can I describe this secret green courtyard in the forest as I saw it this afternoon? The air was heavy with the scent of meadow sweet, not a zephyr moved in the tops of the oaks, and the flies were a torment, following me in a humming cloud.

I pushed my way down a deer track where the grass was waist high, interspersed with brambles, willow herb, and teazel. The forest floor sloped downwards into a hollow. Here was a wide space hedged round with ancient oaks and a few bushes of sallow, most of it 'going back', for the sallow has a short life and, though a strong and fast grower, it seems to outlast its strength and the branches soon die back; I doubt if the life of a full-grown sallow tree lasts more than thirty years. But here in this magic place, where spires of rosebay willow herb stood sentinel, the whole essence of a late August afternoon seemed condensed.

I had journeyed there on my fly-tormented way to search (of course!) for the eggs of the purple emperor butterfly, for this secret clearing is its kingdom. For a number of years I collected their eggs from the big sallows, but now those trees have died off in their nether regions, although higher up they look in full growth and health. I speculated on how many of the coveted eggs were laid up there, far out of my reach. It is true the empress prefers the lower, more shady sprays but I have found eggs high up in a sallow and could only get to them by climbing.

I sat down among the rosebay and endeavoured to deal with the tormenting flies by a whisk of elder which flies detest. And before long my vigil was rewarded, for there appeared over the crown of an oak the floating gliding shape of Iris, that rare and elusive butterfly, the most mysterious of all our British race, a creature of surpassing beauty yet so seldom seen, even in woods where they are known to occur.

Its maddening habit of remaining for hours on end up in the oak crown, where it is far beyond the entomologist's net, is well known to collectors. It is, I believe, the laziest butterfly known, and like the pheasant will not fly unless it is forced to, either by sexual activity or disturbance by birds, which have been known to chase and catch purple emperors. Jays especially have been seen to do this, no doubt attracted by the black and white flicker of the wings. Yet the flight of Iris is perhaps the most striking of all our native species. It is a swift and powerful flight with many soaring glides around the oak crowns. At such times when the sun is shining one can see the pale membrane bands on the dark wings.

I had my powerful glasses with me and was delighted to see my female joined by two others, presumably males. Once she floated down to the top of a high sallow, perhaps to lay an egg, though the time was late. She was no doubt just enjoying herself, a sort of Indian summer before her brief life came to an end.

The sun beat down out of a veiled sky which seemed to intensify the heat much as a tent will do, and in my ears was the continual droning of the flies. The pink spires of the rosebay were motionless, occasionally trembling when they were assaulted by honey-gathering bumble bees and other insects. The oak leaves were dark but showing fresh tufts of reddish green which told, more than anything, how the summer was wearing away. In the hot bleached herbage beside me as I lay in the green shade of a big sallow, I saw the grass blades moving with numerous grasshoppers. This pleased me for grasshoppers, along with frogs and toads, and hosts of other creatures, have been killed by the farmers' sprays.

These purple emperors of mine (they really *were* mine, of my own stocking, for as far as I know Iris did not occur in this forest in recent years) were extremely active, chasing each other about, gliding and floating around the oak crowns far out of reach. I could well imagine the frustration of a greedy butterfly collector who would have loved to secure one of them for his 'cabinet', how he would have groaned with despair of ever catching one with a sweep of his long-handled net. Turtle doves crooned in the deep recesses of the forest, true bird of those quiet thickets and whose companions are the wild deer.

Flitting about among the grasses were numerous gatekeepers, a modest yet warmly flushed little butterfly whose wings, in a certain light seemed to glow. A few meadow browns were with them. How as a boy I used to try and catch them in my fingers! But they always flitted away and I thought they saw me coming out of the round eye on the outside wing. I do not know whether the painted eyes on the wings of butterflies and moths are any deterrent to hunting birds.

The eyes on the peacock's wings are most pronounced. Were the peacock a rare butterfly it would be prized even above the purple emperor for the collector's 'cabinet'. Yet it seems to survive, despite

Haunt of the purple emperor

the fact that nettles are now killed by sprays, for the larvae feed on nettle, usually those that are new growth after the first crop has been scythed.

As I lay in the shade a brilliant blue butterfly went past, so blue that I wondered if it could be an adonis blue, but then that is a butterfly of the downlands of the south. Lying back in the grass and still keeping an eye on the promised appearance of my purple emperors, I could see the hover flies hanging motionless, or seemingly so, as though suspended by invisible threads. The hazy clouds had moved away. I could look up into the ocean of the sky, and across that blue backdrop a white line was drawn as if by a celestial finger. It was the vapour trail of an aeroplane, though the plane itself was so high it was invisible, save through my binoculars.

From *INDIAN SUMMER*

On August 27th, last year I found the egg of a purple emperor butterfly on a sallow leaf in the forest. It was on the very first leaf I looked at on the bush and though I searched the rest of the sallow leaf by leaf I found no others. It looked a little dodgy – not a bright green though it showed the purple waistband. Today, June 28th, a lovely female emerged, a most unusual date as I have never before known Iris to be on the wing as early as June.

Boxing up the newly-emerged female was a ticklish job as when they are active and 'fanning', as this one was, it is easy to damage a wing or leg. However, by slipping the box up against the muslin of the cage, I managed to get the lid in place and straight away bore it up the forest.

The sun was shining when I reached my favourite 'Emperor Ride' and I found the woodcutters busy with their carts. The ride was woefully cut up and furrowed deep by the wheels of carts and tractors. However, I picked my way up the track and, reaching a sunny clearing, I lifted the lid of the box and she darted out with great swiftness, so fast the eye could scarcely follow, and away she went over the oaks.

I hope she finds a nice fresh male, though it is early yet for breeding. I have one more butterfly in my cage. It went into pupation some ten days later, this will probably be a male, as males usually arrive first. We shall see later if any eggs are to be found.

I have written so much about Iris in the past that readers may wonder why this butterfly attracts me so much. It is partly because of its rarity but chiefly because of its habitat, always ancient forest lands which must be extensive. Nowadays so many of our big woodlands have disappeared or been replaced by conifers that its hold is precarious. Not that it stands any danger from butterfly hunters as this insect rarely gives the net a chance – the males keep to the upper canopy of the forest and the females are hard to net among the 'sally gardens' wherein it lays its single purple-banded egg. Also the male has that splendid regal purple flash only seen on the tropical butterflies, a blinding metallic purple in some lights but dark, almost black in others.

The colouring of both birds and butterflies is worthy of study. The outer wings of some of our butterflies are even more beautiful than the inner. That of the painted lady is an exquisite pattern of greenish marblings set off by a blush of glorious warm pink where the forewing joins the lower. The red admiral also has beautiful outer wings, so has the purple emperor.

One of the most memorable butterfly sights I remember is of a sallow bush covered with purple emperors. One year I managed to rear from the egg nearly forty of these lovely, rare creatures. On a hot July morning I took them to the reserve and released them, putting each insect on to a sallow leaf, coaxing it out of its pillbox. The sun was shining, and as I put each insect on its leaf it displayed – the males showing the wondrous purple sheen.

It was as though the whole bush was lit with fairy lamps. How was it I never thought to take a camera to register that unique scene, one that would have made any collector of butterflies slaver at the mouth! One by one the butterflies took wing and soon I was to see males pursuing the females over the tops of the oak trees.

In the first week in August I was introduced to a new and very attractive purple emperor forest. It is always exciting to explore a new locality; Angela and I spent one very hot day with the keeper as guide. I doubt if there is any spot more suitable to this king of butterflies, with wide, well-kept ridings, ancient oaks, and thickets of sallow – so much sallow that it would take days to search and watch for the empress on her egg-laying rounds.

We were given tea by a charming lady who lived nearby, who showed us photographs of a male Iris feeding off sugar on top of a stump. This fine butterfly is always seen around her house each summer and I envied her that true forest retreat. The keeper showed me his pheasant pens, wide and spacious in the forest heart. He regards feeding from bins as a lazy man's way; he likes the poults to find their food which is scattered around.

We were, alas!, too late to see Iris, or to find any eggs, for all was so forward this last summer. I could have spent hours exploring that wonderful wood, but we had a long, hot journey home and we had to leave far too soon, but not before the lady thrust into my hands two bottles of home-made wine, sloe gin, and what she called 'hedgerow wine', brewed from the wild hedge fruits of the forest. Kind souls indeed.

30.

THE QUIET FIELDS

DECEMBER

There had been snow in the night. It still lay in the shadowed parts of the woodland ride, printed here and there with the three-toed spoor of pheasants. The afternoon sun shone upon the naked spires of the larch trees, giving the stems and twigs a golden glow, but where I walked I was in cold shadow from the dark-tasselled firs.

Empty cartridge cases lay in the frosty grass, relics of a recent shoot. The sticks with their numbered labels still fixed in the split tops, showing where the guns had stood, each peg surrounded by a ring of empty cases.

I took a narrow pathway down on my right, glimpsing through the trees the winding river, which was a vivid blue reflecting the clear sunlit sky above. I intended to make my way along the water meadows to the stone bridge close to the empty Hall, standing among its cedars on the opposite hill.

Crawling under the barbed wire I found myself in the spacious green water meadows, peewit haunted, which 'go under' in times of flood. The Nene, even though controlled by locks, still floods the whole valley after heavy winter rains.

I did not progress very far before I was brought up short by quaking boggy ditches filled with dead rush from which snipe arrowed away, exploding from the marshy tussocks with the alarm note 'scaape scaape'. I tried to cross in several places and at last managed to jump one ditch with the help of a sunken log.

Beyond, the grass seemed firm and green but I had not gone more than a dozen yards before the way was barred by yet another slough of despond, so I had to go back into the thick wood, pushing my way

Partridge on the winter stubble

among the rusty stalks of willow herb, burr, brambles, and the white forests of dead nettle stalks.

In summer I could not have found a path through, and as it was I had to fight my way through the briers which were almost as impenetrable as barbed wire. The whipping tendrils of the brier with their armoured spines catch the clothes and hold one fast. But I pushed on, seeing the radiant sun burning before me through the stems of the larches.

Then quite suddenly I came upon the 'Folly' – a towering structure of stone with a high arch above. It had been erected, I suppose, at the end of the eighteenth century, when 'follies' were all the fashion with the big landowners. I suppose the building of them relieved the boredom of those days – possibly the old lord himself designed this 'folly'.

I could visualise him in his warm library with the roaring fire, his dogs about him, pencil and ruler to hand. What a 'phoney' erection it was, this sham ruin! No doubt – on his travels he had seen such ruins when he made the 'grand tour'.

I stood among the brambles looking up at the stone arch above me. Ivy had climbed up it – it stood dark against the tender evening light for now the sun was almost down. Pheasants were cocking up to roost in the larches all about me.

Not far distant, beyond the wood, was the church with its tall spire. Legend has it that this church once stood near the Hall and on Sundays the village, going to worship, had to pass within sight of the Hall windows. So the old lord decided the church should be moved, and so it was, stone by stone, to its new site a mile distant, well out of sight of aristocratic gaze.

Quickly the light in the western sky faded. I fought my way out of the wood at last to the open hill above the river, thankful to leave the tangled wilderness to its rightful tenants, the roosting pheasants, the foxes and the owls who were already beginning to salute the coming night, owl answering owl all along that wooded hill.

Below was the winding river, bright still but no longer blue, a coiling ribbon of paleness set in the quiet fields. A team of ducks went flying against the western sky, a compact bunch, with the location of their night's dinner table firmly in their brains, for they flew with urgency and on a steady compass course.

A day or so to the shortest day! It seemed almost unbelievable, how swiftly my year had gone.

It had been a happy one.

I find, as I grow older, that time takes on a new significance and is something to be cherished. One becomes more aware of the rhythm of the days – night comes too soon for me and I find myself wondering how I have employed myself during the day. Sometimes the precious hours have been wasted, frittered away with no creative work and not even the enjoyment of a good book or country walk.

A lot of time can be wasted in sleep. What a precious thing it is – this 'time' which slips away so inexorably second by second. Clock and watchmakers get so used to the sound of time ticking away that they give the subject no thought at all. I have discussed this subject with them.

When on a Saturday night I wind up the old grandfather clock, I remember my father used to do so for the last forty years of his life. As a small boy in bed on a Saturday night I could hear the grinding noise as the heavy weights were pulled upwards. Now my own child hears that sound. The ancient clock-face – eighteenth century – is a measuring stick which measures life.

I sometimes wish there were no such things as clocks to give audible reminder of the passing seconds and no such things as calendars or diaries. Then I remember the rising and setting of the sun is a measuring stick; each nightfall, a tick of a clock.

Youth, that glorious dawning, does not notice time. We never gave it a thought, and rightly so. To the child, time is non-existent. I have described this realisation in my book *A Child Alone*.

Also published by Merlin Unwin Books

THE COUNTRYMAN'S BEDSIDE BOOK
THE FISHERMAN'S BEDSIDE BOOK
THE SHOOTING MAN'S BEDSIDE BOOK
CONFESSIONS OF A CARP FISHER
THE NATURALIST'S BEDSIDE BOOK